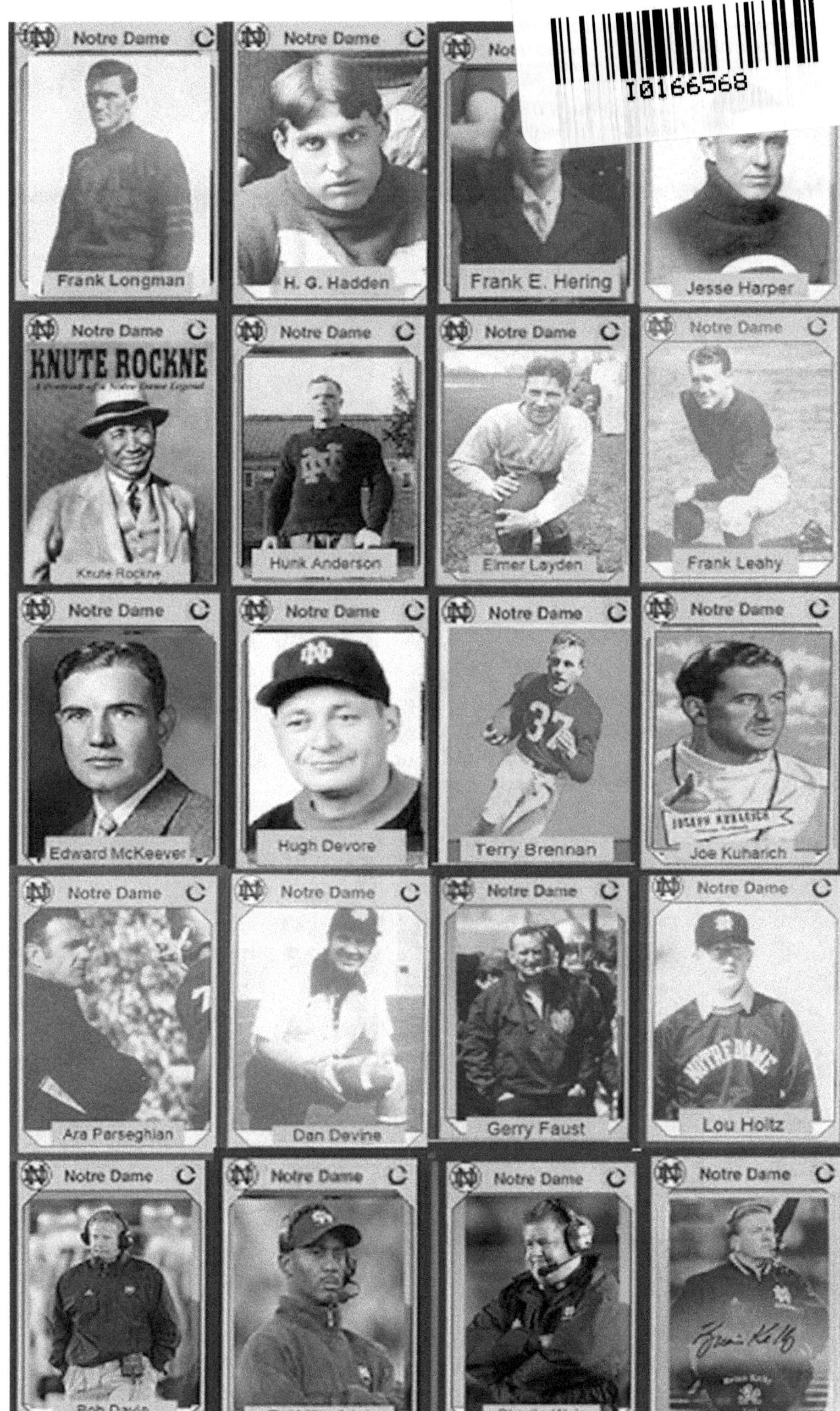
I0166568
Notre Dame
Frank Longman
H. G. Hadden
Frank E. Hering
Jesse Harper
KNUTE ROCKNE
Knute Rockne
Hunk Anderson
Elmer Layden
Frank Leahy
Edward McKeever
Hugh Devore
Terry Brennan
Joe Kuharich
Ara Parseghian
Dan Devine
Gerry Faust
Lou Holtz
NOTRE DAME
Bob Davie
Ty Willingham
Charlie Weis
Brian Kelly

ND FOOTBALL * ND FOOTBALL * ND FOOTB
IRISH

Great Coaches

in

Notre Dame Football

This book begins at the beginning of Football and goes to the Brian Kelly era.

The book is written for those of us who love Notre Dame Football. The greatest coaches of all time trained the greatest coaches of all time and the greatest players of all time for over 126 seasons worth of the greatest football games of all time. All loyal Notre Dame fans are well aware that the words "great" and "greatness" are never misused when describing Notre Dame Football.

This book will light up your sports bookshelf and help make you one of the most knowledgeable ND fans regarding ND's 31 great coaches.

The book first tells the story about the first football game in 1867. From there, the progression leads, to Notre Dame's first football game in 1887, then on to the first Notre Dame coach in 1894, and of course it moves on with the stories of all of the great coaches in ND Football—Rockne, Leahy, Parseghian, Devine, and Holtz, marching through time to the current coach, Brian Kelly.

It takes the reader through stories about Notre Dame's 31 coaches including some stops in the 126 seasons worth of great games (out of 1259 games). Thank you for picking up this book for your own personal reading and/or for that of a great friend or relative.

You will not be able to put this book down

Brian Kelly

 Editor: Brian P. Kelly
Great Coaches in Notre Dame Football Author: Brian W. Kelly
This book begins at the beginning of Football and goes to the Brian Kelly era.

Referenced Material: *Standard Disclaimer: The information in this book has been obtained through personal and third party observations, interviews, and copious research. Where unique information has been provided or extracted from other sources, those sources are acknowledged within the text of the book itself or in the References area in the front matter. Thus, there are no formal footnotes nor is there a bibliography section. Any picture that does not have a source was taken from various sites on the Internet with no credit attached. If resource owners would like credit in the next printing, please email publisher.*

Published by: LETS GO PUBLISH!
Editor in Chief Brian P. Kelly
Email: info@letsgopublish.com
Web site www.letsgopublish.com

Library of Congress Copyright Information Pending
Book Cover Design by Brian W. Kelly

Editor—Brian P. Kelly

ISBN Information: The International Standard Book Number (ISBN) is a unique machine-readable identification number, which marks any book unmistakably. The ISBN is the clear standard in the book industry. 159 countries and territories are officially ISBN members. The Official ISBN For this book is

978-0-9986282-5-7

The price for this work is: **$ 12.99 USD**

10 9 8 7 6 5 4 3 2 1

Release Date: February 2016

Notre Dame Season Records from 1887 through 2015

Year	Coach	Record	Champs	Year	Coach	Record	Champs	Bowl col 2
1887	No coach	0–1		1952	Frank Leahy	7–2–1		
1888	No coach	1–2		1953	Frank Leahy	9–0–1		
1889	No coach	1–0		1954	Terry Brennan	9–1		
1890	No games	0-0		1955	Terry Brennan	8–2		
1891	No games	0-0		1956	Terry Brennan	2–8		
1892	No coach	1–0–1		1957	Terry Brennan	7–3		
1893	No coach	4–1		1958	Terry Brennan	6–4		
1894	J.L. Morison	3–1–1		1959	Joe Kuharich	5–5		
1895	H.G. Hadden	3–1		1960	Joe Kuharich	2–8		
1896	Frank E. Hering	4–3		1961	Joe Kuharich	5–5		
1897	Frank E. Hering	4–1–1		1962	Joe Kuharich	5–5		
1898	Frank E. Hering	4–2		1963	Hugh Devore	2–7		
1899	James McWeeney	6–3–1		1964	Ara Parseghian	9–1		
1900	Pat O'Dea	6–3–1		1965	Ara Parseghian	7–2–1		
1901	Pat O'Dea	8–1–1		1966	Ara Parseghian	9–0–1	Champs	
1902	James Farragher	6–2–1		1967	Ara Parseghian	8–2		
1903	James Farragher	8–0–1		1968	Ara Parseghian	7–2–1		
1904	Louis Salmon	5–3		1969	Ara Parseghian	8–2–1		Lost Cottton
1905	Henry J. McGlew	5–4		1970	Ara Parseghian	10–1		Won Cotton
1906	Thomas Barry	6–1		1971	Ara Parseghian	8–2		
1907	Thomas Barry	6–0–1		1972	Ara Parseghian	8–3		Lost Orange
1908	Victor M. Place	8–1		1973	Ara Parseghian	11–0	Champs	Won Sugar
1909	Frank Longman	7–0–1		1974	Ara Parseghian	10–2		Won Orange
1910	Frank Longman	4–1–1		1975	Dan Devine	8–3		
1911	John L. Marks	6–0–2		1976	Dan Devine	9–3		Won Gator
1912	John L. Marks	7–0		1977	Dan Devine	11–1	Champs	Won Cotton
1913	Jesse Harper	7–0		1978	Dan Devine	9–3		Won Cotton
1914	Jesse Harper	6–2		1979	Dan Devine	7–4		
1915	Jesse Harper	7–1		1980	Dan Devine	9–2–1		Lost Sugar
1916	Jesse Harper	8–1		1981	Gerry Faust	5–6		
1917	Jesse Harper	6–1–1		1982	Gerry Faust	6–4–1		
1918	Knute Rockne	3–1–2		1983	Gerry Faust	7–5		Won Liberty
1919	Knute Rockne	9–0		1984	Gerry Faust	7–5		Lost Aloha
1920	Knute Rockne	9–0		1985	Gerry Faust	5–6		
1921	Knute Rockne	10–1		1986	Lou Holtz	5–6		
1922	Knute Rockne	8–1–1		1987	Lou Holtz	8–4		Lost Cotton
1923	Knute Rockne	9–1		1988	Lou Holtz	12–0	Champs	Won Fiesta
1924	Knute Rockne	10–0 Won Rose	Champs	1989	Lou Holtz	12–1		Won Orange
1925	Knute Rockne	7–2–1		1990	Lou Holtz	9–3		Lost Orange
1926	Knute Rockne	9–1		1991	Lou Holtz	10–3		Won Sugar
1927	Knute Rockne	7–1–1		1992	Lou Holtz	10–1–1		Won Cotton
1928	Knute Rockne	5–4		1993	Lou Holtz	11–1		Won Cotton
1929	Knute Rockne	9–0	Champs	1994	Lou Holtz	6–5–1		Lost Fiesta
1930	Knute Rockne	10–0	Champs	1995	Lou Holtz	9–3		Lost Orange
1931	Hunk Anderson	6–2–1		1996	Lou Holtz	8–3		
1932	Hunk Anderson	6–2–1		1997	Bob Davie	7–6		Lost indep.
1933	Hunk Anderson	3–5–1		1998	Bob Davie	9–3		Lost Gator
1934	Elmer Layden	6–3		1999	Bob Davie	5–7		
1935	Elmer Layden	7–1–1		2000	Bob Davie	9–3		Lost Fiesta

1936	Elmer Layden	6–2–1		2001	Bob Davie	5–6		
1937	Elmer Layden	6–2–1		2002	Tyr Willingham	10–3		Lost Gator
1938	Elmer Layden	8–1		2003	Ty Willingham	5–7		
1939	Elmer Layden	7–2		2004	Ty Willingham	6–5		
1940	Elmer Layden	7–2		2004	Kent Baer	0–1		Lost Insight
1941	Frank Leahy	8–0–1		2005	Charlie Weis	9–3		Lost Fiesta
1942	Frank Leahy	7–2–2		2006	Charlie Weis	10–3		Lost Sugar
1943	Frank Leahy	9–1	Champs	2007	Charlie Weis	3–9		
1944	Ed McKeever	8–2		2008	Charlie Weis	7–6		Won Hawaii
1945	Hugh Devore	7–2–1		2009	Charlie Weis	6–6		
1946	Frank Leahy	8–0–1	Champs	2010	Brian Kelly	8–5		Won Sun
1947	Frank leahy	9–0	Champs	2011	Brian Kelly	8–5		Lost Sports
1948	Frank Leahy	9–0–1		2012	Brian Kelly	12–1		Lost BCS
1949	Frank Leahy	10–0	Champs	2013	Brian Kelly	9–4		Won Pinstripe
1950	Frank Leahy	4–4–1		2014	Brian Kelly	8–5		Won Music
1951	Frank Leahy	7–2–1		2015	Brian Kelly	10-3-0		Lost Fiesta
Total: 892 Wins		314 L	42 Ties	2016	Brian Kelly	4-8-0		

Total Wins 896 Total Losses 320
Total Ties 42 * Prior to Overtime Rules
Stats from 1887 * Through January 2017

In November 2016, it was announced by the NCAA that due to an academic scandal, Notre Dame would be forced to vacate all victories from both the 2012 season and the 2013 season. ND lost 21 wins all-time. We used the NCAA's official Football Records book.

Before vacation of wins:

Rank	Program	Years	Wins	Losses	Ties	Games
1.	Michigan	137	935	332	36	1292
2.	Notre Dame	128	896	320	42	1247
3.	Texas	124	891	359	33	1272
4.	Nebraska	127	889	370	40	1288
5.	Ohio State	127	885	321	53	1248
6.	Alabama	122	875	326	43	1233
7.	Oklahoma	122	870	321	53	1233

After vacation of wins:

Rank	Program	Years	Wins	Losses	Ties	Games
1.	Michigan	137	935	332	36	1292
2.	Texas	124	891	359	33	1272
3.	Nebraska	127	889	370	40	1288
4.	Ohio State	127	885	321	53	1248
5.	Notre Dame	128	875	320	42	1247
6.	Alabama	122	875	326	43	1233
7.	Oklahoma	122	870	321	53	1233

LETS
GO
PUBLISH

Dedication

I dedicate this book to my wonderful wife Patricia; our three wonderful children Brian, Michael and Katie; and our friendly friends—Angel Ben our once very happy dog, and Buddy, our cheerful cat.

Thank You All!

Acknowledgments:

I appreciate all the help that I received in putting this book together, along with the 102 other books from the past.

My printed acknowledgments were once so large that book readers needed to navigate too many pages to get to page one of the text. To permit me more flexibility, I put my acknowledgment list online at www.letsgopublish.com. The list of acknowledgments continues to grow. Believe it or not, it once cost about a dollar more to print each book.

Thank you all on the big list in the sky and God bless you all for your help.

Please check out www.letsgopublish.com to read the latest version of my heartfelt acknowledgments updated for this book. Thank you all!

In compiling my research about Notre Dame, I received some extra special help from many avid Notre Dame supporters including Jack Lammers, Bruce Ikeda, Dennis Grimes, Gerry Rodski, Charles and Marilyn Gallagher, Joseph F. McKeown, Melvin Manhart, Red Jones, Michael McKeown, Wily Ky Eyely, Angel Irene McKeown Kelly, Angel Edward Joseph Kelly Sr., Angel Edward Joseph Kelly Jr., Ann Flannery, Angel James Flannery Sr., Mary Daniels, Bill Daniels, Robert Gary Daniels, Angel Sarah Janice Daniels, Angel Punkie Daniels, Joe Kelly, Diane Kelly, Brian P. Kelly, Mike P. Kelly, Katie P. Kelly, Angel Ben Kelly, and Budmund (Buddy) Arthur Kelly.

References

I learned how to write creatively in Grade School at St. Boniface. I even enjoyed reading some of my own stuff.

At Meyers High School and King's College and Wilkes-University, I learned how to research, write bibliographies and footnote every non-original thought I might have had. I learned to hate ibid, and op. cit., and I hated assuring that I had all citations written down in the proper sequence. Having to pay attention to details took my desire to write creatively and diminished it with busy work.

I know it is necessary for the world to stop plagiarism so authors and publishers can get paid properly, but for an honest writer, it sure is annoying. I wrote many proposals while with IBM and whenever I needed to cite something, I cited it in place, because my readers, IT Managers, could care less about tracing the vagaries of citations. I always hated to use stilted footnotes, or produce a lengthy, perfectly formatted bibliography. I bet most bibliographies are flawed because even the experts on such drivel do not like the tedium.

I wrote 103 books before this book and several hundred articles published by many magazines and newspapers and I only cite when an idea is not mine or when I am quoting, and again, I choose to cite in place, and the reader does not have to trace strange numbers through strange footnotes and back to bibliography elements that may not be readily accessible or available.

Yet, I would be kidding you, if in a book about the great moments in Notre Dame Football, I tried to bluff my way into trying to make you think that I knew everything before I began to write anything in this book. I spent as much time researching as writing. I might even call myself an expert of sorts now for all the facts that I have uncovered.

Without any pain on your part you can read this book from cover to cover to enjoy the stories about the many great moments in Notre Dame Football.

It took me about two months to write this book. If I were to have made sure a thought that I had was not a thought somebody else ever had, this book never would have been completed or the citations pages would exceed the prose.

I used ND Season summaries from whatever source I could to get the scores of all the games. I verified facts when possible. There are many web sites that have great information and facts. Ironically most internet stories are the same exact stories. While I was writing the book, I wrote down a bunch of Internet references that I show you below and when you finish reading this book, you may click and enjoy them.

My favorite source has been the Notre Dame Student Magazine called Scholastic which has been published almost from day one at the university. It stopped publishing football issues under its name for some reason at some point and began different publications that highlight football in the same fashion as Scholastic.

Yearly season football summaries were not included in Scholastic until 1901, so it won't help to look for 1887 articles in this magazine. Articles about football are in many of the many of the older issues of Scholastic that were published each year. As an example, in the April edition of 1931, there is major coverage of Knute Rockne's Tragic Death.

http://scholastic.nd.edu/about/

> *About*
> *Scholastic is the student news magazine of the University of Notre Dame. Founded in 1867, Scholastic is the United States' oldest continuously running collegiate publication. In its history, Scholastic has served first as Notre Dame's weekly student newspaper and now as a monthly news magazine. Scholastic publishes an annual Football Review, printed every February. This issue recaps the Notre Dame Football season with game summaries and in-depth commentary.*
> *Scholastic is a multiple winner of the "News Magazine of the Year" award from the Indiana Collegiate Press Association (ICPA) and the Pacemaker, a national journalism award given by the Associated Collegiate Press.*
>
> *The offices of Scholastic are located in the basement of the South Dining Hall at Notre Dame, and the mailing address is 315 LaFortune Student Center, Notre Dame, IN 46556.*

While I was writing this book, because I was not sure that my citations within the text would be enough, and I was not producing a bibliography, I copied URLs into the book text of areas on the Internet in which I had read articles or had downloaded material and had brought articles or pieces of articles into this book. Hopefully, this will satisfy any request for additional information.

Preface:

I like to begin my books about Notre Dame with this quote:

"We shall always want Notre Dame men 'to-play-to win' so long as there is a Notre Dame to win cleanly according to the rules … because Notre Dame men are reared here on the campus in this spirit and because they exemplify this spirit all over the world , they are the envy of the nation."

- Rev. John J Cavanaugh C.S.C; 14th president of the University of Notre Dame.

Knute Rockne may be the finest coach who ever lived. He is the most revered of all coaches in ND football. Rockne's life was cut short in a plane accident one year after Notre Dame Stadium, aka, The House that Rock Built opened in 1930. There are some historians who suggest that Notre Dame football actually began with Rockne but I beg to differ. I've got some good stories to prove my point.

The Irish played their first game in the new stadium in 1930 on October 4, beating SMU W (20–14). The first Notre Dame touchdown in the stadium was scored by"Jumping Joe" Savoldi on a 98-yard kickoff return. The official dedication was a week later on October 11 against Navy, and Savoldi scored three more touchdowns and was cited as "the first hero in the great lore of Notre Dame Stadium.

Once the stadium was constructed and opened, every Notre Dame Football Team has walked down the same tunnel right before every home game. In the mid-1990s, Notre Dame's red-bricked arena underwent a $50 million expansion and renovation that added more than 21,000 seats. The Campus Crossroads Project is underway now and it will reshape the stadium again about four thousand seats and some great new campus buildings in a mammoth $400 million dollar project

The football program from day one competed under the nickname "Catholics" and for a time it was widely known as the "Ramblers." Coach Harper's and Coach Rockne's teams were often called the

Rovers or the Ramblers and there were no compliments intended. ND would travel anywhere to get a game. They roamed and rambled far and wide, an uncommon practice before the advent of commercial airplanes.

After the 1909 game v Michigan, Sportswriter E.A. Batchelor, who had overheard ND teammates encouraging each other to fight hard because they were Irish and the team needed to fight hard to win the game, is credited with first using the moniker in the written word. University president Rev. Matthew Walsh, C.S.C., officially adopted "Fighting Irish" as the Notre Dame nickname in 1927. So, now, it is official.

You'll learn a lot about Notre Dame and its coaches in this new book by Brian Kelly. It highlights the Great Coaches in Notre Dame Football and it walks the reader briskly through every season in ND history, even a few in which there was not a coach to be seen.

Brian Kelly would like you to know that when football season closes in the second week of January each year, there is now a great football item—this book—that is available all 52 weeks and in fact all 365 days each year…even if the stadium is closed due to a blizzard. It is available for you to add to your Notre Dame football experience and your book collection. Once you get this book, it is yours forever unless, of course you give it away to one of the many who will be in awe, and who will accept it gladly.

The book takes a quick look at all the coaches in Notre Dame history, some famous, and some not so famous. Admittedly, it devotes many more pages for the more famous coaches as well as those who contributed more than their fair share to the Notre Dame legacy that we all appreciate today.

As tough as it may be to believe for some of the more recent Notre Dame supporters, not all Notre Dame coaches are named Rockne or Holtz, or Devine or Leahy, or Parseghian. But, those coaches did win National Championships and just about all ND fans know them. There were 26 other ND coaches—even some who never coached a game.

Lest we forget, it was not just the Championship Teams but all Notre Dame Football teams that were Irish Tough. The teams of these immortal coaches and the others not quite so famous all fought hard for wins as the Fighting Irish. In this book, we look at all 31 coaches who led the Fighting Irish over 126 seasons (28 years) of great Notre Dame football.

The book opens with its first story about the very beginning of college football as a sport in America. It then moves on to the coaches and their seasons—all the way to Coach Brian Kelly's last game. It tells a story about each coach from the first game in 1887 right to the beginning of the 2017 season. It is written for those of us who love Notre Dame Football.

I predict that you will not be able to put this book down

You are going to love this book because it is the perfect read for anybody who loves Notre Dame and Notre Dame Football and wants to know more about the most revered athletic program of all time.

Few sports books are a must-read but Brian Kelly's Great Coaches in Notre Dame Football will quickly appear at the top of Americas most enjoyable must-read books about sports. Enjoy!

Sincerely,

Brian P. Kelly, Editor in Chief
I am Brian Kelly's eldest son

Table of Contents

About the Author

Brian Kelly retired as an Assistant Professor in the Business Information Technology (BIT) Program at Marywood University, where he also served as the IBM i and Midrange Systems Technical Advisor to the IT Faculty.

He is one of the leading authors in America with this, his 104th published book. Brian is an outspoken and eloquent expert on a variety of topics and he has also written several hundred articles on topics of general interest to most Americans.

Most of his early works involved high technology. Later, Brian wrote a number of patriotic books and most recently he has been writing human interest books such as *The Wine Diet* and *Thank you, IBM*. His books are always well received.

Brian's 104 books are all highlighted at www.letsgopublish.com. They are for sale at www.bookhawkers.com, Amazon, Kindle, and other fine booksellers. One day perhaps, even the famous Notre Dame Book Store will agree to host this book for sale.

Brian was a candidate for the US Congress from Pennsylvania in 2010 and he ran for Mayor in his home town in 2015. He loves Notre Dame and was an Irish fan long before some other guy with the same name happened to come to South Bend, Indiana.

Chapter 1 Introduction to the Book

Notre Dame Football in its 128th year.

Brian Kelly, ND Coach Leading the Fighting Irish In Spring, 2012 Game

In 2012, Notre Dame celebrated its 125th year of football. As part of the celebration, the University built a web site that fans of Notre Dame should find quite enjoyable— http://125.nd.edu. The site has many enjoyable items to tickle the imagination and it provides a very real look at Notre Dame over its 125-year history (as of 2012). The very first item that I viewed on this site was at the following web address: http://125.nd.edu/moments/first-game-in-notre-dame-football-history/

Enjoy the Sept 22 2012 125th anniversary game panorama picture at http://125.nd.edu/pano/

This book celebrates Notre Dame's great football coaches and the university's long-lasting impact on American life. People like me, who love Notre Dame, will love this book. Those not quite such admiring fans as I will sneak it off the shelf at their doctor's office and read it quietly in the corner.

We kick off the football part of the book in Chapter 2 with founding of college football and we move on to the founding of the football program in 1887. From there we look at each of the great coaches who helped mold the great football teams in ND history.

In defining the format of the book, we chose to use a timetable that is based on a historical chronology. Within this framework, we discuss the great moments in Notre Dame Football History, and there are many great moments. No book can claim to be able to capture them all, as it would be a never-ending story, but we sure try.

Thanks for choosing to take this fun ride with us through Notre Dame Football History. The great coaches noted in this book are part of the great legacy of Notre Dame University and its world class football program.

Chapter 2 The Beginning of College Football

Lots of playing before playing became official

The official agreed upon date for the first American-style college football game is November 6, 1869. If you can find a replay of this game someplace in the heavens, however, you would find it would not look much like football as we know it. But, it was not completely soccer or rugby either.

Before this game, teams were playing a rugby style similar to that played in Britain in the mid-19th century. At the time in the US, a derivative known as association football was also played. In both games, a football is kicked at a goal or run over a line. These styles were based on the varieties of English public school football games. Over time, as noted, the style of "football" play in America continued to evolve.

On November 6, 1869, the first football game in America featured Rutgers and Princeton. Before the teams were even on the field it was being plugged as the first college football game of all time. Notre Dame did have a rugby team at the time, but nobody at Notre Dame, from what I could find, was even thinking about the game of football.

The first game of intercollegiate football was a sporting battle between two neighboring schools on a plot of ground where the present-day Rutgers gymnasium now stands in New Brunswick, N.J. Rutgers won that first game, 6-4.

There were two teams of 25 men each and the rules were rugby-like, but different enough to make it very interesting and enjoyable.

Like today's football, there were many surprises; strategies needed to be employed; determination exhibited, and of course the players required physical prowess.

1st Game Rutgers 6 Princeton 4 College Field, New Brunswick, NJ

At 3 p.m. the 50 combatants as well as 100 spectators gathered on the field. Most sat on a low wooden fence and watched the athletes discard their hats, coats and vests. The players used their suspenders as belts. To give a unique look, Rutgers wore scarlet-colored scarfs, which they converted into turbans. This contrasted them with the bareheaded boys from Princeton.

Two members of each team remained stationary near the opponent's goal in the hopes of being able to slip over and score from unguarded positions. Thus, the present day "sleeper" was conceived. The remaining 23 players were divided into groups of 11 and 12. While the 11 "fielders" lined up in their own territory as defenders, the 12 "bulldogs" carried the battle.

Each score counted as a "game" and 10 games completed the contest. Following each score, the teams changed direction. The ball could be advanced only by kicking or batting it with the feet, hands, heads or sides.

Rutgers put a challenge forward that three games were to be played that year. The first was played at New Brunswick and won by Rutgers. Princeton won the second game, but cries of "over-emphasis" prevented the third game in football's first year when faculties of both institutions protested on the grounds that the games were interfering with student studies.

This is an excerpt of the Rutgers account of the game on its web site. A person named Herbert gave this detailed account of the play in the first game:

"Though smaller on the average, the Rutgers players, as it developed, had ample speed and fine football sense. Receiving the ball, our men formed a perfect interference around it and with short, skillful kicks and dribbles drove it down the field. Taken by surprise, the Princeton men fought valiantly, but in five minutes we had gotten the ball through to our captains on the enemy's goal and S.G. Gano, '71 and G.R. Dixon, '73, neatly kicked it over. None thought of it, so far as I know, but we had without previous plan or thought evolved the play that became famous a few years later as 'the flying wedge'."

"Next period Rutgers bucked, or received the ball, hoping to repeat the flying wedge," Herbert's account continues. "But the first time we formed it Big Mike came charging full upon us. It was our turn for surprise. The Princeton battering ram made no attempt to reach the ball but, forerunner of the interference-breaking ends of today, threw himself into our mass play, bursting us apart, and bowing us over. Time and again Rutgers formed the wedge and charged; as often Big Mike broke it up. And finally, on one of these incredible break-ups a Princeton bulldog with a long accurate, perhaps lucky kick, sent the ball between the posts for the second score.

It was at this point that a Rutgers professor could stand it no longer. Waving his umbrella at the participants, he shrieked, "You will come to no Christian end!"

Herbert's account of the game continues: "The fifth and sixth goals went to Rutgers. The stars of the latter period of play, in the memory of the players after the lapse of many years, were "Big Mike" and Large (former State Senator George H. Large of Flemington, another Princeton player) ...

The University of Notre Dame did not get into the football act until the late 1880's. At this time, the rules of rugby kept changing to accommodate the infatuation for the Americanized style of "football" play that would ultimately become the American game of football.

Walter Camp: the father of American football?

Walter Camp was a very well-known rugby player from Yale. In today's world, he would have been characterized as a rugby hero. It was his love of the game, his knowledge of the game as it was played, and his innovative mind that caused him to take the evolution of football even further. He pioneered the changes to the rules of rugby that slowly transformed the sport into the new game of American Football.

The rule changes that were introduced to the rugby and association style of play were mostly those authored by Camp, who was also a Hopkins School graduate. For his original efforts, Walter Camp today is considered to be the "Father of American Football". Among the important changes brought to the game were the introduction of a line of scrimmage; down-and-distance rules; and the legalization of interference (blocking).

There was no such thing in those days as a forward pass and so the legalization of interference in 1880 football permitted blocking for runners. The forward pass would add another dimension to the game that made it much different than rugby or association football.

Soon after the early football changes, in the late nineteenth and into the early twentieth centuries, more game-play type developments were introduced by college coaches. The list is like a who's who of early American College Football. Coaches, such as Eddie Cochems, Amos Alonzo Stagg, Parke H. Davis, Knute Rockne, John Heisman, and Glenn "Pop" Warner helped introduce and then take advantage of the newly introduced forward pass. College football as well as professional football, were introduced prior to the 20th century. Fans were lured into watching again and again once they saw the game played.

College football especially grew in popularity despite the existence of pro-football. It became the dominant version of the sport of football in the United States. It was this way for the entire first half of the 20th century. Bowl games made the idea of football even more exciting in the college ranks. Rivalries grew and continued and the fans loved it! This great football tradition brought a national audience to college football games that still dominates the sports world today.

This book has little to do with pro-football or any other sport. However, there is no denying that the greatest college football players more often than not eventually found their fortunes in professional football. Pro football can be traced back to the season that Notre Dame brought forth a real football team after a two-year lapse from its last half-Rugby season in 1889. It was 1892 when William "Pudge" Heffelfinger signed a $500 contract to play for the Allegheny Athletic Association against the Pittsburgh Athletic Club.

Twenty-eight years later, the American Professional Football Association was formed. This league changed its name to the National Football League (NFL) just two years later. Eventually, the NFL became the major league of American football. Originally, just a sport played in Midwestern industrial towns in the United States, professional football eventually became a national phenomenon. We all know this because from August to February, in America, many of us are glued to our TV sets or chained to our seats in some of the most intriguing pro-football stadiums in America.

Rules and Penalties

The big problem players from different teams and different geographies had when playing early American-style football in college was that the style of play was not standardized. The rulebooks were not yet written or were at best incomplete and disputable.

A rule over here, for example, would be a penalty over there. And, so in the 1870's there was a lot of work to try to make all games to be played by the same rules. There were minor rule changes such as team size was reduced from 25 to 20 but of course over the years, this and all other rules continued to evolve. For years, there was no such thing as a running touchdown. The only means of scoring was to bat or kick the ball through the opposing team's goal.

Early rugby rules were the default. The field size was rugby style at 140 yards by 70 yards v 120 X 53 1/3 (including end zones) in today's football game. There was plenty of room to huff and puff and almost get lost. There were no breaks per se for long periods. Instead of fifteen minute quarters, the game was more like Rugby and Soccer with 45 minute halves played continuously.

In 1873 to put some order to the game, Columbia, Princeton. Rutgers, and Yale got together in a hotel in New York City and wrote down the first set of intercollegiate football rules. They changed a few things along the way but the end product was a much more standard way of playing football games. Rather than use the home team's rules, all teams then were able to play by the same rules

Harvard did not to comply with rules

For its own reasons, Harvard chose not to attend the rules conference. Instead, it played all of its games using the Harvard code of rules. Harvard therefore had a difficult time scheduling games. In 1874, to get a game, Harvard agreed to play McGill University from Montreal Cànada. They had rules that even Harvard had never seen. For example, any player could pick up the ball and run with it, anytime he wished.

Another McGill rule was that they would count tries (the act of grounding the football past the opponent's goal line. Since there was no end zone, which technically makes a football field of today 120 yards long, a touchdown gave no points. Instead, it provided the chance to kick a free goal from the field. If the kick were missed, the touchdown did not count.

In 1874 McGill and Harvard played a two-game series. Each team could play 11 men per side. This was in deep contrast to the even earlier days of college football before standard rules when games were played with 25, 20, 15, or 11 men on a side.

The first game was played with a round ball using what were known as the "Boston" rules (Harvard). The next day, the teams played using the McGill rules, which included McGill's oval ball which was much like an American football, and it featured the ability to pick up the ball and run with it. Harvard enjoyed this experience especially the idea of "the try" which had not been used in American football. Eventually, the try evolved into the American idea of a touchdown and points were given when a try was successful.

Not all the rules lasted the duration and some were very strange by today's standards. One of the most perplexing rules was that a man could run with the ball only while an opponent chose to pursue him. When a tackler abandoned the ball-carrier, the latter had to stop, and was forced to kick, pass or even throw away what was called "his burden."

McGill has a great account of this match on their web site. Type ***McGill web site football against Harvard*** into your search engine.

Their players wore no protective pads. Woolen jerseys covered the torso, while white trousers encased the players' legs. Some trousers were short and some were long. It did not seem to matter for the game. A number of the men wore what they called black "football turbans" which were the ancestors of the modern helmet; others chose to wear white canvas hats.

The Harvard players wore undershirts made of gauze. Think about that for a while. They also wore what were called *full length gymnasium costumes*. They also wore light baseball shoes. Most of the team wore handkerchiefs, which were knotted about their heads.

The gauze undershirts were a trick. There was strategy in this choice of top uniform. When a player was first tackled, the gauze would be demolished and the next opponent would have nothing to grab other than "slippery human flesh." Harvard won this game by a score of 3-0

The next go at playing by the rules was when Harvard took on Tufts University on June 4, 1875. This was the first American college football game played using rules similar to the McGill/Harvard contest. Tufts won this game. Despite the loss,

Harvard continued pushing McGill style football and challenged Yale.

The Bulldog team accepted under a compromise rule set that included some Yale soccer rules and Harvard rugby rules. They used 15 players per team. It was November 13, 1875 for this first meeting of Harvard v Yale. Harvard won 4-0. Walter Camp attended the game and the following year he played in the game as a Yale Bulldog.

Camp was determined to avenge Yale's defeat. Onlookers from Princeton, who saw this Harvard / Yale game loved it so much, they brought it back to Princeton where it was quickly adopted as the preferred version of football.

Once Walter Camp caught onto the rugby-style rules, history says he became a fixture at the Massasoit House conventions. Here the rules of the game were debated and changed appropriately. From these meetings, Camp's rule changes as well as others were adopted.

Having eleven players instead of fifteen aided in opening the game and it emphasized speed over strength. When Camp attended in 1878, this motion was rejected but it passed in the 1880 meeting. The line of scrimmage and the snap from center to the quarterback also passed in 1880. Originally the snap occurred by a kick from the center, but this was later modified so the ball would be snapped with the hands either as a pass back (long snap) or a direct snap from the center.

It was Camp's new scrimmage rules, however, which according to many, revolutionized the game, though it was not always to increase speed. In fact, Princeton was known to use line of scrimmage plays to slow the game, making incremental progress towards the end zone much like today during each down.

Camp's original idea was to increase scoring, but in fact the rule was often misused to maintain control of the ball for the entire game. The negative effect was that there were many slow and unexciting contests. This too would be fixed with the idea of the first down coming into play.

In 1982, at the rules meeting, Camp proposed that a team be given three downs to advance the ball five yards. These rules were called the down and distance rules. Along with the notion of the line of scrimmage, these rules transformed the game of rugby into the distinct sport of American football.

Among other significant rule changes, in 1881, the field size was reduced to its modern dimensions of 120 by 53 1/3 yards (109.7 by 48.8 meters). Camp was central to these significant rule changes that ultimately defined American football. Camp's next quest was to address scoring anomalies. His first cut was to give four points for a touchdown and two points for kicks after touchdowns; two points for safeties, and five points for field goals. The notion of the foot in football /rugby explains Camp's rationale.

In 1887, game time was fixed at two halves of 45 minutes each. Additionally college games would have two paid officials known as a referee and an umpire, for each game. In 1888, the rules permitted tackling below the waist and then in 1889, the officials were given whistles and stopwatches to better control the game.

An innovation that many list as most significant to making American football uniquely American was the legalization of blocking opponents, which back then was called "interference." This tactic had been highly illegal under the rugby-style rules and in rugby today, it continues to be illegal.

The more those who know soccer and football find rugby to be more like soccer.

Though *offsides* is a penalty infraction today, *offsides* in the 1880's in rugby was very much the same as *offsides* in soccer. The prohibition of blocking in a rugby game is in fact because of the game's strict enforcement of its *offsides* rule. Similar to soccer, this rule prohibits any player on the team with possession of the ball to loiter between the ball and the goal. Blocking continues as a basic element of modern American football, with many complex schemes having been developed and implemented over the years, including zone blocking and pass blocking.

Camp stayed active in rule making for most of his life. He had the honor of personally selecting an annual All-American team every year from 1889 through 1924. Camp passed away in 1925. The Walter Camp Football Foundation continues to select All-American teams in his honor.

With many rule changes as noted, as American style rugby became more defined as American football, more and more colleges adopted football as part of their sports programs. Most of the schools were from the Eastern US. It was not until 1879 that the University of Michigan became the first school west of Pennsylvania to establish a bona-fide American-style college football team.

Back then, football teams played whenever they could in the fall or the spring. For example, Michigan's first game was in late spring, near the end of what we would call the academic year. On May 30, 1879 Michigan beat Racine College 1–0 in a game played in Chicago. In 1887, Michigan and Notre Dame played their first football game, which did not benefit from Camp's rules.

The first night time game

It was not until September 28, 1892 that the first nighttime football game was played. Mansfield State Normal played Wyoming Seminary in Mansfield, Pennsylvania.

These schools are close to where I live. The game ended at a "declared" half-time in a 0–0 tie. It had become too dark to play.

Wyoming Seminary was not a college and to this day it is not a college. I live about five miles from the school. It is a private college preparatory school located in the Wyoming Valley of Northeastern Pennsylvania. During the time-period in which the game was played, it was common for a college and high school to play each other in football—a practice that of course has long since been discontinued.

The reason that it got too dark to play, ironically was not because the game began at dusk. Mansfield had brought in a lighting system that was far too inadequate for game play. This historical game lasted only 20 minutes and there were only 10 plays. Both sides agreed to end at half-time with the score at 0-0. Though it may seem humorous today, for safety reasons, the game was declared ended in a 0-0 tie after several players had an unfortunate run-in with a light pole.

Mansfield and Wyoming Seminary are thus enshrined in football history as having played in the first night game ever in "college football." History and football buffs get together once a year to celebrate the game in what they call "Fabulous 1890's Weekend." This historic game is reenacted exactly as it occurred play by play just as the actual game is recorded in history. Fans who watch the game are sometimes known to correct players (actually actors) when they deviate from the original scripted plays. Now, that shows both a love of the game and a love of history.

Mansfield and Wyoming Seminary's game added additional fame to both schools when the 100th anniversary of the game just happened to occur on Monday, September 28, 1992. Monday Night Football celebrated "100 years of night football" with its regularly scheduled game between the Los Angeles Raiders and the Kansas City Chiefs at Arrowhead Stadium. The Chiefs won 27–7 in front of 77,486 fans. How about that?

More football history was recorded when Army played Navy in 1893. In this game, we have the first documented use of a football helmet by a player in a game. Joseph M. Reeves had been kicked in the head in a prior football game. He was warned by his doctor that he risked death if he continued to play football. We all know how tough the Midshipmen and Black Nights (Cadets) are regardless of who they may be playing. Rather than end his football playing days prematurely. Reeves discussed his need with a shoemaker in Annapolis who crafted a leather helmet for the player to wear for the rest of the season.

Football conferences

Things were happening very quickly in the new sport of football. Organization and rules became the mantra for this fledgling sport. It was being defined while it was being played. Formal college football conferences were just around the corner. In fact, the Southeastern Conference and the Atlantic Coast Conference both got started in1894.

The forward pass

None of Camp's rules for American Football included the most innovative notion of them all – the forward pass. Many believe that the first forward pass in football occurred on October 26, 1895 in a game between Georgia and North Carolina. Out of desperation, the ball was thrown by the North Carolina back Joel Whitaker instead of having been punted. George Stephens, a teammate caught the ball.

Despite what most may think or surmise, it was Camp again when he was a player at Yale, who executed the first game-time forward pass for a touchdown. During the Yale-Princeton game, while Camp was being tackled, he threw a football forward to Yale's Oliver Thompson, who sprinted to a touchdown. The Princeton Tigers naturally protested and there appeared to be no precedent for a referee decision. Like many things in football including a game-beginning coin-toss, the referee in this instance tossed a coin, and then he made his decision to allow the touchdown.

Hidden ball trick

Some one-time tricks have not survived football. For example, on November 9, 1895 Auburn Coach John Heisman executed a hidden ball trick. Quarterback Reynolds Tichenor was able to gain Auburn's only touchdown in a 6 to 9 loss to Vanderbilt. This also was the first game in the south that was decided by a field goal.

The trick was simple but would be illegal today. When the ball was snapped it went to a halfback. The play was closely masked and well screened. The halfback then thrust the ball under the back of the quarterback's (Tichenor) jersey. Then the halfback would crash into the line. After the play, Tichenor "simply trotted away to a touchdown."

The end of college football?

Football was never a game for the light of heart. You had to be tough physically and tough mentally to compete. Way back in 1906, for example complaints were many about the violence in American Football. It got so bad that universities on the West Coast, led by California and Stanford, replaced the sport with rugby union. At the time, the future of American college football, a very popular sport enjoyed by fans nationwide was in doubt. The schools that eliminated football and replaced it with rugby union believed football would be gone and rugby union would eventually be adopted nationwide.

Soon other schools followed this travesty and made the switch. Eventually, due to the perception that West Coast football was an inferior game played by inferior men when compared to the rough and tumble East Coast, manhood prevailed in the West over the inclination to make the game mild. The many tough East Coast and Midwest teams had shrugged off the loss of the few teams out West and they had continued to play American style football.

And, so the available pool of rugby union "football" teams to play remained small. The Western colleges therefore had to schedule games against local club teams and they reached out to rugby union powers in Australia, New Zealand, and especially, due to its proximity, Canada.

The famous Stanford and California game continued as rugby. To make it seem important. The winner was invited by the British Columbia Rugby Union to a tournament in Vancouver over the Christmas holidays. The winner of that tournament was rewarded with the Cooper Keith Trophy. Nobody in America cared. Eventually the West Coast came back to football.

Nonetheless the situation of injury and death in football persisted and though there was a lot of pushback, it came to a head in 1905 when there were 19 fatalities nationwide. President Theodore Roosevelt, a tough guy himself, is reported as having threatened to shut down the game nationwide if drastic changes were not made. Sports historians however, dispute that Roosevelt ever intervened.

What is certified, however, is that on October 9, 1905, the President held a meeting of football representatives from Harvard, Yale, and Princeton. The topic was eliminating and reducing injuries and the President according to the record, never threatened to ban football. The fact is that Roosevelt lacked the authority to abolish football but more importantly, he was a big fan and wanted the game to continue. The little Roosevelts also loved the sport and were playing football at the college and secondary levels at the time.

Theodore Roosevelt, Jr. after breaking his ankle during a Harvard football game.

Meanwhile, there were more rule changes such as the notion of reducing the number of scrimmage plays to earn a first down from four to three in an attempt to reduce injuries. The LA Times reported an increase in punts in an experimental game and thus considered the game much safer than regular play. Football lovers did not accept the new rule because it was not "conducive to the sport."

Because nobody wanted players injured or killed in a game, on December 28, 1905, 62 schools met in New York City to discuss major rule changes to make the game safer. From this meeting, the Intercollegiate Athletic Association of the United States, later named the National Collegiate Athletic Association (NCAA), was formed.

The forward pass is legalized

One rule change that was introduced in 1906 was devised to open up the game and thus reduce injury. This new rule introduced the legal forward pass. Though it was underutilized for years, this proved to be one of the most important rule changes in the establishment of the modern game.

Because of these 1905-1906 reforms, mass formation plays in which many players joined together became illegal when forward passes became legal. Bradbury Robinson, playing for visionary coach Eddie

Cochems at St. Louis University, is recorded as throwing the first legal pass in a September 5, 1906, game against Carroll College at Waukesha.

Later changes were in the minutia category but they added discipline and safety to the game without destroying its rugged character. For example, in 1910, came the new requirement that at least seven offensive players be on the line of scrimmage at the time of the snap, that there be no pushing or pulling, and that interlocking interference (arms linked or hands on belts and uniforms) was not allowed. These changes accomplished their intended purpose of greatly reducing the potential for collision injuries.

As noted previously, great coaches emerged in the ranks who took advantage of these sweeping changes. Amos Alonzo Stagg, for example, introduced such innovations as the huddle, the tackling dummy, and the pre-snap shift. Other coaches, such as Pop Warner and Notre Dame's Knute Rockne, introduced new strategies that still remain part of the game.

Jim Thorpe, Circa 1915

Many other rules changes and coaching innovations came about before 1940. They all had a profound impact on the game, mostly in opening up the passing game, but also in making the game safer to play without diminishing its quality.

For example, in 1914, the first roughing-the-passer penalty was implemented. In 1918, the rules on eligible receivers were loosened to allow eligible players to catch the ball anywhere on the field.

The previously more restrictive rules allowed passes only in certain areas of the field. Scoring rules also changed which brought the scoring into the modern era. For example, field goals were lowered from five to three points in 1909 and touchdowns were raised from four to six points in 1912.

Star Players

Star players emerged in both the collegiate and professional ranks including Jim Thorpe (shown on prior page,)

Red Grange, and Bronko Nagurski were also big stars. These three in particular were able to move from college to the fledgling NFL and they helped turn it into a successful league. Notable sportswriter Grantland Rice helped popularize the sport of football with his poetic descriptions of games and colorful nicknames for the game's biggest players, including Notre Dame's "Four Horsemen" backfield and Fordham University's linemen, known as the "Seven Blocks of Granite".

The Heisman

Jay Berwanger (below) was the 1st Heisman Winner. In 1935, New York City's Downtown Athletic Club awarded its first Heisman Trophy to University of Chicago halfback Jay Berwanger (left).

He was also the first ever NFL Draft pick in 1936. The trophy continues to this day to recognize the nation's "most outstanding" college football player. It has become one of the most coveted awards in all of American sports.

As professional football became a national television phenomenon, college football did as well. In the 1950s, Notre Dame, which had a large national following, formed its own network to broadcast its games, but by and large the sport still retained a mostly regional following.

New formations and play sets continued to be developed by innovative coaches and their staffs. Emory Bellard from the University of Texas, developed a three-back option style offense known as the wishbone. Bear Bryant of Alabama became a preacher of the wishbone.

The strategic opposite of the wishbone is called the spread offense. Some teams have managed to adapt with the times to keep winning consistently. In the rankings of the most victorious programs, Michigan, Texas, and Notre Dame are ranked first, second, and third in total wins.

And so, that is as far as we will take it in this chapter about the early evolution of football. With so many conferences and sports associations as well as pro, college, high school, and mini sports, something tells me we have not yet seen our last rule change.

Chapter 3 Notre Dame's First Football Team

NOTRE DAME

FIGHTING IRISH FOOTBALL TEAM 1887

1887: Nearly 45 years from the founding

The players coached themselves in the beginning until 1894. On Nov. 23, 1887, nearly 45 years to the day after Rev. Edward Sorin, C.S.C., arrived in northern Indiana, the University of Notre Dame fielded a collegiate football team. There is nobody who can tell the History of Notre Dame Football better than Notre Dame itself. The following brief article was originally published in Scholastic, Notre Dame's internal student magazine.
The quoted narrative from Scholastic describes the scene of the inaugural contest between Michigan and Notre Dame. Following a quick depiction of the game, I have included several additional pictures for your enjoyment and edification. All of these photos are free for the viewing on the Internet.

" For some days, previous to Wednesday great interest had been manifested by our students in the football game which had been arranged between the teams of the Universities of Michigan and

Notre Dame. It was not considered a match contest, as the home team had been organized only a few weeks, and the Michigan boys, the champions of the West, came more to instruct them in the points of the Rugby game than to win fresh laurels.

1887 Champion Michigan Wolverine football team

"The visitors [Michigan] arrived over the Michigan Central RR., Wednesday morning, and were at once taken in charge by a committee of students. After spending, a few hours in "taking in" the surroundings, they donned their uniforms of spotless white and appeared upon the seniors' campus. Owing to the recent thaw, the field was damp and muddy; but nothing daunted, the boys "went in," and soon Harless' new suit appeared as though it had imbibed some of its wearer's affinity for the soil of Notre Dame.

At first, to render our players more familiar with the game, the teams were chosen irrespective of college. After some minutes' play, the game was called, and each took his position as follows:

"**Univ. of M**. – Full Back: J.L. Duffy; Half Backs: J.E. Duffy, E. McPheran; Quarter Back: R.T. Farrand; Centre Rush: W.W.

Harless; Rush Line: F. Townsend, E.M. Sprague, F.H. Knapp, W. Fowler, G.W. De Haven, M. Wade.

"Univ. of N.D. – Full Back: H. Jewett; Half Backs: J. Cusack, H. Luhn; Quarter Back: G. Cartier; Centre Rush: G.A. Houck; Rush Line: F. Fehr, P. Nelson, B. Sawkins, W. Springer, T. O'Regan, P.P. Maloney.

"On account of time, only a part of one inning was played, and resulted in a score of 8 to 0 in favor of the visitors. The game was interesting, and, notwithstanding the slippery condition of the ground, the Ann Arbor boys gave a fine exhibition of skilful [sic] playing. This occasion has started an enthusiastic football boom, and it is hoped that coming years will witness a series of these contests.

"After a hearty dinner, Rev. President Walsh thanked the Ann Arbor team for their visit, and assured them of the cordial reception that would always await them at Notre Dame. At 1 o'clock carriages were taken for Niles, and amidst rousing cheers the University of Michigan football team departed, leaving behind them a most favorable impression." **End of Scholastic Excerpt**

Modern ND Football

Originally posted Sep 4, 2013. http://mvictors.com/teaching-them-modern-football-1887/
Thank you to the Michigan Athletic Association for making this piece, shown in its entirety below, publicly available:

> *"With all the talk on the historical significance of the Michigan-Notre Dame rivalry, I'd thought I'd share a little bit on the original meeting in 1887. Women, prepare to swoon.*

> ### *DeHaven and Harless*

> *So, you've heard that Michigan taught Notre Dame how to play this game. This is true of course, and the details of that meeting are chronicled up front in John Kryk outstanding book Natural Enemies.*

Kryk explains that the origins of the fateful meeting in South Bend over 125 years ago, can be attributed to three men: students George DeHaven, Billy Harless and Notre Dame's prefect Patrick 'Brother Paul' Connors.
In a nutshell, DeHaven and Harless were former Notre Dame students in the mid-1880s who, in 1886, enrolled at Michigan. Both were exceptional athletes and suited up for the U-M 1887 varsity football squad…aka Team 8
While at ND DeHaven had become friendly with Brother Paul, who was a popular administrator on campus and helped run the intramural athletics program. Team 8

DeHaven and Harless (via the U-M Bentley Library)

In South Bend they did have an IM sport which was something like football…but not really. Kryk described it this way: "A hundred boys to a side, all scrambling to get a round ball over the opponent's fence by any means. Kick it, toss it; slap it – whatever. If you want to get technical it was part soccer and part rugby, but mostly it was pure pandemonium."

Michigan didn't play many actual games against opponents back in those days, but they had an appointment for a Thanksgiving Day trip to Chicago to face against Northwestern (FWIW before the game NW would cancel; U-M ended up playing a Chicago-area prep school). In mid-October DeHaven wrote to Connors, shared a few details about this awesome new game and let him know they'd be heading his direction in late November. The missive caught the attention of the sports-loving Brother Paul. Kryk explains what happened next:

Brother Paul wrote back to his friend at Michigan and asked if DeHaven and Harless could convince the Wolverines to make a stop at Notre Dame, on their way to Chicago, and teach some seniors this rugby brand of football.

DeHaven said he'd try, and this morsel of hope thrilled the Notre Dame campus.

"If matters can be properly adjusted," the student newspaper, The Scholastic, announced on Oct. 29, "a match game of football will take place on the senior campus about the 27th of next month… The Ann Arbor boys hold the championship of the West, and are such fine players that they will probably contend with the leading Eastern teams next spring for the college championship of the United States. However, there is good material here for a fine team, and the boys will undoubtedly give the Michigan players a hard 'tussle.'

Eventually a date was set for a meeting and a game. Brother Paul snagged a copy of a football rule book a shared it with a group of seniors who tried, for the most part unsuccessfully, to get a handle on the new sport. Making a stop on their way to Chicago, Michigan arrived at Notre Dame on Wednesday November 23rd at around 9am. After a 2-hour campus tour the Michigan men tossed on their lily-white uniforms and readied for battle. Here's what happened next, as described in Natural Enemies:

At about 11 o'clock the elevens trotted onto the slop, which we can only assume was somehow marked to proper proportions. Before the players were set to have at it, Brother Paul informed DeHaven that the Notre Dame boys – several of them former classmates of DeHaven's and Harless's – had had trouble playing by the book. Brother Paul then suggested the teams at first be mixed for a brief period of hands-on instruction. The Wolverines agreed.

"So, we played gently with them that day," DeHaven recalled, "…and carefully taught Notre Dame how to play modern football."

When the Notre Dame players learned just how physical this brand was, they took to it with reckless abandon. Too reckless, actually. One student in attendance recalled DeHaven and company having to caution their eager pupils against playing too violently.

After this brief tutorial, the players segregated into their proper squads and played a 30-minute game. When both sides finished slipping, rolling, and tumbling in the mud, Michigan tallied two touchdowns (worth four points each) to win 8-0. It was said the Notre Dame players, as well as the students in attendance, appreciated the fact the Wolverines did not try to run it up on their disadvantaged hosts.

So, there you have it. Want this and more? Put Natural Enemies on your shelf.

Now, go impress your friends at your respective tailgates / viewing parties on Saturday night.

Chapter 4 Notre Dame Football – The No Coach Years

Year	Coach	Record
1887	No coach	0–1
1888	No coach	1–2
1889	No coach	1–0
1890	No team	
1891	No team	
1892	No coach	1–0–1
1893	No coach	4–1

Circa 1890 Notre Dame Football Team

1887: As noted in Chapter 3, Notre Dame's football program began in 1887 with an unofficial match against Michigan, a reasonably close team by geography. The ND team was guided by the older players as there was no coach.

Michigan is credited with coming to Notre Dame for the purpose of teaching Notre Dame how to play football. It was a most gracious act; most appreciated by Notre Dame, and highly enjoyed by Michigan. Not unexpectedly Michigan prevailed in the 30-minute contest L (0-8). The scoring was much different than today.

From the moment that Michigan appeared on the field with their spanking new white, almost glistening uniforms, they looked every part the champs that they were that year.

In 1887, football as we know it was not completely defined. Association football, rugby, and even soccer were all having a major influence at the time on the college football rules and game play. For its first seven years, the "fighting Irish" football team had no formal coach. In fact, the whole idea of Notre Dame Football was so tentative that there were two years, 1890, and 1891, which would have been Notre Dame's fourth and fifth seasons. However, they were unable to field a team.

Surprisingly, we have the results of those seasons though not much is known about the fortunes of the early no-coach teams.

1888: Record 1-2; without a coach, Notre Dame sported its own brand new uniforms of brown and black. In muddy terrain, it was hard to tell the players from the ground. That season, the ND team of young men cheered: "Rah, Rah, Rah, Nostra Domina!" They finished the season with two more losses to Michigan L (6-26); L (4-10). The Michigan weekend was special. Michigan looked forward to coming to Notre Dame from how well they had been treated the year before. Notre Dame was a tough team and had just one year of football in them when Michigan came back.

Michigan had kept all of its opponents scoreless until ND scored a total of ten points in two days. The reports of the day say that it was a badly battered team that landed in the crowded Ann Arbor, Michigan train depot coming back from its weekend with Notre Dame. The team "received a proper razzing for breaking a four-year record" No Michigan football team returned to play at Notre Dame until 1942.

First Football Victory Ever for ND

Notre Dame managed to win its first game ever against a Harvard School located in Chicago. The Harvard line was no match for Notre Dame's players, who outweighed their opponent by an average of 23 pounds. Halfback Harry Jewett and captain fullback E.C. Prudhomme helped Notre Dame to a win W (20-0). It was the first football victory in school history. Little did anyone know at the time, that this was the beginning of a storied football program.

The Birth of the Rock

Irishlegends.com says that something else of major proportion was going on far from the football field. In Voss, Norway, Mr. and Mrs. Lars K. Rockne had a new baby named Knute. We Notre Dame fans well know that Notre Dame Stadium of today is the "House that Rockne Built." Well, the house building actually began in Norway.

1889: It was tough getting games in those first five years. With tongue in cheek, however, we can proudly state that in its third season of an infancy program, Notre Dame experienced its first undefeated and untied season. It was 1889. Notre Dame managed to schedule one game that year and won it W (9-0) against Northwestern.

1890, 1891: During the following two years, 1890, and 1891, no games were scheduled and none were played. Shorter than even the first season and the third, these two years brought Notre Dame its two shortest seasons of all time. In 1892, the ND team was back.

1892: Notre Dame came back in 1892 with one victory, one loss, and no ties. The restarting team again had no coach and played just two games. The scores of its games included a victory W (56-0) over South Bend High School on October 19, 1892, and a loss L (12-14) to Hillsdale College on November 24, 1892. It was so hard to get games with other colleges that ND would play high schools. Athletic clubs, and seemingly any group large enough to give them a game.

1893: Coach-less again, the 1893 Notre Dame football team played more games than ever. It was a successful season by any standard.

The 1892 team revived the game after a lapse of two years. Captain Pat Coady with the ball.

The team record was four wins and one loss (4-1). Moreover, Notre Dame had outscored its opponents in aggregate by 92 to 24.

The 1893 Fighting Irish, with almost double the number of players from 1892.
1893 Notre Dame Football Team Record 4-1

Its first four home victories were against Kalamazoo College W (34-0), Albion College W (8-6), DeLaSalle Institute W (28-0), and Hillsdale College (22-10). Then, on New Year's Day, 1894, Notre Dame traveled to Chicago. They played coach Amos Alonzo Stagg's Chicago Maroons. The soon to be "Fighting Irish," lost this one to the Maroons, L (8–0). Hey, folks, it was Amos Alonzo Stagg's team!!!! Few teams in those days would come close to victory v Stagg's boys!

Chapter 5 Notre Dame Football – Five Coaches in the Second Seven Years

Finally, both coaches and scheduled games

Year	Coach	Record
1894	J.L. Morison	3–1–1
1895	H.G. Hadden	3–1
1896	Frank E. Hering	4–3
1897	Frank E. Hering	4–1–1
1898	Frank E. Hering	4–2
1899	James McWeeney	6–3–1
1900	Pat O'Dea	6–3–1

1894 American Football Game

J. L. Morison ND Coach #1

Notre Dame was now established both within the institution and outside with other universities as an independent football school, ready to play a full season and ready to be successful.

The University upped the ante in 1894 by reaching into its finances to hire its first football coach. J. L. T. Morrison was hired in 1894 as the University of Notre Dame's first head football coach.

Morison resigned at the end of the season to become coach of the Hillsdale College "Dales." More than likely, he was asked to donate more than his salary for the good of the institution. Just saying. The football program was not well funded.

Nonetheless, Notre Dame's 1894 football season was its first with a formal head coach. With Coach James L. Morison at the helm, the team record was a very respectable 3–1–1. Notre Dame had outscored its opponents by a total of 80 to 31. The team celebrated victories over Hillsdale College W (14-0), Wabash College W (30-0) and Rush Medical College W (18-6). The team also played two games against Albion College T (6-6). L (12-19)—ending in one tie and one loss.

H.G. Hadden ND Coach # 2

In 1895, ND hired its second football coach. Coach H.G. Hadden took over from Coach Morison and handled the Notre Dame Football squad. Like Morison, Hadden lasted just one year. His team compiled a 3–1 record and overall did quite well, considering all the changes it was experiencing. ND outscored its opponents by 70 to 20. All games were at home in South Bend. The team played Northwestern Law School W (20-0); the Illinois Cycling Club W (18-2); and the Indianapolis Light Artillery L (0-18), and the College of Physicians & Surgeons of Chicago W (32-0). The only loss was in the third game to the Indianapolis Light Artillery.

1896 Frank E. Hering ND Coach # 3

Finally, with the 1896 team, Notre Dame had found a coach who would stay more than just one year. To do this, the university promised the coaching job to Frank E. Hering, who was also a player on the team. But, he was a bona fide coach—even paid for coaching.

In 1896, he became the team's captain and coach. ND compiled a 4–3 record. In the process, it shut out four opponents, and outscored its opponents by a total of 182 to 50. All of its games were played on the campus of Notre Dame.

On the way to its successful season, the team beat South Bend Athletic Club W (46–0), Albion College W (24–0), W Highland Views (82–0), and Beloit College W (8–0). It also lost three games to the College of Physicians & Surgeons W (0–4), Chicago L (0–18), and Purdue L (22–28).

1897 Frank Hering

With former captain and Coach Frank E Hering again at the helm, the 1897 Notre Dame football team enjoyed its second season with Frank E. Hering as coach. The ND squad compiled a 4–1–1 record by shutting out four opponents, tying another and getting a real dousing from Chicago. The team did well in scoring. In fact, ND outscored all opponents by a combined total of 165 to 40.

ND defeated DePauw University W (4–0), Chicago Dental Infirmary W (62–0), St. Viator College W (60–0), and Michigan Agricultural College W (34–6). Notre Dame also tied Rush Medical College T (0-0), and lost handily to the University of Chicago L (5–34).

Every year it seemed at least one team would appear on the schedule that made it difficult for ND to finish the season undefeated.

1898 Frank Hering

In 1898, for the third year in a row, Coach Frank E Hering took the Notre Dame team to a successful season. His team compiled a 4–2 record. In so doing the squad shut out four opponents, and outscored all opponents by a whopping total of 155 to 34.

The teams defeated included Illinois W (5–0), DePauw W (32–0), Michigan Agricultural W (53–0), and Albion W (60–0). Notre Dame was again playing Michigan and did not fare too bad in a 0–23 loss. ND also was defeated by Indiana L (5–11). In many ways, we see the beginning of the Big Ten teams playing Notre Dame. It had been some time since Notre Dame had played Michigan but things were about to change.

1899 James McWeeney ND Coach # 4

Frank Hering coached ND for the first five games of **1899** when the Notre Dame Football team turned over to Coach James McWeeney for the rest of the season. McWeeney was known as being abrasive and it may have had its effect on the morale of the team.

He did fine but stayed just half of one year as coach. His team along with the games coached by Hering compiled a 6–3–1 record. This was the most wins ever for Notre Dame and the most games played by a Notre Dame squad to that point. Football surely had become for real at Notre Dame.

In 1899, Notre Dame shut out five opponents, and outscored all opponents by a combined total of 169 to 55. They defeated Englewood High School, W (29-5), Lake Forest, W (38-0), Michigan Agricultural W (40–0), Indiana W (17–0), Rush W (17-0) and Northwestern W (12–0). They tied Purdue T (10–10), and lost to Amos Alonzo Stag's Chicago team L (6-23), Michigan L (0–12), and also the Chicago Physicians and Surgeons by L (0-5). The Michigan losses were by fewer and fewer scores. Soon Notre Dame was due to win a game from Michigan.

1900 Pat O'Dea ND Coach # 5

The 1900 Notre Dame football team was coached by first-year coach Pat O'Dea. McWeeney had signed up as assistant but his abrasive nature did not sit well with O'Dea and he did not last the full 1900 season. In its first season with Pat O'Dea as coach, ND compiled a 6–3–1 record. The squad shut out six opponents, and it outscored all opponents by a total of 261 to 73. The victories included Cincinnati W (58–0), Rush Medical College W (5–0), College of Physicians &

Surgeons W (5–0). Additionally, the Fighting Irish tied Beloit T (6–6), and lost to Indiana L (0–6), Wisconsin L (0–54), and Michigan L (0–7). The Michigan victories were closer and closer to becoming wins for Notre Dame.

Chapter 6 The First Eight Notre Dame Coaches of the 20th Century

1901	Pat O'Dea	8–1–1
1902	James Farragher	6–2–1
1903	James Farragher	8–0–1
1904	Louis Salmon	5–3
1905	Henry J. McGlew	5–4
1906	Thomas Barry	6–1
1907	Thomas Barry	6–0–1
1908	Victor M. Place	8–1
1909	Frank Longman	7–0–1
1910	Frank Longman	4–1–1
1911	John L. Marks	6–0–2
1912	John L. Marks	7–0

1901 – A Championship Season for Sure

Coach Pat O'Dea's 1901 Notre Dame Team was even stronger in his second year as coach. The 1901 Football season was a real championship season for the ND team. Notre Dame compiled an 8–1–1 record while shutting out six opponents. The team outscored all opponents by a total of 145 to 19.

Highlights of the season included a victory over Purdue W (12–6), Indiana W (18–5), and College of Physicians & Surgeons W (34–0). The team also tied the South Bend Athletic Club Y (0–0), and lost to Northwestern L (0–2).

Though this was not a national championship as this honor would not come until the 1924 season, it was the year (1901) for the most significant Fighting Irish team honor to this point. With an earlier win over Purdue, the Irish clinched the Indiana State Crown with an 18-5 impressive victory against the Hoosiers.

This was a real big deal for the team and the history of Notre Dame Football. In 1901, the Scholastic a great publication of and by Students at Notre Dame began to take a deep interest in football and their reporting over time has been excellent. Please enjoy the following excerpt, written by J. Patrick O'Reilly. It was originally published in the Nov. 23, 1901 issue of Scholastic, the Notre Dame University student magazine.

> *"Nine rahs for Coach O'Dea, Captain Fortin, and the moleskin heroes who struggled so nobly for the Gold and Blue; and on last Saturday won for us the championship of Indiana. For the first time in years, the much-mooted question of supremacy among the Indiana colleges has been satisfactorily settled, Notre Dame winning a clear title by defeating both Purdue and Indiana. The "Big Three" fight aroused great enthusiasm, and the race for the title was closely followed by every football enthusiast in the State.*
>
> *"Despite the drizzling rain which had fallen all morning, the field was in the best of shape. The two elevens were in splendid condition; about equally matched in weight, and both determined to win. The crowd was one of the largest and most enthusiastic of the year, and the rooting was of a high order. All in all, every requisite for a good game was present.*
>
> *"The game was one of the fiercest and cleanest ever seen on Cartier Field. There was no unnecessary roughness, and although every inch of ground was desperately contested, the officials were obliged to inflict penalties but twice. On the defensive, the State representatives displayed a stubborn resistance, but they were unable to impede the progress of our speedy backs, and their offensive tactics availed nothing against our impregnable line and alert ends, never retaining the ball longer than two or three downs. Their only touchdown was in the nature of a fluke, Foster securing the ball on a fumble during a scrimmage, and sprinting thirty yards to Notre Dame's goal while our men were extricating themselves from the heap. In marked contrast to Indiana's poor work was the brilliant defense and offense of our men. The linemen charged well and several times broke through and stopped plays behind the line. Sammon, Doran, Kirby and McGlew were irresistible on the offensive.*
>
> *"Sammon won new laurels by his sensational fifty-five-yard run through a crowded field. His line-bucking and punting were very much in evidence all through the game, and he established himself as a hero with the rooters, but he was not the only one. Pick's fearless tackling and work at center;*

McGlew's clever interfering and accurate passing, and the superb defense of the linemen. Gillen, Faragher, Winter and Capt. Fortin made the hearts of the rooters dance with joy. Doran and Kriby crashed and plunged through and round Indiana's line, making five and ten yards on every attempt, while their work on interference was the best of the season. Lins, Lonergan and Nyere, at the ends, were down the field on every punt and generally nailed the main in his tracks. Foster, Clevenger and Elfers were Indiana's stars. Clevenger and Foster tackled well and were in every play and under every rush."

1902 & 1903 James Farragher Coach # 6

First year Coach James Farragher took over the coaching duties for the 1902 Notre Dame football season. In his first season, Farragher's team went 6–2–1 and outscored all opponents by a total of 203 to 51. In compiling its 6-2-1 record, the team defeated Michigan Agricultural W (33–0), Indiana W (11–5), and DePauw W (22–0), and it enjoyed three other victories. Notre Dame tied Purdue (6–6), and lost to Michigan L (0–23) and Knox L (5–12).

In his second year as coach, Farragher's 1903 Notre Dame Football team had a great year with an 8–0–1 record. The Fighting Irish were at their best and they shut out every opponent, and outscored all opponents by a combined total of 291 to 0. Along the way, the team defeated Michigan State W (12-0), Lake Forest W (28-0), DePauw W (56-0), American Medical W (52-0), Chicago Physicians & Surgeons, W (46-0), Missouri Osteopaths W (28-0) Ohio Medical University W (35-0), and Wabash W (34-0).

1903 Notre Dame football team- The Shutout Season

Notre Dame also played Northwestern to a scoreless tie T (0-0). The defense was obviously at its best the whole season. The offense was led by Louis "Red" Salmon and Frank Shaughnessy with a massive 291 points scored. The following year "Red" Salmon would take over as coach for just one year

1904 Louis "Red" Salmon Coach 77

In his first and only year as Notre Dame coach, Louis "Red" Salmon took the 1904 Notre Dame football team to a a 5–3 record. It was not one of the best seasons for Notre Dame and their new coach. They were outscored by opponents by a combined total of 127 to 94. They had some good moments during the season when the team defeated Wabash W (12–4), Ohio Medical W (17–5), and DePauw W (10–0). However, they lost to Wisconsin (0–58), Kansas (5–24), and Purdue (0–36).

1905 Henry J. McGlew Coach # 8

The 1905 Notre Dame Football team was coached by Henry J. McGlew. The team compiled a 5–4 record and despite its mediocre record, Notre Dame outscored its opponents by a combined total of 312 to 80. The Fighting Irish defeated Michigan Agricultural W (28–0), American Medical W (142–0), and DePauw W (71–0), but lost to Wisconsin L (0–21), Indiana L (5–22), and Purdue L (0–32).

The American Medical game was on Oct. 28, 1905. Notre Dame turned in its greatest offensive performance of all-time, defeating American College of Medicine and Surgery of Chicago, 142-0. The Fighting Irish scored 27 touchdowns, and the game was called after 33 minutes of play, meaning the offense averaged 4.3 points per minute.

1906-07 Thomas Barry Coach # 9

The 1906 Notre Dame football team was coached by another first-year coach, Thomas Barry. Barry coached the team to a 6-1 record with wins against Franklin W (26–0), Hillsdale W (17-0), Chicago Physicians & Surgeons W (28–0), Michigan Agricultural W (5–0), Purdue W (2-0), and Beloit W (29-0). Additionally, ND was defeated by Indiana L (0–12)

This season was the first played under the authority of the IAAUS (now known as the NCAA) and the first in which the forward pass was permitted. There were no national champions declared. Though two teams that had won all nine of their games -- the Princeton Tigers and the Yale Bulldogs were looked upon as the best. The Tigers and Bulldogs played to a T (0-0) tie to end the season.

Thomas Barry again coached Notre Dame in the 1907 Notre Dame College football season. The team won six games again; had no losses and one tie. The wins were against Chicago Physicians & Surgeons W (32–0), Franklin W (23–0), Olivet, W (22–4), Knox W (22–4), Purdue W (17-0), St. Vincent's, W (21-12). The team also played a tie game against Indiana, T (0-0).

Deadly Injuries was of deep concern to the IAAUS. In 1907, the forward pass was used more extensively after being legalized the year before. Despite what some called "debrutalization" reforms, an unprecedented eleven players were killed (9 high school and 2 college). Ninety-Eight others were seriously injured. Yale had the best record that year (10-0-1). Again, no clear national champion was named.

There was already concern that every man was not good enough to start every football game for Notre Dame. And so, in the December 2006 Scholastic, this tribute was written:

T h e Scrubs.

T H E crowd cheers loud for the regulars,
Who have made the Varsity team,
For the men who have swept the football field
And stood in the limelight's gleam,
But little it knows of the silent men,
Of the lads who take the rubs,
Who work their best to advance the team—
Hurrah! for the Varsity scrubs!

The regular man feels well repaid,
When he hears the voices true
Of a thousand lusty college lads,
Who cheer for the Gold and Blue
But they show a love that is deep at heart,
The men who fight like cubs,
When there's no return. And it's ours to shout,
"Hurrah! for the Varsity scrubs."

T. E. B.

1908 Victor M. Place Coach # 10

Victor M. Place became coach of ND in 1908 and directed the team to an 8-1 highly successful football season. Notre dame secured victories against Hillsdale W (39-0), Franklin W (64-0), Chicago Physicians & Surgeons W (88-0), Ohio Northern W (58-4), Indiana W (11-0), Wabash W (8-4), St. Viator W (46-0), and Marquette W (6-0). Always having trouble with rival Michigan, Notre Dame lost the game L (6-12).

The Penn Quakers and the Harvard Crimson both finished the season unbeaten, each with a tie. The LSU Tigers went unbeaten and untied against weaker opposition. Nonetheless all three teams were declared national champions retroactively by various organizations. Only Pennsylvania's Quakers officially claims a true national championship for the 1908 season.

In December, 1908, Notre Dame had been playing football for twenty-two years. The first mention of football in the Scholastic was in 1901, eight years prior. Nobody had taken the time to capture the full story of how football not only got its beginning with the kindness of the Michigan "lads," but also to how the sport had grown in prestige to the 1908 season. Joseph T. Lantry made up for that oversight in this wonderful short piece.

Football History of Notre Dame

From the ND Scholastic Student Newspaper, December, 1908 by Joseph T. Lantry

> *On a November day in 1887, when the husky pigskin warriors of Notre Dame were still in swaddlings, the Michigan University Football Team came to play the local Varsity. This was the first*

contest in which Notre Dame ever engaged. At that time the oval was just being introduced into the University. It was necessary for the men from Ann Arbor to play a preliminary game in order to show the local men the style of game. In this preliminary game the players formed two teams irrespective- of their colleges. This taste of real action which the home men received, seemed to round them into shape, for they held Michigan to an 8-0 score. That same year two games were played between these same colleges. Michigan won both battles, though it is related that the referee won the second contest for the Ann Arbor men.

The following year but one game was played. The Harvard school of Chicago was the opponent of our Varsity in a mediocre contest. In 1889 Notre Dame played its first football game on a foreign field against Northwestern University at Evanston. Our boys' came home with a victory and many battered heads. Cartier, Coady and Prudhomme were the stars for the Hoosiers. In 1892 only one game was played, a tie with Hillsdale on Thanksgiving day. The punting of Quinlan averted a defeat for the Varsity. In 1893 football received a new impetus by the scheduling of more games. Notre Dame succeeded in winning" every contest. Every season since then the Varsity has had a heavy schedule.

The real founder of football at Notre Dame was Frank E. Hering. The team that he built up in 1895 was the one that placed Notre Dame among the leaders in Western athletics. Our noted fighting spirit was born under his captaincy. Acting both as captain and coach he developed such players as Mullen, Farley, Eggeman and Harley. Upon his retirement he was succeeded as coach by McWeeney in 1899. This same true-blue McWeeney still helps to trim up winning teams to battle for the Gold and Blue.

In 1900 a red-headed candidate reported to Coach O'Dea on Cartier Field. Not many days passed before the local critics began to take notice of his work on the scrubs. He was a demon at ploughing through the line, a fierce tackier and a consistent punter. In addition he had the one essential of a great player, brains. The Ann Arbor game as well as the Beloit game elicited high comment upon his work. The following fall the reputation of Red Salmon spread throughout the football world. Every opponent feared and respected him. Against Yost's crack team at Toledo he carried the ball consistently and persistently by short line-bucks from Notre Dame's five-yard line to Michigan's three yard line. The account of every contest from that time to the end of his career is studded with the name of "the mighty Salmon."

When Salmon's term was finished the glory of Notre Dame somewhat declined, due no doubt to the fact that the previous teams were built so closely around that column of strength. After two seasons during which the teams representing the college played fair football, Tom Barry was selected as coach. His achievement needs no comment. Under his skillful direction Notre Dame soon reasserted herself in the list of Western rivals. This year's work under Place [Victor M.] seems only to indicate the victories the future has in store for Alma Mater.

But in the years to come when the bonfires will light up the Brownson campus and the echoes of triumph make the old place tremble, and the men who are to come will celebrate their championship victories over Michigan, Wisconsin .and Chicago, we trust that some of the old-timers at least may recall the memory of the earlier heroes, of a Hering, a Farley, a McWeeney and a Salmon, the men who first set the example of N. D; prowess, and whose interest is still vested in the perpetuation of the honor and success of the Gold and Blue, A Pleasant Race.

Note from President Theodore Roosevelt in ND Scholastic:
Athletic sports, if followed properly, and not elevated into a fetish, are admirable for developing character, besides bestowing upon the participants an invaluable fund of health and strength.
Theodore Roosevelt. North American Review, August, 1890.

1909 Frank Longman Coach # 11

In 1909 Frank Longman took the coaching reins and directed Notre Dame to a 7–0–1season. The Fighting Irish football team's wins were against the following teams: Olivet W (58-0), Rose Poly W (60-11), Michigan Agricultural W (17-0), Pittsburgh W (6-0), Michigan W (11-3), Miami of Ohio W (46-0) and Wabash, W (38-0). Notre dame also played Marquette at the end of the season to a 0-0 tie, spoiling the opportunity for a perfect untied, unbeaten season.

During this 1909 IAAUS football season, the first 3-point field goal was kicked. They had previously been worth four points. Football deaths continued despite attempts to make the game safer. 1909 was one of the most dangerous seasons in the history of college football.

Ten players were killed and 38 seriously injured in 1909. This was up from six fatalities and 14 "maimings," in 1909. Schools in the Midwest competed in the Western Conference became known as the Big Ten. Notre Dame did not join. The teams at the time included Illinois, Indiana, Iowa, Minnesota, Northwestern, Purdue, Wisconsin and Chicago.

In 1910, Frank Longman continued as Notre Dame coach as the fighting Irish played a somewhat reduced schedule. Their record was 4-1-1 which included home victories at Olivet W (48-0), Buchtel W (51-0), and Ohio Northern W (47-0). The Irish also defeated Rose Poly W (41-3) in Terre Haute, IN, lost to Michigan Agricultural at East Lansing, MI L (0-17), and tied Marquette in Milwaukee W (5-5).

In 1910, the association became known as the NCAA and again, there was no clear-cut champion in Division I football.

From the Notre Dame Scholastic Magazine, December 1910

The [1910] Season and the Men.
By ARTHUR HUGHES, II . {Athletic Editor, Scholastic).

The football season for the year 1910 was not as propitious as was the season of 1909.. Last year Notre Dame closed the season Champions of the West. This year she failed in this respect. There were six games played. Out of this number were four victories, one tie game and one defeat. The defeat was suffered at the-hands of the Michigan Aggies. Marquette played us to a 5-5 tie on Thanksgiving Day and we vanquished Olivet, Buchtell, Rose Poly and Ohio Northern. Not a great amount of honor was won through our victories, for the teams defeated were vastly our inferiors in every way as the large scores indicate. In the Michigan Aggies' game at Lansing the team for some reason failed to play up to its standard, and as a result the M. A. C. men pla3'^ed havoc with ever}'- department of the Notre Dame representation. Michigan's cancellation of the Notre Dame game made it impossible for the team to show its strength and ability when playing in its usual form, for there is no doubt whatever but our men would have put forth a far better struggle than they did the week previous at Lansing. The men felt the sting which was administered by the Aggies, and they put in the following week working like demons in order to show their real strength at Ann Arbor. The game with Marquette brought out the ability and power of the team, for in that game ever)'- man in the line-up gave an exhibition which astonished the local fans and spectators at Milwaukee.

Last year the material for a championship team was a great deal more in evidence than was the case this season. While the men got out and fought hard for positions there were not the number of heavy, experienced men in the squad; and it is this that makes teams which get into the first page with their accomplishments. In addition to this, the absence of Billy Ryan and Don Hamilton proved a big factor in weakening the team. Had not Ryan's bad knee and Hamilton's being declared ineligible kept these men out of the game there might have been a different story to relate after the Michigan Aggies' contest. With the end came the close of the football careers of six men on the team: Joe Collins, Ralph Dimmick, George Philbrook, Lee Matthews, Luke Kelley, and John Duffy. The first five of these men were players on last year's team, and they have bade farewell to a branch of athletic sports in which they stood among the best.

1911-12 John L Marks Coach # 12

The 1911 Notre Dame coach was John L. Marks 6–0–2, who would last just two years. The eight-game 1911 schedule featured little glamor but the Fighting Irish were happy to play.

In 1911, the games were against Ohio Northern at home, W (32-6), At St. Viator W (43-0), At Butler W (27-0), Loyola (Chicago) W (80-0), at Pittsburgh T (0-0) and St. Bonaventure at home W (34-0), at Wabash, 6-3, at Marquette T (0-0). Notre Dame out-scored them 216-6. The Big Ten biggies decided to stay away from Notre Dame as they did not want to get beat by such an "inferior team.".

According to Murray Sperber, author of the 1993 book, "Shake Down the Thunder: The Creation of Notre Dame Football," the football program netted a loss of $2,367 dollars, and the total deficit in the athletic department that academic year was $6,472. Notre Dame had little money but an awful lot of heart. Would athletics last at Notre Dame was the question of the day.

In 2012, Notre Dame's John L. Marks in his second season delivered an undefeated and untied 7-0 season… the first. But, there was little room for a major celebration. With the apparent boycott from Big Ten teams that did not want to get beaten by teeny Notre Dame, this 2012 season was less appealing than 2011. The best that ND could do with such a low budget and the disdain of the Midwestern Universities was to add a few local schools such as Adrian and Morris Harvey. But, the ND team played well and won anyway.

The games included St. Viator at Cartier Field W (116–7), at Adrian W (74–7), at Morris Harvey W (39–0), Wabash at home W (41–6), at Pittsburgh W (3–0), at St. Louis W (47–7), at Marquette W 69–0).

1912 Notre Dame Football Team John L. Marks, Coach

Fitting tribute to the team of 1912 as written in the Scholastic:

The Season Just Closed. by
William E. Cotter 'Class of 12, (Manager of Athletics).

Success is intoxicating. And to one intimately associated with those responsible for the successes of the past football season, a review is apt to contain indications of intoxicating influences. Success of the highest grade came to the Notre Dame team of 1912. If the following record of the team's work appears to abound in superlatives, the excusing cause is that nothing less than superlatives can adequately express the conquests of the season. Hailed

Hailed as one of the two or three teams possessing any logical claim to the Western Championship in football; with a record of seven games and seven victories. during the season; • with a total of 389 points scored on opposing elevens against 27 points tallied by opponents; with the championship of Indiana conceded even by prejudiced observers; with our captain recognized as one of the best since the days of Eckersall, Coy, Heston, and Steffen, and our fullback the almost unanimous choice of football experts of the West for the All-Western team; with five Notre Dame men nominated for the All-Indiana team and almost as many picked for second All-Western elevens by a number of different authorities—with all this as the result of the 1912 season, is there any reason why we should not feel triumphant over the work of our football warriors?

With the- exception of the- championship year of 1909, Notre Dame has never had reason to feel so proud over the gridiron efforts of her sons, as during the past season. In many respects, the 1912 season has been more successful than that of 1909. Recognition, long withheld, has been granted in a manner that stamps Notre Dame as one of the football leaders of the West. A foundation has been established in public opinion upon which future teams may build high and strong, secure in the knowledge that 1912 affords the basis for the highest efforts.

In seeking the secret of the season's returns one is confronted by a variety of causes, all of which are deserving of a share of praise. The personal influence of Coach Marks and the willing aid rendered b}' his assistants, Philbrook and Dunbar; the example afforded by Captain Dorais ' and the other veterans who labored indefatigably to perfect the

1912 machine; the loyal strivings of the "scrubs " who bore up under daily scrimmages that meant daily punishments in order that the Varsity might gain strength by their offerings; and the spirit of the students which manifested itself this year in a manner never before beheld at Notre Dame— all of these elements were potent factors in bringing about our success. Not alone to "good football " in the technical sense must our success be credited—loyalty, good sportsmanship, perfect harmony in the squad, willingness to sacrifice personal advancement for the welfare of the team combined to bring to the players of this season the honor that is theirs and to reflect upon their Alma Mater the glory that is hers.

Coach Marks is deserving of more than passing, mention. A Dartmouth player of the present generation, and hailed as one of the best backs in the country during his three years in the eastern school, Marks brought to Notre Dame all the football knowledge the East afforded. Interested solely in the welfare of the team, and sincerely earnest in his desire to develop an eleven worthy of the material at hand, the coach brought out all the strength of all the candidates. His unassuming earnestness won the good will of the players, and his confidence in their ability inspired performances worthy of any team in the land.

Assistant coaches Dunbar and Philbrook rendered splendid service in the drilling of the line, and their work in connection with the second team merits no small credit, because of the important part played by the "scrubs " in strengthening the Varsity.

The Marquette game at Chicago, Thanksgiving Day, provided a fitting end for the football year. Victories over the University of Pittsburg, St. Louis University, and Wabash College heralded a conquest in the closing contest, but not even the most sanguine Gold and Blue follower hoped for the decisive result that ended the three-year tie existing between Marquette and Notre Dame. In Chicago, St. Louis, and Pittsburg our alumni showed their loyalty to Notre Dame in a manner that will be long remembered by the members of the team. Not until • we leave the University can we truly appreciate the love borne by her sons for all associated with her advancement in any field.

Only two members of the 1912 team will be graduated-this year, and the nucleus of experienced players that promises to be here on the field in 1913 insures an eleven that is certain to repeat this year's successes. Crowley and- Rockne are: the men who will go from us in June. • Both have given their best to the "teams of the past three years, and both have -won high honors on the gridiron. All-Indiana nominations -were won by them last season, and this same honor this year, with the additional honor of selection for several All-Western second teams; brings recognition which will give life to the memory of two of the best ends ever developed at Notre Dame.

All said, the year of 1912 will go down in Notre Dame football history as among the most successful ever recorded. We have been fighting against misinterpretation for the past four or five seasons, and so were denied an opportunity to meet our logical opponents. The brighter day that we have been looking for is about to dawn, we feel sure, and Notre Dame will soon come into her own.

The Short Story of a Successful Season.

ND 116	*St. Viator College,*	*7*
ND 74	*Adrian • College, 7*	
ND 39	*Morris -Harvey Col,*	*0*
ND 41	*Wabash College 6*	
ND 3	*Pittsburg University,*	*7*
ND 47	*St. Louis University,*	*7*
ND 69	*Marquette Univ., 0*	
Total 389		*27*

Chapter 7 Coach Jesse Claire Harper

Coach # 13

A Big-Time Notre Dame Historical Hero

1913 Jesse Harper 7–0
1914 Jesse Harper 6–2
1915 Jesse Harper 7–1
1916 Jesse Harper 8–1
1917 Jesse Harper 6–1–1

No money; no football

Many of the facts in this section were derived from the following very informative online article. Check it out when you have the opportunity. http://www.und.com/sports/m-footbl/spec-rel/082913aad.html

Football had surely become a popular sport among the student body as well as the Holy Cross priests in Notre Dame's community. However, the Notre Dame program was going no place nationally and regionally. This brought the future of the team into question. ND Football was at a crossroads.

It was obvious to those who handled the money, the Holy Cross Fathers, the student body, and the folks in South Bend that Notre Dame had to either get out of football or make a full commitment. Eliminating football had become an unappealing if not unacceptable option so the choice was made by simply defining the choices.

Notre Dame President Rev. John W. Cavanaugh opted for the future of the program. He hired the 29-year-old Wabash head coach Jesse Clair Harper as the school's first athletics director. As a small school, the ND athletic department had previously been operated by student managers. Harper would be the first full-time coach in football, baseball, and basketball. He was a great athlete. He would also be the Athletic Director, which was the toughest of all his jobs. His salary, including bonuses, could rise to as much as $5,000 per year.

A young Jesse Harper in his University of Chicago letter sweater. He was a star halfback for Stagg's excellent teams in the early part of the century.

Harper knew sports and he really knew the game of football. He had played for and was a disciple of Amos Alonzo Stagg. Coach Stagg had developed a reputation as college football's grand master in innovation while he coached at the University of Chicago.

Meanwhile, Harper was no slouch. He was a great choice. As head coach, he had been making his own mark at Wabash College, including seeing his out-manned "Little Giants" lose only 6-3 to Notre Dame in 1911.

Harper's secret ingredient for the CSC Fathers was that he had a strong background in business administration. With this background, Harper knew very well that Notre Dame "had to make football pay for itself." He was determined to make the program self-sufficient. Of course, to a bunch of priests with more pocket than wallet, this was music to their ears. They immediately liked Harper's thinking.

Jesse Harper was the right man at the right time for Notre Dame. He was never heralded like the great coaches of the more modern era but he was as responsible for Notre Dame being on the map as much as anybody else in history. He preceded Knute Rockne but in fact, he was the guy who hired Rockne. He stood in the shadows of many but he was responsible for much. He brought a lot of God's sunshine to Notre Dame. He brightened the campus with his positive attitude and can-do demeanor.

He was born close to ND's main campus on December 10, 1883 in East Pawpaw, Ill., just 80 miles west of Chicago. He went to school in Chicago at Morgan Park where he starred in football. He graduated from the University of Chicago, where he was coached by the great Amos Alonzo Stagg.

As good as he was, and he was good—Harper always seemed to be overshadowed by somebody. He played halfback and quarterback at the University of Chicago, He played behind three-time Walter Camp All-American, Walter Eckersall (1904-06). During his senior year in 1905, Chicago was declared the "Big Ten" champion after the team snapped Michigan's 56-game unbeaten streak.

Stagg knew how good of a person and how great an athlete Harper was. When Jesse graduated in 1906, Stagg helped make sure he got the head coaching position for Harper, then 22 years old at Alma College in Michigan. He brought the Alma Scots to a winning season in his second year (5-1-1).

Jesse then coached at Wabash College in Indiana where he eventually encountered Notre Dame in a (3-6) defeat in 1911. Back then Notre Dame was referred to simply as the "Catholics." Though they were always a tough lot and won most of their games, for reasons of the times, the Catholics were not held in high regard by their collegiate "peers."

Notre Dame liked Harper's coaching abilities as they observed in the ND-Wabash game and they also liked the fact that he had a sharp mind and was an astute business man. ND Administration hired the 29-year old Harper as the school's first athletics director.

As noted, he made just $5000 with bonuses and as previously noted, nothing was easy. He also had to coach the basketball and baseball teams and go on their away games Of course for five years, he also coached ND football and did very well from 1913 to 1917.

His football record was (34-5-1). In basketball, it was (44-20) (.686); and baseball (61-28) for an overall 139-53-1 mark (.723). Not too shabby.

Before Brian Kelly, the Irish would have been pleased to have found a Jesse Harper as their head football coach. This Jesse Harper had three other full-time jobs at Notre Dame.

In 1913, with Jesse Clair Harper as the coach, Notre Dame was full of the good kind of pride that continues as its hallmark today. This young coach scheduled some powerhouse games and he directed Notre Dame to an undefeated and untied season (7-0).

Harper had a great player on the team who made All-American that year. The player's name was Knute Rockne. Many would agree that even more important than the great season Harper delivered was the new Notre Dame schedule he had negotiated. Harper worked hard to assure Notre Dame got to play great teams so that its wins meant more.

Jesse Harper enjoyed his time with Notre Dame and he helped the University until he retired in 1917. During his tenure, the Irish stopped playing high schools and trade schools and began playing only intercollegiate games. The Fighting Irish record was admirable with a record of 34 wins, five losses, and one tie.

This period also marked the beginning of the rivalry with Army and the continuation of a rivalry with Michigan State. The objective for

Harper of course was to gain respect for a regionally successful but small-time Midwestern football program.

The new AD / coach was able to schedule games in his first season with national powerhouses Texas, Penn State, and Army. How could Harper have pulled this off? He was smart. He had guts. And most of all, he had a lot of Notre Dame spirit. That is basically it. Jesse Harper did not know the word, "No!"

Two major factors combined to make the 1913 meeting with Army possible. Army had been stiffed by Yale. They were deemed not good enough to compete with Yale by Yale, a major Eastern superpower football team. Yale broke off its series with Army that had been played for 20 consecutive years from 1893 through 1912. Army therefore had a "hole" in its schedule. Jesse Harper knew it was his job to fill that hole with a team named Notre Dame. He did.

Another reason besides Harper's determination was that Notre Dame was in the midst of its scheduling crisis. Once the ND team had finally upset Michigan in 1909, it made the "Catholics" more shunned by the Big Ten. The Big Ten had formed in 1896 and nobody in the BIG Ten wanted to be beat by a little team.

1913 ND v Army

Harper was a diplomat. Through his intelligence and persistence, he eventually broke the Big Ten ice. He added Wisconsin to the 1917 schedule, followed by Purdue in 1918. Indiana and Northwestern were added to the slate by 1920. While Notre Dame's cache of great teams to play was growing under Harper, the great AD and great coach Jesse Harper turned it all over to another great football man, Knute Rockne, in 1918.

Rockne got the reins and the keys in 2018 from his boss, Jesse Harper who was ready to move on in life. Harper's family had a farm and Jesse wanted to go home, which was not too far from the ND campus to enjoy the country living and the occupation he desired.

Though Harper stood tall during his years, nothing is ever perfect. There were numerous and continued rejections and setbacks for Harper during this process of turning around his Big Ten adversaries. Yet, this great man had many negotiation victories that sweetened the experience. For example, Harper gained a $6,000 gate guarantee to play at Nebraska five years in a row from 1916-20. Having a means to finance the team was as necessary as building a great team to help build up the finances.

Scholastic Athletic Notes

This is an excerpt of the athletic notes from the ND Scholastic for November 7, 1913, Jesse Harper's first year as coach. The Penn State Game was ND's closest game played in this year and so here are the game notes:

> *Penn State has been beaten by Washington and Jefferson, Harvard, and Penns3dvania this 3^ear, and b}' larger scores than the Varsity beat them, but all three of Penn's previous losses were sustained in the enemy's territory and to teams unwearied b} ^ wearing travel. Besides this, Penn had determined to make good for its previous poor record in its first big game a t home. Furthermore, it was Penn Day—the big day - for their college. But notwithstanding all Penn's incentive to fight, the Varsity went in to win, and succeeded in doing so, the final count being 14 to 0.*
>
> *The game held particular interest because. Dorais, who is acknowledged to be the best quarterback in the West, was pitted against Miller, the Penn quarterback, who was mentioned by*

several critics last year for All-American. We would naturally be inclined to consider our own man the better, and although we have no doubt of Dorais' superiority, we choose to bring in a non-partisan critic to state our convictions. The following from the Philadelphia Evening Bulletin is our exact sentiment.

BILLY MORICE AT LEAST SEES OVER THE ALLEGHENIES

Billy Morice says that the best quarterback in America is Dorais, the Notre Dame pilot. Morice was a visitor at Franklin Field the other afternoon, and he boosted the little Notre Dame lad to the skies. 'He's the best quarterback in the country,' said Morice. 'I go all over the country officiating, and I will say that he is the king of them all this season. He can toss that pass like a baseball. He throws it, he flings it right at the man; he does not lob it so that while a fellow is waiting to get it, someone else comes along and nails him.

He runs with the ball in front of him like Fred Geig, the Swarthmore coach did when he played. That enables him to shift it to either arm, and-use the other arm to straight-arm off a tackier. He is a great open field runner, and, above all other things, he is a great field general. There is nothing in the East as good as Dorais, and while a few of the critics will not see him play, and they may miss him in their selection, I'll take him as my selection.' — Philadelphia Evening, Bulletin.

Dorais was particularly brilliant in his open field running in the Penn game, returning punts from Tweiit}" to thirty-five yards regularly, and once he caught the ball on the thirty-yard line and carried it the length of the field:—dodging practically every member of the Penn team— for a touchdown, only to be called back because he stepped out of bounds when catching the ball.

Penn State won the toss and kicked to Dorais who returned the ball fifteen yards. The ball see-sawed from one eleven to another, Penn gaining most of its yardage on fake end runs while line-

smashing proved our forte.. The Varsity grew dangerous toward the end of the quarter, but were unable to score.

The second quarter proved to be more exciting. Penn State worked the ball down to midfield only to lose it on downs. Miller punted to Dorais, and after a couple of plays Penn recovered a fumble within striking distance of our goal. Lamb dropped back ' for a field goal, but his trial was smeared by Lathrop who blocked his kick. When the Varsity recovered the ball, it uncorked a little of its old life, displaying the form that won victory for them at West Point. A well-executed forward pass from Dorais to Pliska was carried down the field forty yards. Dorais followed immediately with a thirty'-five-yard end run, and another pass, Dorais to Rockne, put the ball the entire length of the field in three plays for a touchdown.

Even more exciting times were in store during the third period of play. Displaying their brilliant form, the Gold and Blue warriors received the ball from Penn on the kick-off and never lost possession of it until they had carried it all the way down the field for a second score. Line bucks, principally by Eichenlaub, but also some of very material assistance by Pliska and Finnegan, were responsible for three-fourths of the yardage on this wonderful incursion.

Forward passes were almost invariably called back because of oft"-side plays, or were smeared by opposing interference.

A few were successful, however, and these and end rims account for the rest of the distance. Dorais, whom we are beginning to believe infallible with his toe, kicked goal. The Varsity received the kick again and worked, the ball past the middle of the field, but our backs began to tire and the ball was punted to Miller who was downed immediately.

Then a series of fake end runs by Miller, interspersed by line bucks by Berryman and Tobin, brought the ball within fifteen yards of the Varsity's goal, when the only successful Penn forward pass put the home team across our goal for their only score of the da}'-, making the score 14 to 7, where it remained till the end of the game.

Knute Rockne, End & Gus Dorais, QB for Jesse Harper 1913

By1914, Harper had signed even more great teams to road games. Yale was # 1 in the national rankings at the time. ND played Yale at Yale in 1914 but lost L (28-0). Yale had a much better passing scheme that the Fighting Irish, a fact that did not go unnoticed by Harper, an astute coach like Rockne.

ND also played Syracuse on Turkey day at Syracuse and won that game W (20-0). The Fighting Irish have recently renewed their series with Syracuse and are scheduled to play on October 10, 2016 at Met Life Stadium in NJ to accommodate a better crowd.

The Harper 1914 team record was 6-2 with home wins over Alma W (56-0), Rose Poly, W (103-0), and Haskel W (21-7), The Irish won three away games at South Dakota W (33-0), Carlisle, @ Comiskey Park in Chicago W (48-6), and Syracuse in Archbald Stadium at Syracuse W (20-0). The Irish also suffered two big losses -- Yale at the Yale Bowl in New Haven L (0-28), and Army at West Point, NY L (7-20).

The 1915 team record was 7-2 with home wins over Alma W (32-0), Haskel W (134-0), and South Dakota W (6-0), The Irish won four away games at Army W (7-0), Creighton in Omaha W (41-0) Texas at Austin W (36-7) and Rice at Houston TX W (55-2)

1915·Notre·Dame·Football·Season··Coach·Jesse·Harper

The Irish also suffered one very close loss the first time the Irish met the Nebraska Cornhuskers at Nebraska Field in Lincoln, NE L (19-20).

Jesse Harper’s 1916 team record was 8-1 with home wins over Case W (48-0), Haskel W (25-0), Wabash W (60-0) and Alma South Dakota W (6-0), The Irish won four away games at Army W (7-0), Creighton in Omaha W (46-0). Away victories were Western Reserve at Cleveland W (48-0) South Dakota in Sioux Falls W (21-0), Michigan Agricultural in East Lansing W (14-0) Additionally ND picked up its first win on the road ever against the Nebraska Cornhuskers at Nebraska Field in Lincoln, NE W (20-0)

Unfortunately, the one loss in this 8-1 season came against the Black Knights of Army right in the middle of the season, game 5. On November 4, Notre Dame traveled to West Point and lost L (10-30) against Army.

The 1917 team record represented Jesse Clair Harper's last season with Notre Dame. The Fighting Irish were 6-1-1 with home wins against Kalamazoo W 55-0), South Dakota W (40-0), and Michigan Agricultural W (23-0) The three away wins included Army W (7-2), Morningdale in Sioux City, IA W (13-0) and Washington &

Jefferson in Washington, PA W (3-0). They had one loss, which was against the Nebraska Cornhuskers at Nebraska Field in Lincoln, NE L (0-7). The Irish also tied Wisconsin at Camp Randall Stadium in Madison Wisconsin on October 13 T (0-0).

Jesse Harper; coach who hired Knute Rockne

Jesse Harper scheduled the 1918 season's games after he had hired Notre Dame's new Head Coach Knute Rockne, who had been his assistant. Rockne did pretty well in his first year as coach after Jesse moved on.

Years later Harper's son James noted this about his dad: "When he went to Notre Dame he found it difficult to get games with teams in the Midwest because the Fighting Irish had an excellent team and people were afraid to play them." This quote was made long after Jesse Claire Harper had coached at Notre Dame. "He was literally forced to turn to "intersectional games." The son continued:

"Dad was a modest guy. He never wanted to take credit for getting Notre Dame started as a national power. I remember he told me once: 'Well, Lord, I was forced to get a national schedule. No one else would play us around Notre Dame. I had to go someplace where I could get some ballgames." Let's take a break about Jesse Harper briefly and talk about the ND Army Series which continued long after Harper.

The Army Series against Notre Dame would itself make a great book and probably a better movie. We share some of the facts in this chapter. Jesse Harper is the unsung hero who helped Notre Dame's greatest hero, Knute Rockne become a hero. He worked for Notre Dame, the University, Notre Dame, the football team, and Notre Dame the players.

Coach Jesse Harper & ND Player Knute Rockne

This tale is worth telling in a coaches' book

As noted previously, Army needed a game and Notre Dame was willing to travel. Harper was not the only ND coach that had to travel to play Army. In fact, until the 1947 game, Notre Dame's long list of great coaches after Harper agreed to travel every year from 1913 to 1946.

Army was home every game. Sometimes, since the Black Knights had such a small stadium, their home field was often was a larger "neutral" east coast venue such as Yankee Stadium, the Polo Grounds and even Shea Stadium when it was built.

Ironically, the first ND home game in South Bend against Army was in 1947. After delivering two major "home: thumpings in a row at Yankee Stadium L (0-59) and L (0-48) to Notre Dame in 1944 and 1945 right near the end of the war when Army had its best teams, The Black Nights tied the Irish in 1946 T (0-0).

Army went to Notre Dame for the first time ever, after 33 years of "home" play. The teams played every year during this period except for 1918. As we know, World War I ended November 11, 1918. When Army came to Notre Dame in 1947, they were defeated W (27-7).

After the ND home win, following the 1947 season, the teams did not play during what has been called a ten-year hiatus. It has been reported that Army made the decision to end the annual series after 1947 because they felt it was becoming too one-sided in favor of the Fighting Irish. The last game of the series was played in South Bend for the first time and the Fighting Irish prevailed, W (27–7).

This is out of sequence for the book about coaches that is told in sequence, but I think you will enjoy this 1947 story from Scholastic, Notre Dame's Student Magazine. If you like this one paragraph, you may take the link to this issue of Scholastic

http://archives.nd.edu/Football/Football-1947s.pdf for it is without a doubt, a fine book, and a free book for those who want to read more about the fantastic Fighting Irish in their 1947 Championship Season. You may even like it more than this book—well, maybe equally. Here is one paragraph written by Jim Butz, more than likely a 1947 Notre Dame Student, about one game – Army from 1947:

> *"The death knell for Army hopes was sounded in the opening 18 seconds by Terence Patrick Brannan who gathered in Mackmull's kickoff on his five-yard line with a fine over-the-shoulder catch and threaded his way 95 yards down the west sidelines to score. Brennan was aided by some fine blocks thrown by Jim Martin, George Connor, Bill Fischer, and Bill Walsh, but he used each block skillfully and picked his way through until he reached his 25 from where he simply out-ran everyone. Earley added the seventh point as the crowd went delirious with joy at the prospect of an Irish scoring orgy."*

The Army / ND series was picked up again in 1957 and has been off and on ever since with both teams taking turns for home game games. Notre Dame played Army again in 2016 on November 12, in San Antonio Texas. In an otherwise dismal season, Brian Kelly's 2016 Fighting Irish dominated Army 44-6.

Now, let us move on with the Jesse Harper Notre Dame / Army Saga continuing from 1913. Historians and Notre Dame fans admire

Jesse Claire Harper for helping Knute Rockne make Notre Dame Stadium the House that Rockne built. The hard facts suggest that without a sharp guy like Harper coming to Notre Dame when he did, Rockne would have had few materials with which to build the House.

Harper was relentless and there was no email or text messaging back then. So, he did what he could to communicate with the fine teams that he hoped would play the Fighting Irish – home or away. He went on a letter-writing campaign. For 1913, he received positive responses from Army, Penn State, Texas, South Dakota, Ohio Northern, Christian Brothers of St. Louis and Alma, where he had formerly coached. From the eyes of many, Harper had already succeeded.

Let's go back again to Army as this was a real coup and it is fun to recount. The meeting arrangements against powerhouse Army had begun during the spring of 1912. Jesse Harper was the varsity baseball coach. The Notre Dame baseball team had made a successful excursion along the East Coast. From May 9-22, 1912. Harper was finishing up at Wabash until the end of the 2012-2013 Academic year but it did not stop him from writing and writing and writing.

Notre Dame played baseball games at West Virginia, Penn State, Mount St. Mary's, Catholic University, Seton Hall, Brown, Deerfield Academy, Tufts and Vermont before returning home. Harper took over as baseball coach while on the road to book some football games. He was the Notre Dame Head Coach in football, basketball and baseball from 1913-17. He was the baseball coach and he used his baseball contacts to help Notre Dame in all ways.

The Army Cadet (Black Knights) football manager at the time was Harold Loomis. He got his letter from Harper to schedule a contest as soon as possible. Loomis was ready. He offered Harper $600 to come to West Point. Unfortunately, the train ride would cost about $1000 for the Train tickets to transport all 18 members of the traveling squad the 875 miles to West Point. Harper asked for full expenses from Loomis. Loomis reluctantly agreed to pay the $1000 for the 24-hour train ride from South Bend.

"My letter to West Point," Harper recalled later, according to author Frank Maggio, "arrived at a time when the Army-Yale series ended somewhat abruptly. And the Cadets had an open date." Army agreed to a Nov. 1, 1913 game, and offered Harper the $600 revenue guarantee but as noted upped the ante to $1000.00

Chicago Tribune Nov. 16, 1913

JESSE C. HARPER, COACH, TRAINER, AND ATHLETIC "POOH-BAH" AT NOTRE DAME.

When New Director Found Conference Colleges Would Not Grant Football Dates He Scheduled Contests East and West for His Charges.

Article as it looked in the Chicago Tribune – High on Jesse Harper

By the way, Frank Maggio in 2007 wrote a great book about Jesse Harper. Like me, Maggio is impressed with the historical Jesse Claire Harper. His book has a long title: *Notre Dame and the Game that Changed Football: How Jesse Harper Made the Forward Pass a Weapon and Knute Rockne a Legend.*

Though desperately wanting to close the deal for the game, Harper could not afford to lose money on the travel arrangements. The coach knew that he did have one thing that gave him an edge in getting the $1000.00. A number of Eastern college teams had already refused to play Army in light of its admissions policy.

West Point used its own set of rules for recruiting and did not pay attention to the NCAA. After all they were the US Army and the US was in a long war that was just ending. Army recruited football players who had exhausted their eligibility at another college, and to help soldier morale, West Point gave them three more years of varsity play.

Academy officials said they needed the extra time to train officers to fight in wars. Here is an outrageous example: Army halfback Elmer Oliphant played three years at Purdue before graduating in 1914. He was a two-time, first-team All-American at West Point in 1916-1917, and entered the College Football Hall of Fame in 1955.

Army's recruiting practices finally grated on the Naval Academy so badly that in the late 1920s, Navy refused to play Army. How about that for some great half-time trivia at the next ND game? Navy would not play Army!

Harper had a lot of jobs at ND as discussed. As the Athletic Director, the budget was very close to his heart. ND was so strapped for cash that the team had to cover its own "food expenses" when it traveled to Army. They ate sandwiches that were prepared in the Notre Dame campus dining hall.

Additionally, the boys had to carry their own equipment. Things were tough? How tough? It is reported that only fourteen pair of football shoes were made available to 18 Notre Dame players. Many of the substitutes in the two-way (Defense & Offense) player "rotation," had to use the shoes that were on the feet of the players coming out of the game. There was no guarantee that the shoes would fit.

The trip to West Point cost $917, and so ND had in fact made an $83 profit. Using the Alan Shepard quote as a basis to describe this phenomenon, we would characterize ND playing Army as "one small step for Notre Dame ... one giant leap toward helping brand its name, especially with the stunning W (35-13) victory."

THE LIFE OF KNUTE ROCKNE 11

Another view of this same game when Notre Dame defeated West Point 35 to 13.

As noted above, even later in November, Notre Dame would add a great cap to its season with victories at Penn State W (14-7), at Christian Brothers in St. Louis W (20-7) and at Texas W (30-7) to finish 7-0. Because of the great work of Jesse Harper, Notre Dame's football program was literally and figuratively ahead of schedule.

News from the June 1918 Issue of Scholastic

> *—The Faculty Board of Athletic Control recently gave a dinner to Coach Jesse C. Harper, who has resigned and intends to retire to his stock farm in Kansas. Coach Harper was presented with:, a monogram shield, and the board voted to give him the right to wear the Notre Dame-Monogram and elected him.a member of the Notre Dame Monogiram Club. Father Cavanaugh made the only farewell address at the dinner, presenting the monogram and lauding the famous coach, whose work may be judged by the splendid results he has obtained for Notre Dame teams during his five years as coach. Mr. Harper responded with a short talk in which he expressed his gratitude to Notre Dame, and stated that there was no honor in the country which he would appreciate more than the right to wear the N. D. Those present at the dinner, which was held in the Infirmary dining room, were the Faculty Board of Athletic control,— Fathers Quinlan, T. Burke,*

Maguire, Crumley, Professors Farrell, Benitz, and Coach Rockne, Harper's old running-mate, and Fathers Cavanaugh, Schumacher and J. Burke, representing the administrative body of the University.

Just after their return from the Michigan [baseball] games, the baseball team presented Harper with a suitcase, as a testimonial of their gratitude to" the coach that-produced one of the best teams that Notre .Dame has "seen in years.

Jesse Harper waited until June, 2018 to turn in his resignation. It was not like today. ND was not worried about coaches / recruit signing days and such. Why did Harper wait so long to turn in his resignation as the ND head Football Coach? The answer is simple. His job for the year was not finished.

You may recall that Mr. Harper was not only the football coach; but also, the head basketball coach, and the head baseball coach of the University. Not only that but he was the Athletic Director. Today each of these positions has one or several people operating within the positions. Harper was heading back to the family farm in Kansas. Can it be said that after five years of holding four jobs, and with such a great record in football with Knute Rockne and Gus Dorais as his teaching projects, Harper may have been worn out and needed a break?

Chapter 8 Knute Rockne, ND Football Coach— 1918-1930

Coach # 14 --- But, coach # 1 of all time

Three Consensus National Championships 1924, 1929, 1930; Five undefeated and untied seasons!

A Great Record

1918 Knute Rockne 3–1–2
1919 Knute Rockne 9–0 *
1920 Knute Rockne 9–0 *
1921 Knute Rockne 10–1
1922 Knute Rockne 8–1–1
1923 Knute Rockne 9–1
1924 Knute Rockne 10–0 *
1925 Knute Rockne 7–2–1
1926 Knute Rockne 9–1
1927 Knute Rockne 7–1–1 *
1928 Knute Rockne 5–4
1929 Knute Rockne 9–0 *
1930 Knute Rockne 10–0 *

*** == National Champions**
1919 & 1920 National Championships were retroactively awarded to Notre Dame post facto. At the time, there was no one group that had the authority to determine champions right after the season.

Who could ever achieve such a ran overall record, anywhere—even High School?

This inserted piece introduces Knute Rockne to the reader. It was written by Dan Schofield, an analyst for Bleacher Report and the whole article can be found at Http://bleacherreport.com/articles

The True Story of Knute Rockne, College Football's Most Renowned Coach

By Dan Scofield, Analyst
Oct 2, 2009

This piece is a dedication to one of the founding fathers of college football, Knute Rockne. The University dedicated a handsome bronze statue to their legendary coach on Friday, October 2nd 2009 at Notre Dame Stadium.

Knute "Rock" Rockne Famed Notre Dame Coach

"The 'Swede'

This story begins in a municipality of Voors, Norway, a quiet village surrounded by snow-cap mountains, cedar forests, and rivers flowing through valleys.

It is here where a young boy, Knute Rockne, was brought into the world on the evening of March 4th, 1888.

A mere five months later, the Rockne family made their way across seas to begin a new life in the bustling city of Chicago. Here, young Knute was introduced to the game of American Football on the neighborhood streets.

Growing up, Knute had a variety of interests—chemistry being a large one.

With his chemistry books and labs in hand, the Norwegian hopped on a train heading to South Bend, Ind. He would spend the next four years of his life at the University of Notre Dame.

He found his way around campus and soon walked into the office of polymer chemist Julis Arthur Nieuwland. Trying to make his name in the world of chemistry, Rockne took the position of laboratory assistant to the famous chemist himself.

At the time, Rockne attended the university, students were required to participate in a sport. With experience in the game from his high school days at North West Division High, where he played end, it was an easy choice for the underclassman.

1910 marked one of the few times of failure during his life. He was cut from the team for being undersized.

It was one of the turning points in his life, as the man never gave up. He used this rejection as a form of motivation, and from 1911 to 1914, he played left-end for the Fighting Irish.

Rockne left the university w an undefeated playing record, 22-0-2.

The Legend Begins

A year after graduation marked the beginning of the greatest coaching career in the history of college football.

Jesse Harper, whom Rockne played for the previous season, hired him onto the staff as an assistant coach.

The two coaches were seemingly opposite of each other—Harper was more mild-mannered while Rockne had a different attitude than anyone before his time.

Warnings were not a word in his vocabulary book. He believed players would begin to think warnings did not mean much.

Instead, full punishment was given out on the first offense.

Off the field, Rockne became a favorite around campus. Players were soon coming to Rockne's office instead of Harper's with personal problems because of the close relationships the players had developed so quickly with their new "peer" coach.

After a 28-0 defeat, the first Irish loss in four seasons, Harper decided to make a change. He knew Rockne had a football mind like no other, and he used that to the team's advantage.

Before a 1916 game against Wabash, Rockne was asked to fill in for the ill coach. This marked the first time one of Rockne's famous, fiery pep talks echoed throughout the campus. He ended the emotional talk with, "Now go out there and crucify them!"

Notre Dame beat Wabash that day, 60-0.

1918-1930—The Legend Himself

At the end of 1917, Harper called "The Swede" into his office. He gave him the news that he wasn't going to be able to coach the team the next year, and named Knute as his successor.

At 30 years old, Knute Rockne stood on the sidelines of Notre Dame Stadium, clipboard in hand and dressed in full uniform, as the head football coach of the Fighting Irish.

On his first day on the job, he made his mindset known—and loud:

"Win or lose, I'm running this team. Nobody else has anything to say about it's make-up, it's plans, it's type of play. It's my show. If I flop, let 'em pan me. If we're a hit, let 'em say anything they want. I worked

hard around here as an assistant for many years, and seldom saw my name in print. Well, all I want now is the truth".

From day one, the legend began his quest for truth and never looked back.

During his 13-year career, Rockne posted a record of 105 wins, 12 losses, and five ties. He lead the Irish to five seasons of undefeated football with zero ties.

Six of those victories won Notre Dame national championships.

His career record gives him the title as college football's all-time winning percentage leader at 88.1 percent.

The Coached Legends

Throughout his career, he coached players and turned some into legends themselves.

Despite no previous football experience, Rockne recruited George "The Gipper" Gipp to play for his team in 1916.

He finished his career with 83 touchdowns and never let a single pass be completed in his protective zone defense. During his four-year career for the Irish, he lifted the program to fame and notoriety.

Unfortunately, Gipp's career was cut short after contracting a serious strep infection in a game against Illinois. He died a few weeks later on December 19th, 1920.

In a game that seemed almost un-winnable for his injury-decimated team, Rockne delivered one of the most famous speeches in all of sports, "Win One for the Gipper."

Rockne told his team: "The day before he died George Gipp asked me to wait until the situation seemed hopeless—then ask a Notre Dame team to go out and beat Army for him. This is the day, and you are the team."

"One-Play-O'Brien's" scored the winning touchdown as the Irish defeated Army, W (12-6).

Other legends followed in the footsteps of The Gipper.

Don Miller, Jim Crowley, Elmer Layden, and Harry Stuhldreher possibly made the greatest mark during Rockne's time at Notre Dame.

After the "Four Horsemen" led a 13-7 upset win over an elite Army team, Grantland Rice put pen to paper and published some of the most famous journalism lines in college football history:

"Outlined against a blue-gray October sky, the Four Horsemen rode again. In dramatic lore their names are Death, Destruction, Pestilence, and Famine. But those are aliases. Their real names are: Stuhldreher, Crowley, Miller and Layden. They formed the crest of the South Bend cyclone before which another fighting Army team was swept over the precipice at the Polo Grounds this afternoon as 55,000 spectators peered down upon the bewildering panorama spread out upon the green plain below."

The Rock's First Season

1918 Notre Dame Ramblers
With Gipp, Rockne, and Lambeau

Jesse Harper scheduled the 1918 games after he had hired Notre Dame's new coach Knute Rockne. Rockne's first team won its first game against Case in Cleveland Ohio W (26-6). It won its second game against Wabash in Crafordsville, Indiana W (67-7). In the third game against Great Lakes Navy, ND managed a tie T 7-7). Following this game Rockne suffered his first loss as coach of Notre Dame, L (7-13) against Michigan Agricultural.

The team bounced back for its third win against Purdue in West Lafayette, IN W (26-6), Coach Rockne's first team finished the 1918 season with a tie against Nebraska in Nebraska Field, Lincoln, Nebraska. The Knute Rockne legacy was only beginning to begin.

Coach Rockne and ND Players

Here is a perspective from the December 1918 edition of the ND Student Newspaper, Scholastic. This was Rockne's inaugural season and things were not so good but he had the abilities of a great coach, trained by Jesse Harper with his own God-given talents, and he persevered and made it all OK:

From Scholastic, December 1918

Notre Dame Football, 1918. A thing is considered a success if the results are commensurate with the time and energy expended. This fall the Notre. Dame football team had but little time for practice, but used up myriads of units of energy. What have the men of the team to show for this? First of all, they have played a man's game well. In addition they have learned to think; they have forged friendships which will last throughout their lives; and they have developed loyalty, a loyalty to a mother University which can come only from fighting for her. To the football squad for their successful work of the' season the University gives homage. •

After spending the summer at Fort Sheridan Coach Rockne returned for the opening practice in the middle of September. The prospect was only fair. Vohs, Powers, Bader, Hoar, Kennedy, Dooley, and Brandy, men-on whom he had been depending, were all commissioned at Fort Sheridan [WW I]. The loss of these experienced players was a severe one, but the coach went ahead cheerfully to build a .team from almost entirely new timber. Gipp, Bahan, Stine, and Smith were the old men back, and their work, was later the salvation of the team. The rescinding of the freshman rule made every college student in the University eligible, and with this as an impetus the squad began to grow by leaps and bounds. Before the inauguration of the S. A. T. C. there were more than eighty men out in uniform. Most of' these were boys just out of high school.

Practicing twice a day until the formation of the Army units, the squad improved rapidly. Daily scrimmages began to bring out good men, and left the team for the Case game at Cleveland in good condition. •. Case was defeated 26 to 6. This game showed the coach just where the defects in team play were and also who was who in the personnel. Gipp and Bahan were the stars in the backfield; but what was most pleasing to the coach was the stonewall defense of the line. "While the play, as a whole, was more or less crude, it was a team of—possibilities. Their "come-back" in the second half [of the CASE game] showed that they had the make-up of a typical Notre Dame eleven.

With the mobilization of the. S. A. T. C. practice was greatly restricted, but .the boys worked with a will and showed steady improvement. Then began that series of disappointments which for a while threatened- to overwhelm athletics in general. The Educational

Committee of the War Department forbade long trips and the dreaded influenza began to make its presence felt. The West Point and the Washington and Jefferson games were cancelled and the Nebraska game moved back to the 2nd of November. With the scheduling of the great Pier game of Chicago and Camp Custer things began to readjust themselves. On Saturday, October 19, the Pier team made their appearance in South Bend, but there was no game. The influenza epidemic was at its height, and as the medical authorities thought it best to prohibit gatherings of any sort, the game was cancelled. : The game with Camp Custer was also called off. Football practice itself was even prohibited for a few days. Some days later the situation was so much better that the epidemic ban was lifted.

1919 Coach Rockne Year 2

The 1919 team was recognized retroactively as a co-national champion by the National Championship Foundation and Parke H. Davis. It helps to know that there were no championships for years after college football got is start.

When the associations decided that it was time to pick national champions, they also decided to go back and pick some based on their past records. Parke Hill Davis (July 16, 1871 – June 5, 1934) was the person selected to determine who the champions were, post facto. Davis had been an American football player, a coach and he was the historian who got the job to retroactively name the national championship teams in American college football from the 1869 through the 1932 seasons.

In his role, also named co-national champions at the conclusion of the 1933 season. Davis' selections are included in the NCAA's official football record books, as the only championship teams chosen on the basis of research and so they are as official as there is.

1920 Coach Rockne Year 3

The 1920 Notre Dame Fighting Irish football team with Knute Rockne at the helm brought Notre Dame its second undefeated and untied season (9 wins, 0 losses) in a row. The team again was selected retroactively as the 1920 national champion by the Billingsley Report and as a co-national champion by Parke H. Davis. Knute Rockne sure knew how to coach a football team.

The George Gipp story in Notre Dame history goes hand in hand with the Knute Rockne story. Therefore, the Gipp / Rockne story deserves its own spot as we plow through Knute Rockne's thirteen seasons as ND coach. Gipp was born on my wife's birthday, which is also my dad's birthday and my niece Mary DeLucia's birthday.

The Kelly's always celebrate February 18th's birthdays. George Gipp was born February 18, 1895. He died tragically on December 14, 1920 after his last season with Notre Dame's 1920 championship football team. Since this was the last season that Gipp played before his death, we tell his story right here.

George Gipp

Gipp was as good as it gets and he was the first Notre Dame player ever to be declared a Walter Camp All-Americana. He is just Notre Dame's second consensus All-American (of 79). Gus Dorais, class of '14 the QB on the throwing end of Rockne's receptions, was the first. Gipp could play many different positions, but he was used most notably a halfback, quarterback, and punter.

Today, he is considered one of the most versatile athletes to play the game of football. For Notre Dame fans that do not know all of Notre Dame's storied history, who have not seen the movie, Knute Rockne is thought of as the Gipper. Gipp in fact was the subject of Rockne's famous "Win just one for the Gipper" speech. He died at the young age of 25 of a streptococcal throat infection, days after leading Notre Dame to a win over Northwestern in his senior season. May he rest in peace.

Gipp was simply a good athlete, entering Notre Dame to play baseball for the Fighting Irish. He was literally spotted by Coach Rockne during an Irish practice session and the Coach recruited him for the football team. Gipp had never played organized football. The story goes a punt landed out of bounds and a passer-by (Gipp) kicked the ball back onto the field so hard, so high, and so long that Rockne inquired "who was that that did that?"

In his three years of play with Notre Dame under Knute Rockne, Gipp was the leading Irish rusher and passer (1918, 1919 and 1920). His career mark of 2,341 rushing yards lasted for more than more than 50 years until Jerome Heavens broke it in 1978. Gipp's baseball style athleticism made him an ideal receiver for the forward pass.

He not only could catch, he could throw. He threw for 1,789 yards and he scored 21 career touchdowns. He averaged 38 yards a punt. He snagged five interceptions. And he even returned punts with an average of 14 yards per punt return and 22 yards per kick return. Gipp still holds the ND record for average yards per rush for a season (8.1), career average yards per play of total offense (9.37), and career average yards per game of total offense (128.4). What a guy!

In 2002, looking back at the best of the best in football, the NCAA published "NCAA Football's Finest," Gipp was a top entry on the list.

Two weeks after being elected Notre Dame's first All-American by Walter Camp and second consensus All-American overall, George Gipp died of a disease that is totally curable today. As medicine was not as perfected in the US as it is today for diseases such as Staph, the speculation is that after the season Gipp contracted strep throat and pneumonia while giving punting lessons. Since antibiotics were not available in the 1920s, treatment options for such infections were limited and they could be fatal even to young, healthy individuals. What a shame.

Thank God that this will never happen again. I am sure that George Gipp would offer his thanks, and I bet Ronald Reagan, who played George Gipp in the memorable Rockne movie would offer his thanks to God for giving the human race the ability to combat so many one-time fatal diseases.

Next time any of us are in the right place at the right time, let's remember we can always ask anybody to "Win one for the Gipper!" Who could ask for anything more?

1921 Coach Rockne Year 4

The 1921 Notre Dame Fighting with fourth year football coach Knute Rockne at the helm, compiled an impressive 10-1 record with the only loss coming by a score of L (7-10) at Iowa.

At the time, Grantland Rice wrote that "Mohardt could throw the ball to within a foot or two of any given space." Rice noted that the 1921 Notre Dame team "was the first team we know of to build its attack around a forward passing game, rather than use a forward passing game as a mere aid to the running game."

1922 Coach Rockne Year 5

The 1922 Notre Dame Fighting with fifth year football coach Knute Rockne at the helm, compiled another impressive 8-1-1 record with a T (0-0) tie coming on November 11, 1922 at West Point against Army. The team's only loss came by a score of (6-14) in the final game of the season at Nebraska.

1923 Coach Rockne Year 6

The 1923 Notre Dame Fighting Irish football team under Coach Knute Rockne had another great season. For the third year in a row, the team suffered just one loss. This time there were no ties. The loss came to Nebraska, a real nemesis to Notre Dame in the last several seasons.

1924 Coach Rockne Year 7

Among other greats, Rockne's 1924 Notre Dame team had four special people on the team. They were Harry Stuhldreher, Don Miller, Jim Crowley, and Elmer Layden. If their names sound familiar, it is because they played in the backfield on the 1924 Notre Dame undefeated and untied (10-0) season. Together these four great football players are known as the "Four Horsemen." The season topper was the victory over Stanford in the Rose Bowl.

The team was recognized as the consensus 1924 national champion, receiving retroactive national championship honors from the Berryman QPRS system, Billingsley Report, Boand System, Dickinson System, College Football Researchers Association, Helms Athletic Foundation, Houlgate System, National Championship Foundation, Polling System, and Jeff Sagarin.

The 1925 Rose Bowl was Notre Dame's last bowl appearance until the 1969 season. I think it is safe to say that anybody who was anybody in college football slotted the Notre Dame Fighting Irish as the number one football team of 1924 in all of the United States of America.

Notre Dame's Four Horsemen Hamming it UP!

Autographed Picture of the Four Horsemen of ND

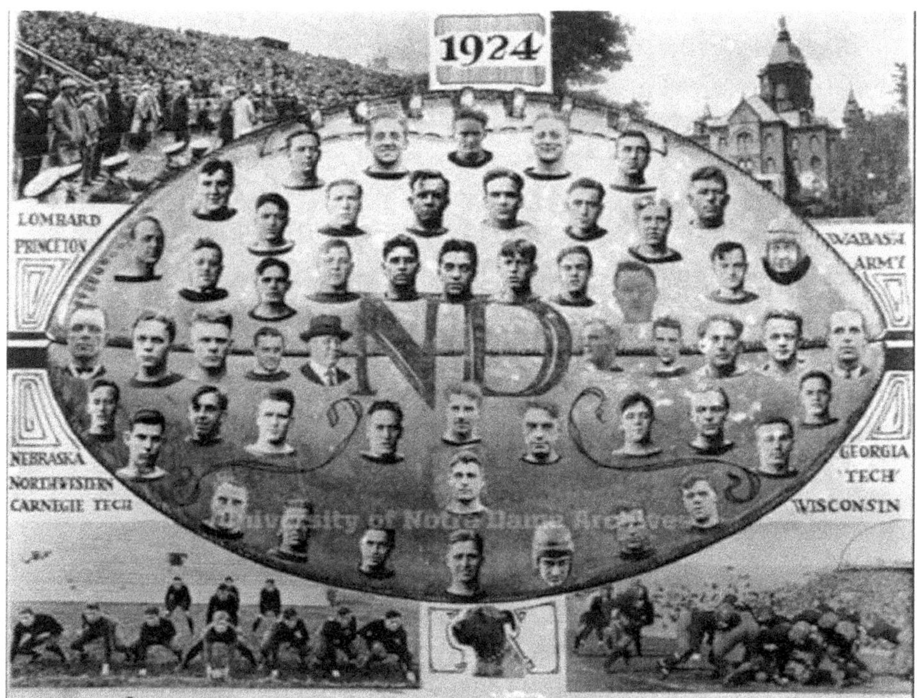

The Fighting Irish topped off its 1924 season in Pasadena California in the 1925 Rose Bowl before 53,000 fans. Notre Dame emerged victorious W (27-10) and finished its season undefeated and untied.

1925 Coach Rockne Year 8

Without the Four Horsemen, The 1925 Notre Dame Fighting Irish showed a respectable record of 7 wins, two losses, and one tie. The team was rebuilding from their consensus national championship of 1924. The Tie was played T (0-0) against Penn State in its new Beaver Field in University Park.

After this two-loss season in 1925, Rockne quietly agreed to take the head coaching job at Columbia for $25,000 - $15,000 more than his Notre Dame salary. When the agreement went public, much to his embarrassment, Coach Rockne decided to stay at South Bend.

1926 Coach Rockne Year 9

The 1926 9-1 Notre Dame Football Season under Coach Knute Rockne fought hard and did very well. An unexpected loss to Carnegie Tech L (0-19) in a game played at Pittsburgh spoiled the undefeated season. The Irish were held scoreless. Let me tell you the whole story about that loss.

Knute Rockne was not only the greatest coach of all time, he made what was known as, "The greatest coaching blunders in history". Instead of coaching his team against Carnegie Tech, as he thought it was in the bag, he put an assistant in charge. Rockne traveled to Chicago while the Carnegie Tech game was being played for the Army-Navy game to "write newspaper articles about it, as well as select an All-American football team. Carnegie Tech used this toward their advantage and won the game 19-0. The loss likely cost the Irish a chance for the national title. They would have been undefeated.

1927 Coach Rockne Year 10

The Rock's 1927 Notre Dame Fighting Irish football team finished at 7-1-1. Based on the difficult caliber of play, it was looked upon as a fine season. Illinois or Georgia was most often selected as the 1927 national champion by the selecting bodies despite the fine year had by Notre Dame. The Fighting Irish did have the distinction of retroactively being named as the national champion by one selector, the Houlgate System.

1928 Coach Rockne Year 11

The 1928 Notre Dame Fighting Irish football team was Knute Rockne's 11th season. It was the toughest, and least productive season since Rockne had become coach in 1918. At (5-4) the team was barely above 500 percent for the first time ever.

This 5-4 record in 1928 was clearly Coach Rockne's worst record ever. Nonetheless some history was made when Coach Rockne delivered his famous "Gipper Speech" at halftime. Rockne was trying to salvage something from his worst season as a coach at Notre Dame. To inspire the players, he told them the story of the tragic death of the greatest player ever at ND, George Gipp. Rockne could really motivate the troops. After this speech, Notre Dame looked like a different team.

Here's how that one went down in history: On November 10, 1928, when Rockne's Notre Dame team was tied with Army 0-0 at the end of the half, Coach Rockne entered the locker room and he recounted the words that he heard from George Gipp's lips while on his deathbed in 1920:

"I've got to go, Rock. It's all right. I'm not afraid. Some time, Rock, when the team is up against it, when things are going wrong and the breaks are beating the boys, tell them to go in there with all they've got and win just one for the Gipper. I don't know where I'll be then, Rock. But I'll know about it, and I'll be happy."

Rockne delivered this short speech as only he could. It fully inspired the team, which then went out and outscored Army in the second half and won the game 12-6. The phrase "Win one for the Gipper" was infused into the lexicon of American society and was later used as a political slogan by Ronald Reagan, who in 1940 portrayed Gipp in *Knute Rockne, All American.*

Rockne's Irish stormed onto the field in this famous game after the inspirational talk. However, it was Army that scored first in the second half. But, ND came right back. Jack Chevigny, who got Rockne's halftime message loud and clear then answered with a 1-yard plunge on fourth down, announcing "That's one for the Gipper!" he yelled out as he plowed into the end zone. Or so legend has it.

Notre Dame is a school blessed with many legends and the 1929 Gipper story is just one of them. But, that did not get the game won After Chevigny's plunge for a TD, ND was still tied 6-6 with Army.

The second legend from this game came when a real speedster from Los Angeles named Johnny O'Brien who had become a track star and held the world record for the 60 yard hurdles got his first chance to play football for Notre Dame. O'Brien was on the football team, but seldom played. He was on the bench for the whole game, until, in an inspired moment, Rockne turned to the fleet Johnny, and with the score 6-6 sent his speedster onto the field. Nice call, there, Rock.

The ball was snapped, the quarterback retreated and threw it in the general vicinity of Johnny O'Brien. Johnny got under the ball, caught it, and then quite literally, he sprinted as only he could into the end zone for the final 12-6 margin of victory.

Therefore, on this one day that the Irish won one for the Gipper, Johnny O'Brien made that ONE PLAY that ever after labeled him Johnny "One Play" O'Brien.

1929 Coach Rockne Year 12

Knute Rockne's 1929 Notre Dame Fighting Irish football team therefore made up for any losses from the prior year (5-4) and then some. During the season, Coach Knute Rockne fell ill, Tom Lieb, assistant coach in 1929, became in some respects the de facto head coach at times. Lieb helped Rockne's boys throughout the season to achieve their high success.

!929 ND National Champions

The team at 9-0, was undefeated and untied and it was selected as the 1929 national champion by Billingsley Report, Boand System, Dickinson System, Dunkel System, College Football Researchers Association, Helms Athletic Foundation, National Championship Foundation, Poling System, and Jeff Sagarin's ELO-Chess system. It was not an undisputed all-consensus championship but it was just about as good as it gets. It should have been consensus but various organizations had their favorites.

So, during the next season (1929) Notre Dame made a great comeback from 1928. But Coach Rockne got sick. He was diagnosed with life-threatening phlebitis in his leg. Consequently, he missed some games and at times directed the team from a wheelchair or a cot. As noted, the team went 9-0, punctuated by a 13-12 victory over powerful USC, and won the national title. Notre Dame followed up with a 10-0 record and another national championship in 1930 as Rockne regained his health.

Picture to the left: Former Notre Dame Star Jack Chevigny, who scored the winning touchdown in the Irish's famous 1928 "Win one for the Gipper" game against Army, later became Texas' head football coach.

The Story of Cartier Field, Rockne, & Notre Dame Stadium

Every football team needs a place to play. Cartier Field was a stadium in Notre Dame, Indiana. When it was apparent that Notre Dame was keeping football, as played the American way, it adopted Cartier Field as its football spot.

This tradition-rich field hosted the University of Notre Dame Fighting Irish football team from 1900 to 1928. It held just about 30,000 people at its peak. Considering that there were games before 1930 played at Soldier Field, that had actual attendance of 120,000, it was clear that a stadium that could just about hold 30,000 was inappropriate for a team that was reaching for the stars if not the heavens.

Notre Dame always had a problem with finances though Coach Jesse Clair Harper's five years helped Notre Dame's sports programs become self-sufficient. However, even Jesse's financial acumen could not squeeze one more person into Cartier Field even when it was clear that twice to four times that number of tickets could be sold per home game.

Moreover, when Coach Rockne was hired by Harper and took over the team, he knew that for the ND program to grow, its stadium needed to grow. This became known as Rockne's dream. The coach worked very hard to achieve his dream. He loved and appreciated Cartier stadium and would not let it disappear while he was at Notre Dame.

The Cartier stands had to be torn down after the 1928 season to make room for Notre Dame Stadium, which opened in 1930. Notre Dame, while building its new stadium had to play its entire 1929 schedule away from campus. Chicago, ninety miles north of South Bend, promised to help.

And, so, all Notre Dame home games were played at Chicago's huge Soldier Field. Nonetheless the Rockne led team went 9-0 and won the National Championship. At Coach Knute Rockne's insistence, Cartier Field's grass was transplanted into Notre Dame Stadium. Think about that.

For more than 30 years after the football team moved out, Cartier Field remained the home of Notre Dame's baseball and track and field teams. In 1962, as the University was growing and growing and it needed space, the original Cartier Field was replaced by a quadrangle adjoining the Memorial Library, which opened in 1963. Showing the sentimentality for the field, a new facility named Cartier Field was opened east of Notre Dame Stadium.

Since 2008, the Notre Dame Fighting Irish football team has held outdoor practices at the LaBar Football Practice Fields, and indoor practices at Meyo Field in the Loftus Center. Things change, mostly for the good.

By the way, one of the most integral athletic buildings on campus today is the Loftus Center, which serves as an indoor practice facility for several Irish varsity sports (football, track and field, rowing, women's soccer, men's soccer, women's lacrosse, men's lacrosse, baseball and softball). It also hosts competition for the track and field teams and lacrosse teams. The Center also features Meyo Field, a 100-yard Field Turf field with end zones surrounded by a six-lane track one fifth of a mile long - making it as large as any indoor track in the nation

Cartier Field had originally been named after Warren A. Cartier, an 1887 civil engineering graduate and former member of the football team. He had purchased 10 acres (40,000 m2) and donated it to the University for Establishment of the Field. He also paid for furnishing the lumber required to enclose the Field with fencing and furnished the lumber required for a grandstand. These human-interest stories that get to the heart abound in the Notre Dame archives.

The 1929 Football Review, a publication by Notre Dame officials, included a dedication by Reverend Charles L. O'Donnell, C.S.C., Ph.D., President of The University of Notre Dame. This Dedication commemorates the generosity and the appreciation of the dream of Coach Knute Rockne that ultimately resulted in what the world now refers to as The "House that Rockne Built."

Thousands of generous donors combined their efforts over the years prior to 1929 to make possible the new Notre Dame stadium, begun in 1929 and scheduled to be opened for the 1930 season.

Here is the President's dedication:

"*Every man who ever wore the Blue and Gold ·of Notre Dame, every member of the faculty, every member of the coaching staff, every loyal Notre Dame student, every faithful Notre Dame follower has done his share since the founding of the school to make this dream of Coach Rockne's a reality. To the known and unknown heroes ·who have contributed their bit in bringing about this new house for the warriors of Our Lady we offer our heartfelt thanks, and to these do we dedicate this account of the 1929 team, worthy successors to Notre Dame teams of the past.*"

Cartier Field in the 1920's

As previously noted, Notre Dame struggled to a 5-4 record in 1928. It was the team's worst mark ever in Knute Rockne's tenure as head coach. In 1929, Notre Dame came roaring back with more fight than ever. During the 1929 season, the Fighting Irish did not lose a single game and finished up at a perfect 9-0 record. The team could not play at Cartier Stadium because the construction of Notre Dame Stadium was set to begin.

Despite playing all nine games away from South Bend. Notre Dame outscored its opponents, 132-38. The Fighting Irish closed the season with a W (7-0) over Army at Yankee Stadium. In 1929, the Irish were one of four teams to end the season undefeated. Notre Dame finished before Dickinson in the rankings to earn its second national championship. This was the first of two consecutive titles.

Respect your Elder

On the und.com web site, Notre Dame posits a question for its readers: "What is the most overshadowed, underrated or overlooked play in Notre Dame Football history?" The writers answer their own question by suggesting that a good answer would be Jack Elder's school-record 100-yard pass interception return for a touchdown in the Nov. 30, 1929, Notre Dame-Army game. It is available to watch on You Tube https://www.youtube.com/watch?v=svDz5fxtyKk.

In the clip, Notre Dame's Jack Elder intercepts a pass from Army's Chris Cagle and returns it 100 yards for the touchdown and the 7-0 win against Army.

Notre Dame lists a number of factors that make this game special. Without the interception for example, ND may have tied Army and 1929 may not have been a championship season. Ironically this obvious fact is not the most unique factor noted.

Here is what ND has to say:

> "Think about all the factors in that contest where so much was at stake:
>
> 1. Last game of the season in front of a capacity crowd of 79,408 fans in New York City's esteemed Yankee Stadium.
>
> 2. The opponent was the archrival, the Army Cadets, whose coach, Biff Jones, had announced his departure after the 1929 season. Army was determined to send him out with a victory.
>
> 3. For the 8-0 Fighting Irish, who had played every game away from campus while Notre Dame Stadium was under construction, it needed to defeat Army to clinch a consensus national title.

The play by Elder tends to be overshadowed because too many other games in Notre Dame-Army lore seem to supersede it:

1930 Coach Rockne Year 13

The 1930 season the 13th year by Knute Rockne. No coach prior to this had ever coached so many consecutive years. This would be Rockne's last season. Everybody loved Knute Rockne and he could have coached at Notre Dame forever. This was another championship season as the Fighting Irish again were undefeated and untied and hailed a championship style 10-0 record. The Irish were consensus national champions.

Notre Dame was very excited and ecstatic about playing the 1930 season because the team now had a stadium that looked as good as the revered stadiums of its most staunch foes. This was the first year that the Fighting Irish played its home games in Notre Dame Stadium, which quickly became nicknamed as *The House That Rockne Built!*

Early the next year in March, Knute Rockne received a lucrative offer to help in the production of a Hollywood movie, "The Spirit of Notre Dame." It would not take him away from coaching per se, and it would more than likely be good for the school. Traveling to Los Angeles on March 31, Rockne was killed when his plane crashed in a pasture near Bazaar, Kansas. Knute Rockne was 43.

Rockne Plane Crash March 1931

With all the research, I accomplished about Jesse Harper and then Knute Rockne, I was actually brought back to this past era as Notre Dame first struggled for its identity in football and then it mastered the game and became champions of the United States, which by the way was the only country playing American style football.

I studied each of Coach Rockne's seasons and I first noticed that the 1929 season had no home games before I realized that Rockne's dream of a Notre Dame Stadium instead of the rag-tag Cartier Stadium was about to happen. All the while, I knew that the beloved coach had passed away for real in a plane crash in 1931 after the 1930 National Championship season—the one season played at Notre Dame Stadium. The one which we just discussed.

Brian Kelly's Personal Note on Rockne Tragedy

By Brian Kelly the author, not the ND Coach

"Like watching the Titanic when we all know the plot and how it ends, I knew the plot when I first began this part of my research. I knew that at the end of one of these great Notre Dame Football seasons, though I enjoyed the research about each one, the great coach—the star of all these seasons—would meet his fate.

"I knew from the start that Knute Rockne, a great man, whom I had begun to know well from the history that I was learning, would one day go down in a field in Kansas. I knew that his era at Notre Dame would end while his legacy continued. It made me sad and weepy just thinking about it. And, finally, the moment I dreaded most so far in writing this book is here. I now have to write about it. Knute Rockne is dead! Long live the memory of this great human being and great coach!"

Knute Rockne had been a very celebrated and highly successful coach at Notre Dame. Many to this day say he was one of a kind, and they are right. After being hired by Jesse Clair Harper, whose also a great coach but whose expertise clearly was in being able to schedule big games when ND was reasonably unknown, Rockne was able to shine his own light and the light of Notre Dame.

The "Rock" continued Harper's tradition of playing the best teams in the nation and he brought home a number of undefeated and untied seasons as well as more national championships than anybody ever if we can claim all the disputed titles for US, the ND faithful. There was nobody like Knute Rockne and though great ND coaches have come and gone over the years since Rockne, there still have been none who were as consistently great.

Tribute Picture from the April Edition of ND Scholastic Student Magazine

In March 1931, head coach Knute Rockne (ND class of 1914) boarded Transcontinental and Western Air Flight 599. It was headed to Los Angeles so that the coach would be able to participate in the production of a new movie titled, "The Spirit of Notre Dame." Tragically, the plane went down a few miles west of Bazaar, Kansas, killing Rockne and the other seven on board.

After leading Notre Dame to back-to-back national championships, Rockne's death, every citizen in the United States knew him. The news devastated the university community and shook the United States. President Herbert Hoover declared it "a national loss."

Irish head coach Ara Parseghian when interviewed about Rockne's death recalled that in his own childhood, at the time he found out about the Irish coach's passing, was distraught. Like everybody else in the nation, the young Parseghian was devastated. One of the finest coaches ever, Parseghian's days at Notre Dame were yet to begin."

A Review of Knute Rockne's life:

In 1918, that little guy born in Vonn Germany that we discussed earlier in this book, had now grown to be a man. He was living in South Bend, Indiana. His name of course is Knute Rockne, and he came to town to make sure Notre Dame kept playing great football.

Knute Rockne was one of Jesse Harper's players on the Notre Dame team in the famous 1913 season. Rockne signed up for a Notre Dame education almost four years earlier. He had taken a four-year hiatus after dropping out of high school and like many in those times, he worked to survive.

Though he did not graduate from high school because he had a habit of cutting class to practice his track skills, four years later, he was able to enroll at Notre Dame. During those four years, Rockne worked in the Chicago post office as a mail handler and dispatcher. Two of his friends were about to enroll at Notre Dame University in South Bend, Indiana, and they encouraged him to join them at the Catholic school.

An intelligent and talented student, and much more mature four-years out of high school, Rockne was accepted and worked as a janitor in the chemistry department to help pay his expenses. Soon, he began to play for the football team in 1911 as a fullback and left end. After four years of chemistry and football, he would graduate from the University of Notre Dame magna cum laude in chemistry, one of the toughest majors.

Though Rockne was mortified as a freshman when he was deemed not good enough to make even the scrubs and he was cut from the football team, the Rock kept at it. Along the way, in spring 1914, he broke a few records on the Track Team. The following autumn, he tried football again and made the team. After that, he excelled as a player in football and track at Notre Dame. He was an end but played other positions also. Rockne was an athlete.

In his senior year in 1913, he won All-American honors under Coach Jesse Harper. Rockne spent a lot of time as an older player on the team, working with quarterback Charlie Gus Dorais on various innovative forward pass techniques. The two practiced all the time. During the summer of 1913, both were preparing for their senior year. They practiced the forward pass while working as lifeguards on a beach in Ohio. Rockne had a mission that came directly from coach Harper. He had to learn how to catch the ball with his fingers.

Receivers in football are taught that the ball should not bounce against the arms and chest when a pass is received. They learn quickly that there are too many opportunities for fumbles that way. Moreover, such a catching technique forces a cut in stride and it limits the opportunity to advance during / after the catch. Jesse Harper watched Rockne catch the ball and he knew that "Rock [naturally caught] the ball in his stomach, and I told him he had to learn to catch it with his hands"

Jesse Harper took some issue with those telling the story of the dedication of QB Dorais and End Rockne practicing their passing on the beach. He countered that it was not really passing on the beach. Yes, Harper admitted the two would practice on the beach for hours at a time, running the ball mostly in the sand. This toughened their leg muscles. Though they did toss the ball around a bit on the beach, overall, they perfected their passing act on a turf field nearby. Practicing on the turf helped them not only learn how to pass and catch as a cohesive unit, it also helped to get their timing down pat—just like it would have to be in a game.

With Harper's instruction, Rockne thus patterned himself after a baseball player. Through hard work, he learned how to catch the ball with his fingers. Rockne often repeated the phrase like a litany: "Mobility, Mobility and change of pace. That´s what we need. They're not going to know where we're going or when we get there". Ask the 1913 Army team.

In other words, unlike an outfielder in a baseball game camping out for a fly ball, receivers had to be moving and shaking around the field so the ball could be caught in full stride with open relaxed hands. Willie Mays' breadbasket catch would not do nor would "medicine ball stuff."

Dorais and Rockne worked hard all the time to be the best they could be. They established timing patterns in their pass routes so they knew where the other and the ball would be. They knew if there would be a curl back or a dead stop. Practice makes perfect. Nothing worth having or doing is easy. With the forward pass, itself in such an infancy in football, more than likely, nobody ever saw as many possibilities for passing options as much as Dorais and Rockne. Eventually, the duo believed that there were infinite possibilities. Army in 1913 simply did not see it coming

On Nov. 1, Notre Dame met Army for the first time in West Point, N.Y. Led by head coach Jesse Harper, the Irish debuted the forward pass. Their offensive scheme surprised the Cadets and shocked the sporting world. It helped counteract Army's size advantage. Dorais was almost perfect, completing 14 of 17 attempts to Rockne for 243 yards

Notre Dame literally stunned the much bigger and more experienced Army Cadets with an offense that featured both the expected Notre Dame powerful running game but also their new and innovative long and accurate downfield forward passes from Dorais to Rockne. Dorais was a smaller player but he had a powerful, accurate arm, and Rockne had taught himself how to catch the ball with perfection. This game was the first major contest in which a team used the recently legal forward pass throughout the game so frequently that it secured their victory.

Rockne as a student and student lab technician, and lab mop-up guy, at Notre Dame was educated as a chemist. He graduated in 1914 with an advanced degree in pharmacy, without ever getting a high school diploma. After graduating he was the laboratory assistant to famous polymer chemist Julius Arthur Nieuwland at Notre Dame.

While making a buck in this profession. Rockne helped out with the football team.

Rockne loved football and rejected further work as a chemist after receiving an offer to coach football. Coach Rockne used his chemistry background to come up with the formula to create a great football strategy. Each year, with a new class of recruits and lots of solid veteran players, the coach got to perfect his formula.

Rockne's coach, Jesse Harper stepped down as head football coach after the 1917 season, announcing in 1918 after baseball season was completed. Harper returned to ranching in his home state of Kansas. Jesse also found oil on his ranch. His land was not far from where Knute Rockne's plane crashed in 1931.

Harper was so close and such a friend of Knute's that he accompanied Rockne's body on the train from Kansas back to South Bend, Indiana, for the funeral and burial. The University of Notre Dame immediately asked Harper to fill Rockne's role as athletic director. Harper agreed to help out Notre Dame. He held the position until 1934, when Elmer Layden, one of Rockne's "Four Horsemen" became ready to become head football coach and athletic director.

Rockne was assistant coach; played professional football after graduation

When Rockne finished his college football playing days and graduated magna cum laude in chemistry at Notre Dame in 1914, Jesse Harper hired him as assistant coach, a position he held until he became head coach in 1918. Since the pros played on Sunday, Rockne was able to play professional football.

It will make more sense reading the next few paragraphs if I tell you first about *Peggy Parratt,* admittedly a strange name for a male football legend. George Watson "Peggy" Parratt, was born March 21, 1883; and died January 3, 1959. He was a professional football player and coach when Rockne was a college player. Parratt played in the "Ohio League" prior to it becoming a part of the National Football League.

Over the years, Parratt played quarterback for the Shelby Blues, Lorain Pros, Massillon Tigers, Massillon All-Stars, Franklin Athletic Club of Cleveland, Akron Indians and the Cleveland Tigers between 1905 and 1916. He was a player, coach, owner, and promoter. Perhaps he was best as a promoter.

His interest in Knute Rockne came in 1914 when Rockne could no longer play college ball. At this time, Parratt changed the name of the Akron Indians to "Parratt's" Indians. With Peggy as player, coach, and owner-manager, the name change was natural. Parratt employed a number of ND players on his team. They got paid and that is why it is called professional compensation. By the end of the 1914 season, the whole left side of Parratt's line were former ND players.

In 1914, while working at Notre Dame, Knute Rockne, as noted, could have been a chemist or full-time pharmacist. He permitted himself to be recruited by Peggy Parrat to play professional football for the Akron "Parrott" Indians. While playing for the Indians, Parratt moved Rockne around and had him playing both end and halfback.

Rockne helped Akron learn to love the forward pass and it worked on several successful plays during their title drive. Rockne eventually wound up in Massillion Ohio, and he was able to team up with his Notre Dame team-mate Dorais.

Rockne's career as a pro player in Massillion Ohio was enhanced with his former team-mate Dorais pitching the pigskin for the professional Massillon Tigers. The two brought the forward pass to professional football from 1915 to 1917 when they led their team, "the Tigers" to the championship in 1915.

Rockne "toyed around" with continuing to play professional football during these years before coming back to Notre Dame as a serious head coach. In trivia at the time of "the Rock,", the rumor mill noted that Rockne got his worst loss ever as a pro coach. They say he led the "South Bend Jolly Fellows Club" when they lost 40-0 to the Toledo Maroons.

After Rockne took over the head coaching job at Notre Dame that was it for pro-ball, and that was it for big losses.

Knute Rockne is Dead! Long Live His Memory!!

As with all of the great coaches with a number of years' credit at Notre Dame, I have chosen to find an article of the times to display as both a reminder of what they were when they arrived and what they were when they left Notre Dame. This was the first time that I have selected an obituary as a closing article in this book as of course it is the first time, and hopefully the only time that a Notre Dame coach's career is interrupted by death. This piece is from the New York Times as written by columnist Robert F. Kelley.

OBITUARY

April 1, 1931
http://www.nytimes.com/learning/general/onthisday/bday/0304.html

Knute Rockne Dies with Seven Others in Mail Plane Dive

Date of Death: March 31, 1931
By ROBERT F. KELLEY

From his days as a player Knute Rockne made his influence felt on the trend of football. As captain of the 1913 Notre Dame team, he figured at end in the most successful exhibition of forward passing the game had seen up to that time; and from that date on the forward pass grew steadily to its present importance in the game.

As a coach, he brought the shift play to its highest state of perfection and made it such an important factor in offensive football that the rules committee finally passed legislation designed to take some of its power away.

That shift development, the back-field hop, was the most important of his contributions to the coaching of the game, but he added others, notably the reshaping of the line. Prior to Rockne, linemen were big men inevitably. Rockne brought the idea of using linemen, particularly guards, in interference [blocking], and demonstrated that the small, fast lineman could hold his own with the big man and outplay him where the big man was not as fast.

Changed Strategy of Touchdown

He worked for the perfection of a team as a whole and his last two teams won game after game through the successful application of what came to be called "the perfect plays." In these, every individual carried out a part of the blocking, and when no man failed to carry out his job the play often went for a touchdown.

This perfect play did a great deal to wipe away the idea of aiming first for scoring territory and then the score. Rockne always said that every play, if perfectly carried out, would go for a touchdown from wherever it was started. His last two teams usually started their scoring with long runs from scrimmage.

In coaching he tried always for perfection and spent hours in teaching the art of blocking. Simple plays, well executed, were his idea of the way to win football games. He had small use for any so-called trick plays. There were only seven places in a line to send a man with a ball, he said, and there ought not to be many more than seven plays.

Hard work was another of his slogans. "The best thing I ever learned in life," he said last June during a visit to Poughkeepsie for the intercollegiate boat race there, "was that things have to be worked for. A lot of people seem to think there is some sort of magic in making a winning football team. There isn't, but there's plenty of work."

Suddenly Developed the Pass

As a player and captain of the 1913 Notre Dame team, the first to ever beat the Army, Rockne began his shaping of football's destinies by bringing the forward pass suddenly and dramatically into the front of the game. Army that season had scheduled Notre Dame as a "breather" game on its schedule. Only a small crowd turned out, and they stood amazed as Notre Dame defeated Army, 35 to 13. Gus Dorais, now coach at Detroit, threw seventeen passes in that game and thirteen were completed, and a great majority of these went to the short, chunky end, Knute Rockne.

The forward pass had been more or less of a haphazard thing until that time. The success of this Western team with it amazed the football world. Dorais and Rockne remained behind at West Point for a few days after that game to show the Army how it was done. One of the results of that was the famous Pritchard to Merrillat combination of Army teams.

In that first success was an indication of the capacity for taking pains which Rockne owned. That game was the direct result of the Summer before. Dorais and Rockne had obtained vacation jobs together at a mid-West beach and included a football in their baggage. All that Summer they got out on the beach and threw passes. The success against Army was no accident. It had been carefully planned.

Remarkable Record as Coach

As a coach, of course, Rockne's record is one of the most remarkable that any coach of any sport has ever piled up. Nearly all of his teams have been in the front rank of the game, despite the fact that they always played hard schedules. Five of them were undefeated. Taking over the head coach job, after helping instruct in the chemistry department of Notre Dame, in 1918, Rockne had almost immediate success. His 1919 team was undefeated and his 1920 team was one of the greatest that he had.

To the game in general Rockne brought the high development of the backfield shift and a new conception of line play. He never claimed the invention of the shift play. But there can be small argument with the idea that under him Notre Dame's players brought it to its highest perfection.

So successful were his teams with the shift that three years ago the football rules committee, fearing the offense of the game would overbalance the defense, began ruling against it and this last year finally insisted that a full second, in which an official might count five, must come between the close of the shift and the start of the ball.

Rockne never was reconciled to this and never lost an opportunity to defend his favorite style of play. Legislating against the shift, he said, was like taking the feinting out of boxing and leaving in only the slugging.

Rockne organized coaching schools in which coaches might gather during the off seasons and study the methods of others. He assisted with Summer schools all over the country and in 1928 even conducted one at sea when he chartered a ship and took a party of coaches and athletes to the Olympic Games of that year.

Developed Famous Players

Perhaps his greatest teams came in 1920, 1924, 1929 and 1930. On the first was George Gipp, who was named by Rockne as the greatest player he ever had. The coach told the story of seeing Gipp, who was not trying for the team, throwing a ball and kicking on the campus and of inducing him to join the squad. Gipp died a few weeks after the close of the 1920 season of a throat infection, with Rockne at his bedside.

The 1924 team was the one of the famous Four Horsemen, Harry Stuhldreher, Jimmy Crowley, Don Miller and Elmer Layden. As a combination, they have not been excelled in modern back fields and they had a great line in front of them, led by the famous Adam Walsh at centre, who is now assisting with the coaching at Yale. That team of the Four Horsemen won all over the country, beating Princeton at Princeton with a temperature of 10 above zero, and several weeks later journeying to the Coast to defeat Stanford in a temperature of 70 degrees.

The records and names of the members of the two recent teams are still fresh in memory, Frank Carideo, Marchmont Schwartz, Marty Brill, Joe Savoldi, Bucky O'Connor, Moon Mullins. And the 1930 team came very near to being the best. Northwestern, Army and Southern California were played on successive Saturdays. One Saturday, in Chicago, Army was turned back in ice and cold rain and the following week the highly regarded Southern California team was badly beaten on the Coast.

Provided Coaches for Nation

If there were any doubt of the influence of Rockne on football, the list of head coaches for the past year might remove it. There were, throughout the country, North, South, East and West, twenty-three head coaches of football from Notre Dame without naming the assistants here and there. Notable among them are Walsh and Rip Miller, who has this year been elevated to head coach at Navy.

The mere record of his work fails to bring out for those who did not know him the biting, incisive, clear-cut character and personality of the man. Dramatic in everything he did, even to his death, Rockne became a sort of god to the boys who played for him. A great talker, a keen wit, he had a balanced, sane philosophy of life and a keen knowledge of psychology.

There are numerous instances in the near legends which have sprung up about him of his use of the latter element in dealing with his boys. The year that Army and Navy played in Chicago, in 1926, he went to Chicago to watch the game, confident his strong team would beat Carnegie Tech without too much trouble in his absence. They did not.

Used the Delayed Criticism

The coach returned to South Bend. The next week the team was to play on the Pacific Coast. All week, Rockne coached without mentioning the defeat. The players kept waiting for him to say something. He did not. But when they boarded the train and opened their baggage, each player found a carefully clipped account of the lost game in his baggage. They won on the Coast.

This year, before the Army game, Rockne sat in the dressing room with his players, waiting for the time to go out on the field. The players sat silently, waiting for him to say something. The minutes ticked off in the quiet room, and finally an official came to tell them to come out. Rockne nodded, stood up and said, "Come on, boys." That was all.

He has given words to the vocabulary of the sport as well, some of which fit exactly the army of people who criticize the players and coaches after a defeat, waiting until the day after to display their wisdom. "Sunday morning coaches" was Rockne's name for this class.

A polished story-teller and a constantly interesting companion, Rockne made friends wherever he went, and was almost as much at home at the colleges he played against on his numerous visits as he was at his own. At these places he will be greatly missed as a friend.

Here are some more thoughts about the feelings at Notre Dame just several weeks after Rockne's death. They are taken from the same April issue of Scholastic. They surely touch the heart:

The April edition of The Scholastic put together this edition as usual but it was far from usual. Even the writers were affected, and the writers not specifically assigned to the Rockne story had an even more difficult task in writing their every week articles about life at ND. Many of the Student Paper's pages were dedicated to paying tribute to a man that many, if not all of the people in this college community truly loved and admired:

From Scholastic

It has often been said that Time is the great healer of all wounds. Perhaps, but the wound that Notre Dame has suffered by the death of her most loved man will never be healed completely. Even now, after the nation has partially recovered from the passing of one of its greatest citizens, it is hard to realize what the loss of "Rock" means to us all.

Notre Dame without Rockne ... the United States without Rockne. What does it mean? We hardly know, yet. The thousands of telegrams and letters received by the University are only partially indicative of the grief felt by the entire nation. It "mattered not whether the newsboys in San Francisco or New York or Florida knew "Rock" personally; he was a friend to everyone and they loved him.

We at Notre Dame were closer to Rockne than anyone else; his vert appearance on the campus made the world look brighter; his kind face, his soft smile, his cheery hello gave a thrill to all who spoke to "Rock." And no one was ever intentionally snubbed. Rockne was that kind of a man—"a. man's man."

Father O'Hara received a letter from the father of a crippled boy, who last year asked for a photograph of Rockne and got it, personally autographed. The little fellow heard the announcement of the air crash over the radio. He turned the radio off. When his father came home, his small son—with tears in his eyes, asked: "Daddy, will there be a Notre Dame now?" That is typical of the question asked by millions, young and old. And the only answer to the question is: "There will be a Notre Dame, a greater Notre Dame, because the spirit of the man-who made Notre Dame famous will inspire her sons to greater heights, will drive them on to preserve the high ideals which their leader always advocated, because '"Rock" will be watching, guiding, and praying for them to "carry on" where he left off—at the pinnacle of success."

We shall remember Rockne because he wanted us to do the right things in the right way. Always clean, always fair, always fighting for the highest things in life. That was Rockne.

722 The Notre Dame Scholastic

ROCKNE FUNERAL IMPRESSIVE

Father O'Donnell In Inspiring Eulogy Describes Rockne's Character, Ideals

Sad Throngs Visit Campus to Attend Final Services in Sacred Heart Church.

Sad Throngs Visit Campus to Attend Final Services in Sacred Heart Church.

On Wednesday morning, April 1, after the reports of the death of Knute Rockne the day before had been verified, a solemn and grave student body filed into Sacred Heart church to kneel at Mass for the repose of his soul. The Reverend Charles L. O'Donnell, C.S.C, president of the University, sang the Mass that daj', and the Reverend John O'Hara, C.S.C, prefect of religion, began the distribution of Communion with the entrance of the celebi-ant. To a man the students at the Mass received the sacrament as their spiritual tribute to the man they had last seen the Saturday before.

Students and friends of Knute Rockne packed Sacred Heart church again on Saturday morning, April 4, the day of the funeral, to assist at a Mass sung by the Reverend Francis Wenninger, C.S.C, assisted by

Father Thomas Kelly and Father Joseph McAllister. The brothers and priests of the Congregation of the Holy Cross, and nuns of the order from St. Mary's college all received Communion at this Mass, paying a last tribute to Rockne.

Noon found the crowd beginning to assemble for the funeral services. Students who had left on vacations returned; sorrowing admirers of Rockne lined the walks and spread over the quadrangle. Rockne's closest friends, his associates, filed into the church to be with him for the last time, while the great bell in the steeple tolled at short intervals. The balcony of the Administration building was packed with clergymen, faculty members, and newspaper men, and students strained eyes from the roof of the Sorin hall porch.

Just before three o'clock, the long funeral cortege appeared past the statue of Father Sorin, and made its way over a hushed campus to the church, while the crowd on the quadrangle edged closer to the ropes that formed the roadway. The long cortege came to a stop at the church door, and the casket was lifted out and borne into the church by six of Rockne's 1930 football stars, bowed now in grief at the death of their leader. These were Larry Mullins, Marty Brill, Marchmont Schwartz, Tom Yarr, Frank Carideo, and Tom Conley, captain last season. They were weeping grimly as they consigned the casket to Father O'Hara.

Inside the church, Rockne's friends listened to Father O'Donnell's splendid eulogy of his beloved friend, while out on the campus the crowd pressed around the loud speakers which carried to them the message and the solemn chanting of the funeral dirges by the Moreau choir. Heads were bared and some knelt on the grass in prayer.

The service over, the funeral cortege wound slowly out of the grounds and through the city towards Highland cemetery, on the western outskirts of the city, where Rockne was to be interred. Streets along the route of the procession were packed and all traffic was suspended while the crowds stood silent to honor Notre Dame's coach.

At the cemetery police fought the crowds which attempted to get a last glimpse of the casket. Men and women pressed about the grave where relatives and close friends of the great man stood in mourning. Father O'Donnell conducted the simple and touching burial services, and the casket, with its monogram blanket for mantle, was lowered into the grave by those six teammates who had played their best for their coach. Rockne was buried as he had lived, simply and earnestly, with his men and his friends gathered around him.

Above Picture from Scholastic

A better picture of Rockne's funeral at the Basilica

Catholics are very lucky people. We believe in an afterlife and we believe that our lives are guided by Jesus Christ, our savior and by his mother Mary. So, we have a cushion to lie on at death and that is the understanding of a rewarding afterlife.

Father O'Donnell's message us a holy recount of the Rockne Funeral. It is presented here to help us all, who feel for the loss of Notre Dame family, and the Rockne family, in 1931.

Father O'Donnell's Comments:

This piece is from http://faith.nd.edu/
The specific link which I found is:
http://faith.nd.edu/s/1210/faith/interior.aspx?sid=1210&gid=609&calcid=32056&calpgid=15918&pgid=15920&crid=0I

> *Each year, the Basilica holds funerals for deceased alumni and for members of the Holy Cross community of priests and brothers. The most famous funeral in the Basilica happened in 1931.*
>
> *When famed football coach Knute Rockne died in a plane crash on March 31 of that year, the Notre Dame community was crushed. The students had lost a pillar of their community, and were overwhelmed with sorrow and grief. They packed hall chapels and organized campus-wide prayer.*
>
> *News of his plane crash captivated the country. The funeral was broadcasted on radio nationwide and loudspeakers were attached to the exterior of Sacred Heart Church for the thousands who gathered outside. The entire city of South Bend came to a standstill.*
>
> *Rockne was buried on April 3, Holy Saturday, with a rosary in his hands. In his eulogy, University President Father Charles O'Donnell, C.S.C., said that Rockne loved his neighbor with "genuine, deep love":*
>
> > *"He was quite elementarily human and Christian, giving himself, spending himself like water, not for himself, but for others... he cast away to the deep, he has lost his life to find it.*
> >
> > *"He might have gone to any university in the land and been gladly received and forever cherished there, but he chose Our Lady's school, Notre Dame. He honored her in his life as a student, he honored her in the monogram he earned and wore.*

He honored the ideals he set up in the lives of the young men under his care. He was her own true son.

"To her we turn in this hour of anguish and of broken hopes and hearts laid waste. She is the Mother of God, and Mother of God's men, we give him into thy keeping. Mary, Gate of Heaven, we come to thee, open to receive him. Mary, Morning Star, shine upon his sea. Mary of Notre Dame, take him into thy house of gold. Our life, our sweetness—(and here, Father O'Donnell's voice broke with a hoarse, choking sob so that it was difficult for him to finish the sentence) our hope, we lay him in thy bosom."

Some other appropriate Rockne headlines

This is not a book about Knute Rockne but clearly he is the most well-known hero coach of Notre Dame football, and his legacy has made many happy just to know Notre Dame and that the "Rock" once stood tall in South Bend.

The students of Notre Dame had seen "Rock" for every year they were there. His last two years were their last two years and they meant national championships. Why would an ND student or any ND anything from janitor to president ever think it should be any other way? The campus was in disarray and reading the US headlines at the time, things were not right.

The country itself was in disarray as the finest coach who had ever lived had died. It was like a President dying. The nation mourned and Notre Dame mourned the most. Please let me capture some of the headlines from the period as written in the Scholastic. There is no need to look for headlines outside of the University as theirs in this edition of the Scholastic reflected the pain of all.

724 The Notre Dame Scholastic

NATION MOURNS ROCKNE'S DEATH IN CONDOLENCES TO UNIVERSITY

Telegrams And Letters Pour Into Notre Dame As Thousands Express Grief

MASSES, COMMUNIONS FOLLOW ROCKNE DEATH

Students and Alumni All Join in Tribute to Dead Coach.

The news of Knute Rockne's tragic death found the campus silent in tribute to the man. One of the first

726 The Notre Dame Scholastic

NOTABLES IN THRONG AT ROCKNE FUNERAL

Many Prominent Figures at Burial Rites.

ROCKNE GRAVE DRAWS THOUSANDS OF PEOPLE

Burial Ground Jammed With Sorrowful Crowds.

PLAN ROCKNE MEMORIAL

Committee Considers Project For Commemoration.

The Notre Dame Scholastic 733

COLLEGE PARADE

NOT ONLY NOTRE DAME . . .

A COACH WHO BELONGS TO THE AGES

Knute Rockne possessed natural leadership and a magnetic personality which undoubtedly would have made him an outstanding figure in any field of work that he might have chosen . . . His death robs the nation of a dynamic figure. His influence in sports will be felt for years to come.

—*Daily Illini*

A MAN HAS GONE

The Greatest Coach of them all saw fit to beckon Knute K. Rockne to the sidelines for all times . . . and the nation mourns one of its most colorful and outstanding figures — a man whose football wizardry was legend, a man to whom full grown men and callow youths alike looked upon with respectful awe.—Stanford *Daily Cardinal*

THE MASTER MENTOR

Football and Knute Rockne—always in the same breath and always allied in the minds of football hungry fans and players. Now a sudden tragedy sweeps the master mind of the gridiron from the coaching fields and leaves the realm of the pigskin and sport-loving, sport-respecting Young and Old America desolate.—*Daily Texan*

AMERICA'S COACH IS DEAD

THE GAME IS OVER

In a highly publicized game such as football myths are apt to overshadow the actual personality of the best known leaders of the sport. In the case of Knute Rockne, whose untimely death takes away one of the greatest coaches in the history of the game, such was not true. This glamorous figure in the ever shifting gridiron spotlight was a man revered as much for his ability and character as for the success of his athletic teams that he coached . . . His name will go down in the annals of gridiron history as the finest coach, football's greatest exponent, and a man whose sterling character honored his game, his university, and his country.—Minnesota *Daily*

KNUTE ROCKNE

The news of Knute Rockne's death has been received here, as everywhere, with considerable surprise and sorrow . . . To those who had the privilege of being personally acquainted with Rockne, he was a fine man and a good friend. To the thousands of others who knew him as football coach of Notre Dame, he was the greatest figure in present-day sport.

—*Daily Princetonian*

ROCKNE WILL REMAIN AN INSPIRATION

And, of course there were more headlines about Knute Rockne here, there, and across the globe. Knute Rockne was the "man" before the notion of "***the man***" ever existed. He still is **"THE MAN."**

His thirteen years of greatness at Notre Dame gave the University the idea that a guy like Rockne would always be available to the University of our Lady of the Lake. I like to call Rockne one of the first immortals because his first coaching boss, Jesse Harper would also be on that list along with Frank Leahy, Terry Brennan, Ara Parseghian, Lou Holtz, and now, the real Coach Brian Kelly, not the writer of the great 2016 book about Notre Dame.

Every now and then God had to send a regular good or OK coach to Notre Dame so that the leaders of the University would understand the gift from God when one of the real immortals or one of the immortals to-be began to show up for work on the campus fields every day.

REQUIESCAT IN PACEM: That is how the coach who survived the 1925 conversion to Catholicism would have heard our final tribute to him: RIP Rest in Peace.

Please Lord, give Coach Rockne a fine place with the stars as he has helped many of your people be stars on earth. And, so it ends!

Chapter 9 Post Rockne: Coach Hunk Anderson 1931-1933Era

Coach # 15

Not too bad after 2 championships in a row

1931	Hunk Anderson	6–2–1
1932	Hunk Anderson	6–2–1
1933	Hunk Anderson	3–5–1

Hunk Anderson started off OK as ND coach.

1931 Coach Hunk Anderson Year 1

The 1931 Notre Dame Fighting Irish football team, coached by Hunk Anderson in his first year did reasonably well, but with a record of 6-2-1, it was clear that Anderson's team was either readjusting or rebuilding after two consecutive national championship seasons under Knute Rockne.

Yet, Notre Dame still was able to finish with a rank of #11 in the country. Rockne had helped Notre Dame not only gain respect but gain the benefit of the doubt.

1932 Coach Hunk Anderson Year 2

The 1932 Notre Dame Fighting Irish football team with second-year coach Hunk Anderson finished the season with seven wins and two losses (7-2). This was the second football season since the passing of Knute Rockne in a shocking accident and it brought Hunk's team the pride of being ranked # 4 in the Country.

1933 Coach Hunk Anderson Year 3

The 1933 Notre Dame Fighting Irish football team with third year coach Hunk Anderson, finished the season with three wins, five losses, and one tie. It was Notre Dame's worst season ever and the fans were expecting a new coach for 1934. It goes without saying that this year's Fighting Irish were unranked.

Scholastic Magazine, run by ND Students always had something insightful to say about what is / was happening at Notre Dame when it is / was happening. They do not like writing anything negative.

Hunk Anderson as all ND coaches was not a bad guy at all. He may even have been a good coach if there were somebody to help him out just a bit. But, he did not measure up to his promises. He had one really bad season.

As we will see as we move forward in time. Ara Parseghian will define the whole rationale of being a successful coach at ND. He will reduce it to one word: *WIN!* I added the exclamation mark.

Scholastic Magazine, a student-run, administration controlled positive influence on ND faculty, students, alums, and friends did not have much to say about Hunk Anderson. Here it is:

> *Elmer Layden, '25, last Saturday morning signed a contract to become head football coach and Athletic Director at Notre Dame. At the same time, announcement was made by the Reverend John F. O'Hara, C.S.C, vice-president of the University, who completed negotiations with Layden, of the official acceptance of the resignations of Heartly W. Anderson and Jesse C. Harper, head grid coach and Director of*

Athletics respectively. Layden will take over his new duties here on February 1st. The new Notre Dame athletic head has just completed his seventh season as head football coach at Duquesne University in Pittsburgh, where his teams, especially the 1933 eleven, compiled excellent records.

Summary of the "Hunk" Anderson Years:

Heartley "Hunk" Anderson Coach 1931-1933

There is a notion that when a person is looking for a top job, such as CEO, they can leverage their opportunity for success by coming after (meaning after in time) somebody who has done a poor job; was incompetent, miserable, could not get along with people, and that most people in the company would be tickled if the old guy had left lots sooner.

The worst scenario for success is when the old guy is terrific; has great business acumen, great results, a great personality, and everybody loves the guy and are sorry to see him gone. Though everybody from new coaching prospects, alumni, the CSC Fathers, and the Notre Dame faithful knew that nobody would be able to replace Rockne and succeed, somebody still had to gain the appointment for the job.

'HUNK' ANDERSON IS OUT AT NOTRE DAME

SOUTH BEND, Ind., Dec. 8 —(AP)— Elmer Layden, one of the famous "Four Horsemen," will replace Heartly "Hunk" Anderson as head football coach at Notre Dame next fall as a result of a drastic shake-up of the University's athletic staff.

Jess Harper will also retire as athletic director. Harper's successor will probably be named within the next two weeks.

The most persistent rumor, however, was that Layden would hold both the director's and coaching jobs. He is now coach at Duquesne University.

In the 13 Rockne years, Notre Dame had been taken from a school in which most of its coaches lasted no more than three years to a university in which the last coach not only lasted thirteen years, he was at the top of his game for almost every one of those years. Not only that but he had three recognized national championships and five unbeaten and untied seasons including one in his last time out.

The notion that "Success breeds success" may not be the proper analogy but a derivative of that does apply: "Success breeds the demand for success." At Notre Dame, post Rockne, there was little room for failure and there was no apparent hesitation to oust unsuccessful Rockne successors. It can be called the downside of a winning culture.

As discussed, there was nobody who was unaware that following Rockne as coach would be a nearly impossible task. Almost immediately after the coach's death, university president Father Hugh O'Donnell put the squeeze on Jesse Harper to return to South Bend to help out.

Harper loved Notre Dame but agreed only to take on the role of Athletics Director. He had no interest in being the predecessor and successor to Rockne. He knew of the major pressures and there were many. Despite the risks being well known, there were several candidates who nonetheless were confident enough to be interested in the job.

Heartley "Hunk" Anderson, Rockne's assistant was offered and accepted the job. He played and coached for Rockne and besides that, he was a five-sport letterman. Anderson was extremely athletic and very talented. While an assistant at Notre Dame, he was still playing pro ball for the Chicago Bears.

Anderson had no limit to his athletic aptitude and he could spot talent in others. He added the right amount of passion, commitment, love of football, and a drive to win to his overall package. He was without a doubt, a great paper choice to be head coach of Notre Dame. What he did not have, unfortunately for him, and it mattered in the end was Rockne's affable charm, but few do. Few could. The Rock was the whole deal.

Anderson had a knack of getting the most from his young players, but he did not have a style that helped him be successful when dealing with adults in high places. Rockne had a way of being able to control his inferiors and his superiors. The Rock was a great schmoozer.

Nobody can put a top US college team on the field without free tuition for many players. Rockne figured out how to get them what they wanted outside the bounds of the university's limited scholarship program. He would find various grants in aid and his relationships with wealthy boosters prompted financial help for student players.

When Anderson became coach. ND VP Father Michael Muclaire made clear that the new era would be different. The priests would subject the program to more oversight. Though Anderson had the same basic amount of scholarship packages from the school that Rockne had been given, that was it. Because Anderson was not Rockne, lots less students could get free rides to Notre Dame.

The "Hunk," failed to maintain the network of unofficial booster relationships to provide things such as off-campus jobs for ND players. That system had enabled Rockne to continually bring on more and better players. Additionally, Jesse Harper was the AD after Rockne. It was not Coach Anderson.

Rockne did everything and basically controlled everything, including the administration. He served as Notre Dame's athletic director, business manager, ticket distributor, track coach and equipment manager while concurrently being the Head Football Coach. Anderson did not have the connections or the chutzpah to be like Rockne where interpersonal activity mattered and so the gravy-train dried up and nobody can field a great team without a shot at the best players.

"Hunk" was an aggressive task master as assistant and motivated players with his grit, not his charm. The ND head coaching job required both skills. Despite not having the structure to bring in more and more talent, there are analysts who have concluded that his teams did not lack talent.

Rockne had recruited them and the Rockne deals were not taken away from students. There were three Rockne classes coming back the first year, then two, and then one, Anderson also had his own recruits but his seniors were Rockne's. The conclusion was that even in the early years when the team had few defeats, Notre Dame was too often out-coached in times that the team lost.

For example, in the 1931 USC game in which the Irish were ahead 14-0, Hunk pulled the starters and USC began a comeback and overtook the Irish for a 16-14 Trojan win. Substitution rules back then were like intramural Soccer. A player pulled from the game could not be returned within the same quarter. In the USC game, ND starters were sitting on the bench watching USC win the game against the scrubs. Rockne's teams lost games, sometimes. But they were never out coached—ever.

The 1931 season finished with a 12-0 road loss at Army. Losing the last game in a season is a "no-no" for coaches wanting to keep their jobs. Onlookers with football knowledge believed that somehow Army had been "listening" and understanding Notre Dame's play calling as the ND team performed so poorly.

So many people cared and watched closely every time Notre Dame took the field that the murmurs and rumors and whispers of Hunk's inadequacy began, even after season one with what ND fans and alumni considered a not unrespectable 6-2-1 finish. The Student Newspaper, Scholastic reported that Hunk would be retained because he "was a Notre Dame man."

Hunk's second season was another pressure cooker after the team had won three straight against small poor performing schools. When better schools came to play, ND did not do so well under Anderson. After the Pitt game, a 0-12 loss, a reporter openly criticized the game effort: “A Notre Dame team, its assurance and cohesion absolutely destroyed, passing wildly like a bunch of high school kids in a demoralized effort…”

It got so bad that Jesse Harper, serving as Athletic Director had to explicitly address the situation. He told reporters that Anderson would be coaching at ND the following year: “The fact that he lost one game is no reason to fire him. We at Notre Dame feel he has done a fine job.”

Hunk Anderson did not handle the press well and the press began their own private war against the coach. Priests always were treated special when visiting Notre Dame. Anderson just did not get the importance of being nice to people who have the ears of the administration.

The Coach actually banned visiting priests from watching pre-season practices unless they came with letters of clearance from their bishops. The reaction was expected and bitter. When ND opened the season with a miserable 0-0 tie against Kansas, jaws dropped, wondering what all the secrecy was about. The Irish had won its season opening games forever from 1901.

The South Bend Tribune had become fully annoyed with Coach Anderson from many angles. They wrote: “This fellow Anderson may be a coach, but if he is, I’m ready to accept my post as ambassador to China.” Audacious and irreverent attacks from the press and from ordinary fans became par for the course. Like Jimmy Johnson from his days as Miami U and Dallas, head coach, Heartly "Hunk" Anderson became persona non-grata. He became the ND coach everyone loved to hate.

In year three, the roof Anderson had seemly built to protect himself from criticism was crumbling down. His 1933 team began losing games to poor opponents. Notre Dame would not accept excuses even when a victorious opponent was worthwhile. Games played against good teams were crucial to success and needed to be won. Nobody even conceived of losing to mediocre and poor teams.

Anderson's team mantra seemed to become that it's OK to lose to anybody, good and bad alike. That was too much to handle for any university. Everybody wanted the 1933 season to end quickly.

End it did and ND had finished 3-5-1. It was the school’s first losing season since it had played Michigan three times and lost all three in 1887—its very first year of football. A bad team that is purged takes with it a lot of lumber that is no longer needed. Just one week after the season had ended, Notre Dame announced that both Jesse Harper and "Hunk" Anderson had ‘resigned’

Chapter 10 Coach Elmer Layden 1934-1940

Coach # 16

Elmer Layden, New ND Coach

1934	Elmer Layden	6–3
1935	Elmer Layden	7–1–1
1936	Elmer Layden	6–2–1
1937	Elmer Layden	6–2–1
1938	Elmer Layden	8–1
1939	Elmer Layden	7–2
1940	Elmer Layden	7–2

Layden Signs Contract as ND Coach & Athletic Director

The University of Notre Dame broke its silence on the football coaching situation and from this came the appointment of Elmer Layden, coach of Duquesne university at Pittsburgh, as director of athletics and head football coach. Layden will take up his duties on Feb. 1, 1934

As director, Layden, one of the famous Four Horsemen of Notre Dame's In 1924, succeeds Jesse Harper, one time coach of all four major sports at Notre Dame, who took over the post of director for the second time upon the death of his former pupil. Knute Rockne, in 1931.

As football coach, Layden succeeds Heartly (Hunk] Anderson, who has directed the destinies of the Irish football team since the season of 1931.

Signs in Indianapolis.

Confirmation of Layden's appointment and the resignation of Anderson and Harper came from the Rev. Charles L. O'Donnell, president of the university, during a brief visit in Chicago; from an announcement released at the office of the Rev. John F. O'Hara, vice president, in South Bend; and from a conference between Father O'Hara and Layden in Indianapolis, where Layden formally signed a two year contract which placed him at the head of what Is generally recognized as the greatest collegiate athletic activity in the country.

At the same time, Father O'Hara announced that Joe Boland, reserve tackle on the 1924 Notre Dame team on which Layden starred and until recently coach at St. Thomas college in Minnesota, - had been appointed as assistant to the new coach. -No other assistants have been named.

Neither Father O'Hara nor Layden would discuss the salary terms under which Layden returns to his alma mater.
"That part is sacred to the persons concerned," Father O Hara said.

It is understood, however, that the consideration is in the neighborhood of $10,000 for his first year in both positions.

Release Scaled Statement.

The official statement announcing the changes in the athletic administration at the university was left with his secretary by Father O'Hara before his departure from South Bend on Friday to meet Layden at Indianapolis. It had been held in a sealed envelope and was to have been released late yesterday afternoon, but after the conference between the vice president and the new coach, it was made public. It follows:

> *" The University of Notre Dame has accepted the resignations of Jesse Harper and Heartly Anderson as athletic director and head football coach and has signed Elmer Layden for a contract that covers both positions. The university also has approved the se- lection of Joseph Boland as assistant football coach.*
>
> *"In accepting these resignations, the university wishes to pay high tribute to the men who, three years ago, on the tragic death of Knute Rockne, assumed the very difficult task of carrying on his work.*
>
> ***Rockne's Methods Unique.***
>
> *For Mr. Harper, it meant perfecting a new organization. Knute Rockne was a keen business man, but his methods were unique. Mr. Harper installed a new and very efficient system for the direction of athletics at Notre Dame. This is deeply appreciated by the university, and will be by Mr. Harper's successor.*
>
> *Mr. Anderson threw his whole soul into the work he inherited from his old teacher, and he brought to it not only a great knowledge of football but a remarkable devotion and loyalty as well. No alumnus of the university was ever more honest and sincere.*
>
> *"It is with great regret that Notre Dame bids farewell to these two men whose service has carried her over a critical period in an extra-curricular activity which commands much public attention."*

> *Father O'Hara vigorously denied "reports that negotiations had been opened with Joe Bach, Layden's present assistant at Duquesne University in Pittsburgh, or with Mal Elward, assistant to Noble Kizer at Purdue."*
>
> *The status of the present Notre Dame Freshman coaches has not been taken under consideration as yet, Father O'Hara said.*
>
> *"We have no need for freshmen coaches until next fall, since the present freshmen will work under the varsity coaches in spring practice," he said. "There is still plenty of time to take care of these positions."*

...

Layden Good Leader.

Layden is taking over the biggest, If not the hardest, coaching job in the country. Notre Dame football teams have been making history since 1913 when Harper brought the name of the Irish into the headlines throughout the country by placing on the field, an eleven which upset a powerful Army largely through the use of a marvelous passing combination of Gus Dorais and Knute Rockne, which pioneered the pass in the east. Since then, under first Harper, then Rockne, and lastly Anderson, Irish teams have been the most consistently successful of any teams in the United States.

Layden was one of the brightest of the Notre Dame stars of a decade ago. As a fullback who weighed only 160 pounds he was considered the greatest offensive threat in the four horsemen back field and its greatest defensive player. After graduation in 1921, he played one year of professional football in the south and then coached for one season at Columbia college in Dubuque, IA. He went to Duquesne in 1927 and has had better than average success with the football teams there, where his qualities of leadership were even more highly appreciated than his coaching abilities.

...

Head coach Elmer Layden (left) had a sterling .770 winning percentage but left after seven seasons when no national title was produced.

1934 Coach Elmer Layden Year 1

With Elmer Layden, the fullback in the famous 1924 Four Horsemen ND backfield, as the head coach of the 1934 Notre Dame Fighting Irish football team, Notre Dame was able to pick itself up, dust itself off and come back roaring and fighting for excellence. Having gone through a miserable 3-5-1 season, the Irish were ready to win some football games. Layden's Irish finished at 6-3-0

1935 Coach Elmer Layden Year 2

The 1935 Irish finished the season at 7-1-1. Things started really nice for Elmer Layden's boys as the Irish won their first six games starting at home.

Scholastic: Wayne Miller, All American, One of Layden's Power Men in 1935

1936 Coach Elmer Layden Year 3

Elmer Layden's third season as ND's head coach began very strong with three home wins at Notre Dame Stadium. Notre Dame finished the 1936 season at 6-2-1 and earned a national rank in the AP of # 8.

1937 Coach Elmer Layden Year 4

Layden's 1937 Notre Dame Fighting Irish football team, picked Joe Zwers. The team compiled a record of 6-2-1. For this effort, they were selected as the AP's #9 ranked team.

1938 Coach Elmer Layden Year 5

In 1938 with Jim McGoldrick as its Captain and Elmer Layden at the Helm, the Notre Dame Fighting Irish football team looked like it was going to have an undefeated and untied season until the final game at the University of Southern California. The game was played in Los Angeles at the huge Coliseum.

The Irish were undefeated and untied going into the game. USC, always a spoiler, did it again. The Irish lost in this last game of the 1938 college football season L (0-13). For its great season, ND was ranked # 5 by the Associated Press (AP) when all was said and done.

1939 Coach Elmer Layden Year 6

The 1939 Notre Dame Fighting Irish football team finished (7-2) but started off undefeated for its first six games. Captain Johnny Kelly led Elmer Layden's team and it looked for a while that this would be another championship season for ND before the Irish traveled to Iowa on November 16. Iowa's Hawkeyes beat the Irish in a close match L (6-7). Notre Dame played its season finale at home against rival nemesis USC, and the Trojans again defeated Notre Dame L (12-20).

Notre Dame home game victories were all nail-biters and they came against Purdue W (3-0), Georgia Tech W (17-14), SMU W (20-19) and Northwestern W (7-0. Away victories included Carnegie tech W (7-6), Army W (14-0), Navy W (14-7) at Cleveland. The AP ranked the Notre Dame Fighting Irish # 13 for 1939.

Navy team captain Alan Bergner led the way for Navy's all-out effort against Notre Dame. The game ended in a close win for ND and a disappointing 14-7 loss for the Middies.

1939 Notre Dame v Navy in Cleveland's Municipal Stadium

1940 Coach Elmer Layden Year 7

1940 ND captain Milt Piepul was the player charged with leading Elmer Layden's seventh and last Notre Dame Fighting Irish team in the 1940 season. The team had another finest season finishing 7 wins, 2 losses with no ties.

The Fighting Irish were ranked # 2 at mid-season but after a close game at Navy and losses in two games in a row, the 10-6 victory in Los Angeles against USC did not help in bringing Notre Dame into the national rankings.

Notes about Elmer Layden

Nobody was asking for Elmer Layden to resign. He looked pretty good even next to the immortal Rockne and those immortals to come, but his record was not 100% wins and he had no undefeated seasons. He was a great coach and he was a great person and that is why the NFL snatched him away from Notre Dame.

Because he did not succeed in the way Rockne succeeded, he was perceived as a "not-so-great" coach. Nonetheless, it was Layden himself who got to decide when he would leave Notre Dame. I think he would have kept getting better; would have brought in a championship or two but like most, he too would have tired out from all the pressure. Maybe he thought so too.

He would not have been fired because he succeeded an OK coach, Hunk Anderson. He did not immediately succeed Knute Rockne, an outstanding coach. Either way, Layden was a fine coach.

Elmer Layden Steps Down.

This piece is taken from:

Notre Dame Alumnus Magazine March 1941.

This section reflects the words as printed in the Alumnus Magazine with very light editing.

> *On February 4, 1941, Elmer Layden, LL.B. '25, Notre Dame Director of Athletics and Head Football Coach since 1934, resigned his post to accept the newly created post of Commissioner for Professional Football, at an announced salary of $20,000 per year. Layden signed a five-year contract. Frank Leahy, B.S. in Phy. Ed. in 1931, for the past two years head coach of the Boston College football team, was announced on February 15 as the successor to the post vacated by Layden.*
>
> *Alumni hardly require details of the latest Notre Dame shift. Papers, magazines, moving pictures hastened through their various channels to elaborate the succinct and startling scoops that rolled from the national radios during this historic eleven days. Significant to alumni are several points. First, Elmer Layden leaves a remarkably fine record written in words as well as in figures. His seven seasons produced 47 victories, 13 defeats, and three ties, against a schedule that grew in intensity under his guiding hand. [47–13–3]*
>
> *Attendance steadily reflected a continued national admiration for Notre Dame football. These are figures, and vital ones at Notre Dame. But even deeper, and more vital, was the widespread good will, the genuine admiration which Layden won personally and which Notre Dame shared. Old rivalries were preserved in a spirit of healthy competition,*

tempered with manifest sportsmanship and mutual respect and admiration.

New competitors appeared on the schedules over the seven seasons, and in the several seasons ahead, opening new vistas of interest and influence for Notre Dame and Notre Dame followers. Nor should the work done in his capacity as director of athletics, in the promotion of a balanced program of major and minor sports, varsity and intra-mural schedules, and the general welfare and interests of the students in all forms of athletics, be omitted in this brief summary of Elmer's crowded Notre Dame career. Second in significance, Notre Dame retains its conviction that the Notre Dame system of football, so integral a part of the Rockne Tradition, is still self-sustaining.

In all the speculation of the short interim between resignation and appointment, it was simply a question of which one of the many outstanding Notre Dame coaches would be selected. As usual, the Board in Control of Athletics weighed the arguments carefully, if rapidly. The result has been followed by nation-wide acclaim.

Frank Leahy was the type of student and athlete in which the campus has always taken particular pride. Success, and he had that in a great era — the '29 and '30 undefeated teams — made him no more known or liked than the period when injuries kept him out of the game. He was a combination of serious student, rugged player, and pleasant companion. Off the field and on the field, his influence was good, and consistent.

Frank is immediately limelighted by his spectacular success at Boston College, which was climaxed by his team's victory over Tennessee in the 1940 Sugar Bowl. But the two years of his ascendancy in the Boston school were, characteristically, prefaced by years of hard work on the fundamentals of his profession, first as line coach for Tommy Mills (now director of the Rockne Memorial) at Georgetown, and then as line coach with Jimmy Crowley, first at Michigan State, and then at Fordham. His success at Boston College, for those who had followed his work, was merely the added revelation of a great personality in this young man whose coaching ability had long been outstanding in the major leagues of the sport.

A five-year contract with Boston College, signed the day before Elmer's resignation was announced, was, by mutual action, set aside in favor of the obvious logic of Leahy's succession to the Layden post at Notre Dame.

Third in alumni interest is perhaps the disposition of the assistants involved in the shift. The splendid staff of Notre Dame men, with whom Elmer Layden had worked at Notre Dame was, in the nature of Layden's move, automatically disbanded in one sense. Their ability makes the nature of this state temporary at most. Joe Boland, '27, for example, has already been signed with Mal Elward as assistant coach at Purdue University, and the next ALUNUS Magazine expects to announce new connections for the remaining members of the staff, Chet Grant, Bill Cemey, and Joe Benda.

Leahy's loyalty to his own assistants has been a growing tradition in the two short years at Boston, as has their loyalty to him. And the record speaks for itself as to the efficacy of the foursome. Ed McKeever, assistant to Leahy, is himself a Notre Dame man, 1929-32, who left N.D. to finish his college work and to play football at Texas Tech. Line coaches Johnny Druze and Joe McArdle are Fordham graduates, products of Leahy's own line-coaching of the Blocks of-Granite era. McKeever reported at Notre Dame on March 1, and Leahy was expected March 7, as this issue of the ALUMNUS goes to press.

Elmer Layden will continue to occupy his home, under present plans, on Ironwood Drive, South Bend, until the children finish school in June. He will open an office in Chicago in April, and Mrs. Layden and the family expect to move to Chicago during the summer.

Alumni regard the record of Elmer Layden as a personal tribute to his ability and a definite contribution to the athletic and general welfare of Notre Dame. By the same token, alumni welcome his successor not as a stranger, but as a fellow-alumnus who, like Elmer, will without question, win new personal laurels, and at the same time continue to preserve and to promote the phase of Notre Dame which, more than any other, has won the University a loyal nation-wide and uncounted following.

The Notre Dame tradition definitely wins. Elmer leaves for new worlds to conquer, but remains a part of it. Frank Leahy comes to it, not a stranger, but himself already a part of it.

Chapter 11 Coach Frank Leahy 1941-1953

Coach # 17 Frank Leahy
Coach # 18 Edward McKeever
Coach # 19 Hugh Devore

Four National Championships 1943, 1946-47, 1949

1941	Frank Leahy	8–0–1	
1942	Frank Leahy	7–2–2	
1943	Frank Leahy	9–1*	
1944	Edward McKeever	8–2	Coach # 18
1945	Hugh Devore	7–2–1	Coach # 19
1946	Frank Leahy	8–0–1*	
1947	Frank Leahy	9–0*	
1948	Frank Leahy	9–0–1	
1949	Frank Leahy	10–0*	
1950	Frank Leahy	4–4–1	
1951	Frank Leahy	7–2–1	
1952	Frank Leahy	7–2–1	
1953	Frank Leahy	9–0–1	

From the Website, which hosts the tribute sculpture from 1997

Coach Frank Leahy

The tribute to Leahy at the base of the monument reads as follows:

> ***Frank Leahy came to Notre Dame to play football for Knute Rockne. After suffering an injury his senior year, he became a student of Rockne's and entered the coaching profession himself.***
>
> ***Coach of the Fighting Irish from 1941-43 and 1946-53, he led the Irish to six undefeated seasons, five National Championships, and an unbeaten streak of 39 games in the late 1940's.***
>
> ***Selected for the College Football Hall of Fame in 1970, this sculpture commemorates Coach Leahy, and was unveiled next to Notre Dame Stadium in 1997.***

Leahy learned success from Rockne & ND

Before Coach Leahy coached at Notre Dame, he graduated from Notre Dame. He attended the University of Notre Dame, where he played football as a tackle on Knute Rockne's last three teams (1928–1930). He graduated from the university in 1931. He learned the notion of success from both Notre Dame and Coach Rockne. He learned the notion of love from a loving family and the many friends who loved him, even though for most of his life, he was a workaholic.

Like Rockne, whose coach was Jesse Harper, and Frank Leahy, whose coach was Knute Rockne, successful people need lots of help and lots of love in their lives. Very often, these otherwise tough people are too busy to notice or to understand their own need. Harper, Rockne, and Leahy were great family men and they benefitted immensely from a lot of love. They were self-inspired and encouraged to do well in life by their life experiences for sure, but it was not all them! Yes, even self-made men can fail when they are alone and when there is no loving support system.

Frank Leahy was a great coach and a great man. He loved his family deeply and kept increasing it in numbers until—well, let's just end it at until! He was tough but fair. He was also kind and good, and though not sloppy or gushy, he was very loving. Men do not want to think of Frank Leahy as *the family man* but it was his family that gave him his strength. Most men wanted to look up to him as an iron-man coach!

I did not know him personally but I would have liked to have met him. The research I have done showed me Leahy the man, Leahy the husband, Leahy the dad, and Leahy the coach. All aspects of Frank Leahy are worthy of admiration. We could use a few more!

So, maybe I do know him. I have spoken to people who have known him or knew those who knew him, and I have read a lot about him. So, I say I know Frank Leahy! I would not want to cross him for all his goodness. As I was finishing up this book, tidying up some wording, I found a great Sports Illustrated article from 1955. I am providing the link below. It is worth a look.
http://www.si.com/vault/1955/10/31/596398/subject-frank-leahy

In this book, I have borrowed the public words of others in print or on the Internet and have given them attribution as I cannot superimpose myself onto the 1887 Notre Dame campus, nor can I sit down with the ten Leahy's and have dinner followed by the Rosary. So, I use the words of others from the past to help me.

The words immediately below are excerpts from Bill Dwyre a great columnist for the LA Times
http://articles.latimes.com/2012/oct/19/sports/la-sp-dwyre-notre-dame-20121020.

Bill Dwyre's piece was titled: "Frank Leahy always had Notre Dame standing tall and up straight."

Dwyre was interviewing Fred Leahy, the coach's # 6 child of 8. In this part of the piece, Leahy's son, Fred creates a quick snapshot of the coach and his family in this excerpt:

> *"Fred's summary of life in the Leahy family is a classic of all-encompassing brevity.*
>
> *"Dad belonged to the world, and mom had eight kids," he says.*

Fred says Frank Leahy never turned down an autograph request and drilled into his family the need to treat people equally and well.

"He wore the famous bow tie all the time," Fred says, "and that wasn't for any image reason. He knew, when he was out eating dinner, somebody would come over to the table, he'd get up and reach across to shake their hand and his tie would fall into the soup.

"When we went out to dinner, he'd eat ahead of time. People wouldn't leave him alone to eat, and he'd never turn anybody down. When dinner ended, he'd disappear into the kitchen and shake the hands of all the helpers."

A writer, seeking to characterize the presumed terror of failure with which Leahy's players existed, once asked star quarterback Johnny Lujack what Leahy was like after a loss. Lujack pondered the question and said, "I don't remember ever losing."

1941 Coach Frank Leahy Year 1

In 1941, Frank Leahy coached the Notre Dame Fighting Irish football team for the first time. Like Elmer Layden and Knute Rockne, and Jesse Harper, Frank Leahy was a natural coach on strategy and on motivation. He made everybody around him want to do their best.

Whereas Knute Rockne had the Four Horsemen, even before Frank Leahy got to BC or Notre Dame he was a famous coach. As a lineman, himself, he was a line coach at Fordham. While at Fordham for five years, Leahy was an excellent line coach. His job was to develop the Fordham line.

He did, and then some. He developed a solid Fordham line that were so tough, they became known as the "**Seven Blocks of Granite**." One of those "Blocks of Granite" was an intense, studious, blocky, raven haired young man named Vince Lombardi. That's right, great coaches teach great coaches. Rockne taught Leahy; Leahy taught Lombardi.

In Leahy's first season, Notre Dame was at its best. Its record was (8-0-1). It could have been a National Championship but for the tie against Army.

1942 Coach Frank Leahy Year 2

The 1942 Fighting Irish football team was coached by Frank Leahy in his second season with the Irish. Leahy was already a successful Notre Dame coach with his 1941 team. At # 6 in the AP rankings at the end of the season, the (7-2-2) 1942 team also received much acclaim. Leahy was a natural coach in the order of other Notre Dame greats. The 1942 Notre Dame football and those Leahy coached until 1953 responded well to his great coaching talents.

1943 Coach Frank Leahy Year 3

The Coach Frank Leahy's 1943 Notre Dame Fighting Irish football team ended its season with 9 wins and 1 loss, winning the national championship. This was the fourth Irish team to win the consensus national title and the first for Frank Leahy.

Led by Notre Dame's first **Heisman Trophy** winner, Angelo Bertelli, Notre Dame played and beat seven teams ranked in the top 13 and played seven of its ten games on the road. Despite a devastating season ending loss to Great Lakes, a recent powerhouse comprised mostly of military men, Notre Dame was awarded its first national title by the Associated Press.

The war years were special years. The service academies and the semi-pro teams from the military were at their best. Because of Notre Dame and Navy's cooperation to educate midshipmen, the 1943 Irish team included 14 Navy apprentice seamen.

Sophomore quarterback John Lujack was one of those players. Lujack would win the 1947 **Heisman Trophy** after helping steer the Irish to a third national title under coach Leahy. Other seamen on the Irish roster included powerful lineman / left tackle Jim White -- who finished 9th in the 1943 Heisman balloting, and other starters including left end Paul Limont, center Herb Coleman and his backup Frank Szymanski, plus fullback Jim Mello.

Back to Notre Dame in the WWII Years

Notre Dame was a major participant in the Navy's V-12 program. The V was for victory. The 12 mean that it was not the first try. During World War II. The "V" designation was often used to mean that the program was to help insure an Allies victory. The V-12 Navy College Training Program was put together to supplement the force of commissioned officers in the United States Navy during World War II.

Navy units use the Notre Dame Football field
To train during World War II.

Between July 1, 1943, and June 30, 1946, more than 125,000 participants were enrolled in 131 colleges and universities in the United States. The program was mutually beneficial to the Navy and to the colleges and universities. Academia willingly participated to assure an American victory. In many ways, it was mutually beneficial as it saved College Football from extinction. Ask Gonzaga!

There was a major V-12 military program on Notre Dame's campus that lifted attendance at the University from 3000 to about 4500. Among them were 12 transfers who were part of the Marine branch of the V-12. There were some already famous football players among them. For example, there was starting right halfback Julius Rykovich. After the war, he would transfer and star at the University of Illinois before going on to an eight-year NFL career.

Notre Dame was proud to have 17 Marine privates, among them were future College Football Hall of Fame inductees Ziggy Czarobski at right tackle, All-American right end John Yonakor, starting left guard Pat Filley and, of course, 1943 **Heisman Trophy** winner Angelo Bertelli at quarterback.

The football game was very serious in 1943 as was the war effort. Notre Dame had players involved in both.

On Nov. 1 during the 1943 season, after leading Notre Dame to a 6-0 record, QB Bertelli got his military orders and he departed for officer's training school in Parris Island, S.C. Johnny Lujack filled in more than capably to finish the national title run.

Angelo Bertelli Heisman 1943 & Johnny Lujack Heisman 1947

There also was one NROTC man, Jack Zilly, who would later serve as an Irish assistant coach from 1956-58.

The 1943 National Championship Notre Dame team was like no other. It defeated the teams that finished No. 2 (Iowa Pre-Flight, a semi-pro World War II outfit), No. 3 (Michigan) and No. 4—none other than the Naval Academy located in Annapolis, Md.

There are only two college football teams in history to defeat the teams that were the final #s 2-3-4 in one season. They are the 1943 Notre Dame Fighting Irish and the 1971 Nebraska Cornhuskers.

Furthermore, the 1943 Irish overpowered the teams that finished #9 (Northwestern), #11 (Army) and #13 (Georgia Tech). Beating six teams that placed in the final AP Top 13 might never again be achieved in college football again.

It is difficult to believe that such a team could ever be beaten. The Fighting Irish went into the game with a 9-0 record against the Great Lakes Blue Jackets, a great team loaded with outstanding military personnel. This team knew how to play the game of football.

The home of this great Navy team was different from what we know. Its home was the Blue Lakes Naval Station and that should say it all. In addition to the 1943 football team, it is still the home of the United States Navy's only boot camp, located near North Chicago, in Lake County, Illinois. Important tenant commands include the Recruit Training Command, Training Support Center and Navy Recruiting District Chicago.

Naval Station Great Lakes is the second largest military installation in Illinois and the largest training station in the Navy. Nobody thought this game would be easy, but Notre Dame had a great team.

This 9-1 season ended with a defeat L (14-19) by the Great Lakes Bluejackets, on a "Hail Mary" touchdown pass. Notre Dame pundits like to ask if this were "the one way any school named after Our Lady should never lose -- with 33 seconds remaining." --A Hail Mary Pass--

To emphasize the Bluejackets talent and skill, note that Notre Dame neither required nor gave any excuses for the defeat. It helps to recall that Great Lakes, which finished #6 in 1943, was a semi-pro operation during the war years comprised of seamen (hence Bluejackets) that included future 1946-49 Notre Dame leading rusher Emil "Six Yard" Sitko—another member of the College Football Hall of Fame.

The Coach, staff, & the team go to War

After the 1943 season, Notre Dame head coach Frank Leahy and his entire staff volunteered for active duty in World War II. They joined—what else? —the Navy. That is why Leahy was not the coach in 1944 or 1945. He was fighting in World War II.

Picture Courtesy Notre Dame Archives Leahy, Right, takes Oath

1944 Coach Edward McKeever Year 1

Since Frank Leahy and a number of the coaching staff joined the Navy after the 1943 Championship Season, Notre Dame asked Edward McKeever to coach the 1944 Notre Dame Fighting Irish football team. McKeever had attended Notre Dame from 1930-1931 and transferred to Texas Tech, where he played football from 1932-

1934. McKeever had been a very successful backfield coach in 1935 through 1938.

He was hired by Frank Leahy while Leahy was at Boston College from 1939-1940. He joined Notre Dame with Leahy in 1941 even though he had been offered head coaching job at BC.

He coached for Leahy through the 1943 season and agreed to be head coach in '44 when Leahy went into the Navy. Coach McKeever got a great offer from Cornell and he became their head coach after his one year stint with Notre Dame. Eventually, he moved to the front office and became general manager of the Boston Patriots in 1960.

McKeever guided the Irish to a very nice 8-2 season and a ninth-place finish in the AP final poll. The 1944 team won its first five games. as

The 1944 Army ND Game

It had been thirteen years since Army had beaten Notre Dame. In fact, the last time Army had scored against the Irish was in 1938. The Irish were the defending national champions, but lost many key players to graduation and the armed services. The Irish even lost head coach Frank Leahy to military service, and were now being led by Ed McKeever.

Notre Dame went into the game 5–1 and ranked No. 5, coming off the 32–13 loss to Navy. The Army squad was being led by Glenn

Davis and Doc Blanchard. The Cadets also had a quarterback named Doug Kenna, and a transfer from the University of Texas, sprinter Max Minor.

Army overwhelmed the Irish. When asked by a reporter about the score, Army halfback Doc Blanchard said "If there was anyone to blame for the size of the margin, it was Notre Dame, which fired our desire to win with its long humiliation of Army teams."

1945 Coach Hugh Devore Year 1

Hugh Devore coached the 1945 Notre Dame Fighting Irish football team to a 7-2-1 record. It was his one season as interim coach while the Irish were awaiting the return of Lieutenant Frank Leahy from active duty.

Devore had graduated from Notre Dame in 1934. He had played end and was Irish co-captain as a senior. He stayed at Notre Dame as freshman coach under Elmer Layden for one year before he moved on and held various coaching positions.

Devore, shown on left came back to Notre Dame in 1943 as Frank Leahy's end coach and left after his interim head coaching assignment in 1946. He held numerous head coaching positions at highly rated schools and was assistant coach for the Green Bay Packers in 1953 and head coach for the Philadelphia Eagles. In 1958 he returned to Notre Dame as Terry Brennan's freshman coach and assistant athletic director and he remained on the staff when Joe Kuharich took over the following year.

As interim head coach at Notre Dame in 1945 and again in 1963, Devore had a record of 9-9-1. He filled in for Leahy in '45 and he filled the gap in '63 between the Kuharich and Ara Parseghian eras.

1946 Coach Frank Leahy Year 4

Returning Navy Lieutenant Frank Leahy's 1946 Notre Dame Fighting Irish football team ended the football season with 8 wins and 1 tie, winning the national championship for the second time in Leahy's tenure as coach.

This was the fifth Irish team to win the national title and the second title for Leahy. The 1946 Irish is the first team/season what is considered to be the Notre Dame Football dynasty, a stretch of games in which Notre Dame went 36-0-2 and won three national championships and two Heisman Trophies from 1946-1949.

The 1946 team was as good as it gets. It was cited by Sports Illustrated as the part of the second-best sports dynasty (professional or collegiate) of the 20th century as well as the second greatest college football dynasty. The season also produced one of college football's "games of the century," the famous 0-0 tie with Army at Yankee Stadium.

1946 Army ND Game

Considering that the last two Army encounters at Yankee Stadium in 1944 and 1945 resulted in Army wins of (0-59) and (0-48), one might have expected drama in the Army game, and there was exactly that. Both the Irish and the battle-hardened Army team came to win; yet the defenses were so good that neither could score.

The 1946 Army / Notre Dame game goes down as one of the best games of all time. The stakes were the highest. Army began the season favored to win its third straight national title. They were not even counting Notre Dame as they had trounced the Irish when the two interim coaches took over for Leahy the two prior years. The Cadets were riding an 18–game winning streak and they still had Doc Blanchard and Glenn Davis. Clearly. Nobody could beat Army or so it seemed and Army Coach Red Blaik's squad would have to be beaten to lose its status as the No.1 team in the nation.

Well, not exactly!

Frank Leahy had coached Notre Dame to a national championship in 1943, then left South Bend for the Navy and spent his duty time in the South Pacific. He returned to Notre Dame in '46 and he had a great bunch of lettermen-turned soldiers who still had playing eligibility remaining. The Irish were loaded and determined to win. Leahy's Irish not only wanted to get back their No.1 ranking, but they were none too happy about the trouncing the team received in the prior two years. They were ready to avenge the 0-59 and 0-48 losses to Army in 1944 and '45.

For years of matchups from 1913 to 1946, no games had ever been played at Notre Dame Stadium. So, it was a given that the game would be at Army, which played its home games against Notre Dame at Yankee Stadium.

The wartime gravy train of talent was over for Army, and no significant new players contributed in 1946. After two national championships, the Army team was still great at 7–0 and Notre Dame was 5–0 when the two met on November 9. The #1 Cadets came in averaging 30 points a game while the No.2 Irish averaged 35. Final score: T (0–0).

> **By the way:** The 1941 ND / Army game in Frank Leahy's first year at ND, was also a 0-0 tie. The Irish finished 1941 at 8-0-1. It was the only blemish on the record and it prevented Notre Dame from winning a mythical national championship (MNC).

Army's 25–game winning streak was over but the Cadets were still unbeaten. They won their last two games, but had to struggle past Navy. Meanwhile, Notre Dame shut out Northwestern and Tulane and beat Southern Cal by 20.

A week later, the final AP poll gave the championship to the Irish. Nonetheless the end-of-season polling was not always 100% accepted and there was no BCS. Army still claims what is called an

MNC for 1946, giving them a trifecta. The MNC stands for Mythical National Championship.

As several other games over the years, the Army-ND game of 1946 This 1946 special game featured some outstanding statistics:

> *3 Heisman Trophy winners, 3 Outland Trophy winners, and 10 Hall of Famers, not counting the Hall of Fame coaches on each side. Notre Dame claims MNCs for 1943, 1946, 1947, and 1949, and Army claims MNCs for 1944, 1945, and 1946. This was a true clash of the titans, an intersection of 2 of the greatest runs in college football history: Army going 27-0-1 1944-1946 and Notre Dame going 36-0-2 1946-1949.*

Pictured above is the defining play of 1946's "Game of the Century" :Notre Dame's Bill Gompers turning the corner on 4th down and heading for Army's goal line. But alas, he didn't make it. He didn't even reach the 2 yard line for a first down, and this game saw no other serious scoring threats, ending in a 0-0 stalemate. I do not have the link for the required cite below.

Jim Martin (38), Larry Coutre (24), Leon Hart (82) and Emil Sitko (14) arrived with the 1946 class. Up front is quarterback Bob Williams. Notre Dame.

1947 Coach Frank Leahy Year 5

The 1947 Notre Dame Fighting Irish football team was another leg of the Notre Dame dynasty coached in the second year of Frank Leahy's second stint since the War. The 1947 team ended the season with 9 wins and no losses. They were unbeaten and untied and for the second time in a row for Leahy and the sixth time in history, Notre Dame won the national championship.

Let me repeat as it sounds so good, and ND fans do not get to say good things so often any more—this ND squad was the second team in what is considered to be the Notre Dame Football dynasty. This is a stretch of games in which Notre Dame's record was a whopping 36-0-2 and the university football team won three national championships and two Heisman Trophies from 1946-1949. This team was cited by Sports Illustrated as the part of the second-best sports dynasty (professional or collegiate) of the 20th century and the second greatest college football dynasty.

The idea of the second greatest college football dynasty as of 1946 puzzled me. Was it Minnesota or Army? The 1944-49 Army team was simply outstanding and they whooped Notre Dame two times by large scores during this period. Notre Dame did not often play Minnesota

In 1933, the Minnesota Gophers won their first conference title since 1927 with a 4-0-4 record, but 1934 was the real beginning of the dynasty. During the 1934 season, Minnesota really took off, winning its first-ever national title, obviously along with its second straight conference title, with an 8-0 record.

Minnesota then won two more consecutive national championships and finished 23-1 over that three-year span. The Golden Gophers went 54-9-1 and won six conference titles while adding five national championships as well— two came before the modern AP voting era. From 1925 to 1938, Notre Dame and Minnesota played five games. One was a tie and Notre Dame won the other four games. So, I remain puzzled for in this time period, Rockne was in the middle of a mini Notre Dame dynasty.

Right after the Minnesota dynasty happened, Army and head coach Red Blaik took over college football's elite status, winning at an unbelievable clip. From 1944-46, the Black Knights were 27-0-1 and had three national titles under their belt — which happened to be the only three "official" claimed national titles in school history.

It is hard for many of us to think of national titles for West Point with the current state of the program not being Army's best. During this time period, however, the Black Knights finished 57-3-4 as one of the most dominant runs in college football history. Army finished as one of the top two teams in the final AP poll four times as an Independent.

1948 Coach Frank Leahy Year 6

The 1948 Notre Dame Fighting Irish football team was coached by Frank Leahy. Notre Dame won its first nine games and then at the end of the season, the Irish visited Southern California, a long-time rival and always a very good football team. Southern Cal tied the Irish T (14-14).

But for this one faux pas, Notre Dame may have had its fourth National Championship in a row in 1949. Instead the AP selected the Fighting Irish as the #2 team in the country. The Michigan Wolverines were #1 based on strength of schedule.

The 1948 NCAA football season finished with two unbeaten teams. The Michigan Wolverines and the Clemson Tigers were both unbeaten and untied. Ultimately, Michigan was the first-place choice for the majority (192 of the 333) voters in the AP Poll. Michigan could not play in the postseason because of a no-repeat rule for Big Nine schools.

Notre Dame, which finished 2nd in the AP Poll and tied USC 14-14 at the end of the regular season, did not participate in any bowl per university policy at the time. The Northwestern Wildcats went to the Rose Bowl, and handed California a 20-14 loss. Clemson would defeat Missouri in the Gator Bowl but it did not seem to affect the Gators final ranking. Clemson came in #11.

Some other good news did happen for Notre Dame on January 30, 1948 in Wilkes-Barre PA. A future King's College student and avid Notre Dame Fan was released by the Stork at Mercy Hospital in Wilkes-Barre, PA. His name is Brian Kelly. He is not the coach as the coach is a younger man. He is, however, the proud author of the book you are reading. This is his 104th book.

1949 Coach Frank Leahy Year 7, Nat. Champs

The 1949 Notre Dame Fighting Irish football team, coached by Frank Leahy for the seventh time, won the national championship for the third time in four years, The Irish, ended the season with 10 wins, and no losses. ND was undefeated and untied. This 1949 squad became the seventh Irish team to win the consensus national title and to repeat, the third in four years.

Leon Hart and James Martin, l to r… Hart was known as a 21-year-old "Monster" who had established himself as one of the great ends in Notre Dame history. This 245-pound stripling, moved swiftly on offense, blocks and tackles sharply to earn fully his All-America rating. Martin moved to the tackle post from his old end position this season, Jungle Jim has carved a name for himself in the Irish forward wall. A senior, Jim at 27 years old was heavyweight boxing champ at Notre Dame in 1947.

The Fighting Irish were led by **Heisman winner** Leon Hart throughout this championship season. Hart was a 6' 5" 260-pound end at time when they did not grow them that big. ND outscored its opponents 360-86.

This was the last Irish team to be considered part of the Notre Dame Football dynasty, a stretch of games in which Notre Dame were 36-0-2 and won three national championships and two Heisman Trophies.

This Irish team received many honors including a citation from Sports Illustrated as the second-best sports dynasty (professional or collegiate) of the 20th century and second greatest college football dynasty of all time.

Frank Leahy's teams after the war were the best of the best. But for the tie in USC against the Trojans in 1948, this would have been Notre Dame's fourth undefeated season in a row.

1950 Coach Frank Leahy Year 8

The 1950 Notre Dame Fighting Irish football team, coached by Frank Leahy during his eighth year at Notre Dame, ended the season with 4 wins, 4 losses, and one tie. There were some sportswriters who blamed this season on a cutback by over ½ of player scholarships. Because Notre Dame as most colleges lives well from the munificence and beneficence of its alumni, the problem of the football team being short on scholarships would be self-correcting, regardless of the academic standards of the institution.

Besides a lack of scholarships to replace the greats who had moved on. The gravy train of servicemen who had come and who played football at Notre Dame after had stopped. Coach Leahy had met with many while he was in the service and had gained commitments for ND football. Now it was 1950, four years later and they were all gone. They had either finished with football or had graduated. These were new days for Notre Dame.

Though ranked #1 in the preseason AP Poll, while serving as defending National Champions, the 1950 team– without Heisman Trophy-winner Leon Hart and other standouts, who had graduated in the spring, the Irish barely achieved a .500 record for the season. Hart had been drafted by the NFL's Detroit Lions with the first overall pick. It was a significant loss for ND in 1950.

1951 Coach Frank Leahy Year 9

Coach Leahy and Captain Jim Mutschwller brought the Notre Dame Fighting Irish back from 4-4-1 to a respectable # 13 ranking and a 7-2-1 record in 1951.

1952 Coach Frank Leahy Year 10

The 1952 Notre Dame Fighting Irish football team, coached by Frank Leahy fought to a 7-2-1 season record. In the AP and the coaches poll Notre Dame was recognized as the #3 top team in the USA.

1953 Coach Frank Leahy Year 11

Let's begin our look at the 1953 season with a great introduction from the December 1953 edition of ND's Scholastic Magazine:

December 11, 1953 Notre Dame, Ind. To OUR READERS: When eleven members of Notre Dame's 1953 pigskin squad lined up for the first whistle down in Norman, Oklahoma, earlier this Fall, they were opening up the sixty-fifth season of Irish competition in intercollegiate football.

And they were conscious of the fact too, that their predecessors—in the 64 seasons before them—had built a reputation for Notre Dame as one of the oldest and most consistently hard-to-beat football powers—in the nation. They carried quite a number of impressive laurels into that first game with them:

Notre Dame teams had brought the National Championship back to South Bend seven different times—a feat no other school had equaled in the long history of collegiate football. Notre Dame teams had also won six Western Championship titles, and they had amassed a total of 17 undefeated seasons—ten of them, untied. They had established a record with modem college football's longest string of unbeaten games at 39.

The Fighting Irish had also turned out more Ail-Americans than any other college or university in the nation. The prowess of Gipp, Crowley and Brown previewed the performances of the immortal four horsemen and their rampage that set the nation's gridirons afire in the early 1920s. Since then, the roster has grown with the names of men like Carideo, Brill, Connor, Lujack, Fischer and Hart.

This year's team has done it again—in performances and personalities.

They have plowed through a suicidal schedule with what we consider as a powerful precision that matches any previous team in Notre Dame's history. At times, when the odds were stacked, they produced the stuff that has earned for them the national recognition which they justly deserve. Although not every one of them got All-American honors, every one of them played like it.

You've noticed, for example, that Notre Dame seldom shook one of its backs loose for long touchdown sprints this season; but they tore opposing teams to shreds with steady power plays and tricky tosses until they finally hit pay dirt. This is the story of teamwork ... the story that always ends well.

Looking back, we can truthfully say that it has been another great season. Most people say that this year's team will go down in the record books as one of our greatest. Only time will tell. One thing we do know, however, is that it was made up of the same stuff 64 teams before it had—the will to win.

We're again reminded of the words former Irish captain Jack Alessandrini once said at a pep rally before a game with Pittsburgh: "We can't be beat when we won't be beat." It's the same principle that wins National Championships and molds All Americans. As Knute Rockne put it: "I don't want a man to go in there to die gamely—I want a man to go in there fighting to live!"

Not -- Notre Dame plays so hard—not because she hates to lose, but because she loves to win.

Patrick Carrico
Editor, the Scholastic.

In 1953, The Notre Dame Fighting Irish football team played its last season for Coach Frank Leahy who retired for health reasons. The Irish were undefeated again under Leahy with a record of 9-0-1, which got Notre Dame a #2 finish in the national standings.

Leahy Superstar: Johnny Lattner

Leahy guided John Lattner to win the **Heisman Trophy**. It was Leahy's fourth player to win the Heisman. Lattner was an all-around great player. He did not lead the Irish in passing, rushing, receiving or scoring. However, Lattner held the Notre Dame record for all-purpose yards for twenty-six years until Vagas Ferguson broke it in 1979.

Lattner claimed the Heisman Trophy during his senior year. It was the second-closest Heisman balloting in history. It bears repeating that Lattner did not lead the Irish in rushing, passing, receiving or scoring. He was a jack of all trades who barely nosed out Minnesota's Paul Giel for the award.

Lattner clearly benefitted from helping Leahy's final Notre Dame team to a 9-0-1 record and having the Irish win the national title recognition helped the balloting. Johnny received the Maxwell Award as the top collegiate player as both a junior and senior and finished fifth in the Heisman voting as a junior behind Oklahoma's Billy Vessels.

Frank Leahy's Post Script

BELONGED UNDER GOLDEN DOME AS FRESHMAN TO GRIDIRON COACH

Chicago Daily Tribune February 1, 1954

Our sincere thanks to the Chicago Tribune for permission to print this well-written, tremendous tribute to Frank Leahy

BY EDWARD PRELL

From the time that he was elected president of his freshman class. Frank Leahy belonged at Notre Dame. And he will continue to belong under the golden dome despite his retirement.

In 1927 he was a big, rugged youngster from the plains of South Dakota and Nebraska, who, after a mental tug-o'-war, had decided to enter college against seeking his fortune in the professional prize ring.

No fame that might have come his way as a boxer could have matched that which he gained in his brilliant career as football coach of the Fighting Irish. He was the modern Knute Rockne whose teams had the scoring magic in the clutch which had distinguished Notre Dame under the Norwegian from Chicago.

A Picture Coach

Leahy is a picture coach in physique and mannerisms. Six feet tall and weighing 190 pounds, he is a striking figure. A firm jaw, topped off with blue eyes and brown hair help make his face strong and handsome.

He became the dominant coach of his time. His success was built upon a zealous devotion to Notre Dame and his job. Four times his teams were rated national champions. Six times in his 11 year term the Irish were undefeated. Countless of his lads—that's what Leahy called his athletes—won All-America acclaim.

A Family Man

Leahy, the coach, also is a family man. He was a member of Fordham's coaching staff when, on-July 4, 1935, he married Florence Reilly of Brooklyn. The ceremony was performed in St. Patrick's church in the Bronx.

The first of eight children, Frank Jr., was born on April 28, 1936. Others born to the union are Susan Marie, 15; Florence, 13; Jerry, 10; James, 6; Frederick John,4; Mary Patricia, 2, & Christopher, 1.

Leahy was born on Aug. 21, 1908, in O'Neill, Nebraska, the son of Frank and Mary Leahy. He is one of eight children-four boys and four girls.

At Winner [S.D.] High school he won football, basketball, and baseball letters for three years under Coach Earl Walsh, who had been a mono gram winner at Notre Dame in 1920 and 1921. An after dinner speech by Rockhe and by Coach Walsh convinced the youngster that Notre Dame was the place for him.

In his senior high school year, Leahy captained three sports teams at Central High school in Omaha, after his parents had. moved to the' Nebraska metropolis.

Played Center in 1928

In the fall of 1927, when he reported for freshman football at Notre Dame, Leahy's coach was Tommy Mills. As a sophomore in 1928, Leahy played in two games as a center. The following season he was regular tackle on Rockne's national champions, but a knee injury in pre-season practice kept him out of action in 1930, his senior year.

Rockne was so attracted to the earnest, soft spoken youngster that after the 1930 season he invited him along to the Mayo Clinic for repairs. Rockne underwent treatment for a leg ailment, which had almost cost his life in 1929. Leahy submitted to a. knee operation and a two week course in inside football as hospital roommate of Rockne.

Aid at Georgetown

In 1931, after receiving his bachelor of science degree in physical education, Leahy immediately moved into the college coaching ranks as assistant to Mills at Georgetown university. Against Jimmy Crowley's [one of the Four Horsemen] Michigan State eleven that season, Georgetown was beaten by only 6 to 0. The Georgetown line, coached by Leahy, made such an impression on Crowley that he persuaded the youngster to join him the following season at Michigan State.

Wins in Sugar Bowl

When Crowley moved to Fordham in 1933, he took along Leahy, who promptly began his most monumental job as a line coach-that of fashioning the famous "Seven Blocks of Granite." This line kept Fordham from defeat on all but two occasions in 1935. 1936, and 1937. His coaching apprenticeship-ended after the 1938 season when he was appointed head coach at Boston College.

Leahy's 1939 Boston eleven won nine, losing to Florida, 6 to 0, and to Clemson, 6 to 3. The next season brought a clean sweep, climaxed by a 19 to 13 upset of Tennessee in the Sugar bowl.

In the 11 games, Boston scored 339 points to 55 and six of the victories were shutouts.

Since Rockne's death in an airplane accident over Kansas early in 1931, Notre Dame's head coaching succession had passed to Heartly [Hunk] Anderson and Elmer Layden. Layden, one of the fabled Four Horsemen, had taken over in 1934. At the end of the 1940 season he resigned as athletic director and head coach to become National Football league commissioner.

Return of Leahy

Once again Notre Dame was looking for a coach. But it was a short search. Two weeks after Layden' s resignation, Leahy, then 32, was announced as the new athletic director and head coach. The date was Feb. 15, 1941.

He took charge in spring football practice on March 12. On the same day he was given a tremendous ovation by several thousands of students in the-Notre Dame Gymnasium.

"This is a trip back home," he responded. "We [he often used the editorial 'we' instead of 'I'] hope, with the guidance of the faculty, good material, hard work, and with the support of the student body, to produce a team comparable to those that have preceded."

Accepts the Challenge

"The student body is the 12th man on our team and it will be the best 12th man in the United States. We accept the challenge of this appointment. Perhaps we can make in a small way a return on the tremendous debt we owe our alma mater."

Leahy brought along his three Boston assistants - Ed McKeever, John Druze, and Joe McArdle. None had played football at Notre Dame except McKeever, who transferred to Texas Tech after his freshman year.

Of the three assistants he brought to Notre Dame from Boston, all stayed except McKeever. It was McArdle who took command during the 1953 season when Leahy's attack of Pancreatitis Between halves of the game against Georgia Tech on Oct. 24 forced him to the sidelines.

Coached Over TV

Before returning to the practice field on Nov. 4 for the match against Penn, Leahy directed the squad from his bed in St. Joseph's hospital when a closed television circuit was rigged up at Cartier field, more than a mile away.

Leahy started repaying his "debt" to his alma mater in the 1941 season when the Irish won eight and tied one. The deadlock was a scoreless tie with the Army. Leahy was named the Coach of the Year in the annual poll of the New York World-Telegram. His team had beaten three rivals from the Big Ten-Northwest ern, Indiana, and Illinois.

The strain of Leahy's terrific coaching pace first developed in the 1942 season when he left on Oct. 9 for a checkup at the Mayo clinic. It was not uncommon for Leahy to summon his aids to staff meetings as early as 5 a. m. He worked far into the night.

Passes Team to McKeever

"I have reached the point physically where I am of no value to the Notre Dame he said. "For this reason I have decided to leave the squad in Ed McKeever's hands."'

Leahy, after treatment for what was diagnosed as spinal arthritis, returned three weeks later for the game against Navy which Notre Dame won, 9 to 0.

In discussing his condition, Leahy recalled he had suffered a back injury as a youngster in diving and that in his freshman season at Notre Dame several vertebrae were injured in a head-on tackle of Marty Brill.

Lost to Great Lakes

The Irish won seven, lost two, and tied two in this hectic 1942 campaign. Losses were to Georgia Tech, 13 to 6, and to Michigan, 32 to 20. In 1943, Leahy's stature increased with a 9 to 1 tabulation. The defeat was inflicted by Great Lakes in the final game and in the final minute of the season by a desperation pass from Steve Lach to Paul Anderson, making the score 19 to 13.

On May 19, 1944, Leahy was sworn into the Navy in Chicago as a lieutenant. After eight weeks of indoctrination at Princeton, he was assigned to Admiral Charles Lockwood, Pacific submarine commander. Leahy's duties were to organize and supervise athletic activities and recreation for submarine crews returning from combat patrols.

Long Term Contract

When he left the Navy service late in 1945, Leahy was a Lieutenant-Commander. He came back to the Notre Dame campus in November of that year. Months before, the Rev. Hugh O'Donnell, C. S. C., president of Notre Dame, had announced the signing of Leahy to a long term post-war contract.

Leahy punctuated the resumption of his coaching in 1946 with his second unbeaten season at Notre Dame—eight victories and the inevitable scoreless tie with Army.

Johnny Lujack was his quarterback that season, as he had been in 1943 and was to be in 1947. Lujack was the first string quarter back in 22 of the games in those three seasons.

Wins All-Star Game

Leahy began the 1947 season as head coach of the College All-Stars, who won a smashing 16 to 0 triumph over the Chicago Bears-their first defeat in the colorful spectacle. The Notre Dame coach went on to an undefeated, untied season which included nine victories. Most spectacular, perhaps, was the 59 to 6 shellacking of a Tulane team which came to South Bend with all Dixie predicting a victory.

After 1947, Leahy's Irish elevens had won 41 games, lost three, and tied four. The phenomenal record brought him rich offers, including one to join the Detroit Lions.

Leads All-Stars Again

Leahy, again the College All- Stars' head coach in 1948, saw his forces beaten by the Chicago Cardinals, 28 to 0. Players from Notre Dame and Michigan predominated. The Irish played the T formation, the Wolverines the single wing. Leahy felt it only fair to divide his squad into units playing the two different systems. In so doing, he might have sacrificed his chances for victory or for a closer game.

The Irish rolled on in '48, winning nine straight until held to a 14 to 14 tie by Southern California in the final game.

On March 22, 1949, Leahy relinquished the athletic directorship to Ed [Moose] Krause, basketball coach, who had been a great all- athlete at Notre Dame. The action was taken at Leahy's request.

A Two Man Job

"With increased enrolment and increases in all athletic problems it would be prudent for the university to have these two important p o s i t i o n s handled by separate individuals," he told the Rev. John J. Cavanaugh, C. S. C., president of Notre Dame.

"We have now come to the realization that too much has been demanded of Frank Leahy," said Fr. Cavanaugh. "As a result of performing the duties associated with both positions, he has more often than not had to put in working days lasting from 16 to 18 hours."

Always the pessimist in public statements on Notre Dame's victory chances, Leahy said in the spring of 1949: "We'll have the worst team Notre Dame ever had. We'll lose seven games."

Won 10 Out of 10

It developed into Leahy's most whopping season with the Irish winning 10 out of 10- the first a 49 to 6 rout of Indiana, the last the spectacular 27 to 20 triumph over Southern Methodist.

Leahy's reward was his selection by the Football Writers of America as football's Man of the Year. The Washington Touchdown club gave him a similar honor. Emil Sitko was rated the nation's outstanding back. Leon Hart won the Rockne Memorial trophy as the nation's best lineman, an honor which had been won by Bill Fischer in 1948 and Bob Dove in 1942.

A Big Strain

Commenting on the strain of coaching during the 1949 season, Leahy said:

"When you are a coach at Notre Dame you don't control your personal life. You belong to the people, to the priests, to the radio. I notice now that I become fatigued a little earlier each day. My family would be happy if I decided to discontinue coaching. During the fall I get home twice a week. The other nights I stay at the university. In 1947, during the winter months, there was one stretch when I was home only six nights in 90. The rest of the time I was out, speaking."

Only once did Leahy publicly blast officiating at a game in which his team competed. This was in 1949 after a 27 to 7 victory over Washington in Seattle.

"How could it be a good game when we had to play four extra men?" he asked. "They tried to even up the game. They wouldn't even explain to our captain the penalties they called."

The Irish had an unbeaten string of 38 games when the 1950 season started. They defeated North Carolina in the opener, 14 to 7, but this was the end. The next Saturday they were walloped by Purdue, 28 to 14. This was to be the only dismal season in Leahy's career. Notre Dame lost three more times and wound up with a 4-4-1 record.

At Best In 1951

Leahy's greatest coaching challenge came in 1951. He had perhaps the youngest squad in Notre Dame History and even the staunchest supporters of the Irish were not prepared for a spectacular comeback. He perhaps showed his greatest genius as a coach in directing the team to a 7-2-1 season.

The defeats were inflicted by Southern Methodist, 27 to 20, and by Michigan State, 35 to 0. But after this latter loss the Irish rebounded to trounce North Carolina, Iowa, and Southern California.

In the 1952 season, Notre Dame was the underdog in at least five of its games. These five opponents either won or tied in their conference races. One of them, Michigan State, was national champion in '52.

Sixth Unbeaten Season

Again the Irish posted a 7-2-1 record. They lost to Pittsburgh in the third game, 22 to- 19, and to Michigan State, 21 to 3, in the eighth contest of the year. Then they walloped Iowa, 27 to 0, and Southern California fell, 9 to 0.

Then came Notre Dame's sixth unbeaten season in 1953, climaxed with a 48 to 14' crushing of Southern California. Only a 14 to 14 dramatic tie with Iowa prevented another all-victorious campaign.

Here is the wrap-up to Frank Leahy from the Chicago Daily Tribune:

http://archives.chicagotribune.com/1954/02/01/page/1/article/leahy-resigns-at-notre-dame

Feel free to take this link and many more in this edition of the Chicago Tribune from 1954. There are many Leahy articles in this edition from the day after Coach's resignation from the University of Notre Dame

Leahy Resigns at Notre Dame

Ill Health Ends Coach's 11 Year Reign
Will Rest, Then Enter Business
By Arch Ward The **Chicago Daily Tribune** February 1, 1954

Frank Leahy, the most successful college football coach of his time, yesterday resigned from the University of Notre Dame.

Leahy's decision to abandon his position was necessitated by ill health. He never has recovered fully from the acute pancreatic attack he suffered during the Notre Dame – Georgia Tech game Oct. 24.

Plans Business Career

University Authorities concurred in the recommendation of Leahy's physician that he withdraw from an activity involving the emotional and physical strain of football coaching. Leahy, 45, who had two more years remaining on a ten year contract, plans a business career after a long rest.

Notre Dame Executives have given no hint as to Leahy's successor, but it is expected he will come from the present staff. Joe McArdle, who had had charge of Notre Dame's defense, Rober McBride, who has set up the offensive patterns, Johnny Lujack, Bill Early, John Druse, Wally Ziemba, and Terry Brennan all are qualified for the assignment.

Only Unbeaten Major Undefeated Team

Leahy in his last season produced the only major undefeated college football team in the United States. Notre Dame was tied by Iowa, 14-14, but defeated the other nine opponents on its schedule. It was rated # 2 behind Maryland in the Associated Press poll.

Chapter 12 Coach Terry Brennan 1954-1958

Coach # 20

Coach Terry Brennan Was Just a Kid

1954	Terry Brennan	9–1
1955	Terry Brennan	8–2
1956	Terry Brennan	2–8
1957	Terry Brennan	7–3
1958	Terry Brennan	6–4

Intro from Chicago Tribune:

Brennan, who at 25 [was] the youngest of the Notre Dame corps, was the only one with extensive experience as a head coach. His Mount Carmel High School teams won the Chicago Championship three straight years – 1950, 1951, and 1952.

Coach Terence Patrick Brennan, who was born June 11, 1928, and was just 26 years old when appointed Notre Dame Head Football Coach in 1954, took over after Frank Leahy retired.

Notre Dame was beginning to believe in its own magic. Leahy worked sixteen hour plus days and (living 30miles away) never went home in order to bring winning seasons to Notre Dame. There was no magic in his results—just hard work. At 45 years of age, Frank Leahy had gotten old too, too quickly and he was feeling old when he retired.

Terry Brennan was a good man and always a good coach but Leahy, almost like Rockne before him, was so extra good that even today many expert analysts looking back consider him as a souped up coaching version of Knute Rockne. Notre Dame always has the highest expectations for all of its coaches. Rockne for thirteen and then Leahy for eleven spoiled Notre Dame into thinking wins came simply by being Notre Dame. Who, after Leahy could make anybody think that a loss or a tie was acceptable? Nobody!

When Leahy moved on, Notre Dame was so accustomed to winning that it had begun to take winning for granted in the appointment of Terry Brennan, a good man and a good coach but with just high school experience. Brennan took on the most major leadership collegiate football coaching role in the US at age 26. He did fine but then again it was Notre Dame and all those expectations.

Some say Parseghian pulled a Leahy later on in ND history with all of his success. He helped the University again to take winning for granted. After Parseghian & Dan Devine, University officials again blindly trusted another great HS coach, Gerry Faust, a championship HS coach of the highest caliber, to bring in the bacon. Said differently, the University repeated the Terry Brennan mistake by bringing on a high school coach after Parseghian and Devine, even though they had been forced to fire Brennan, whose record was actually not bad at all.

So, we ask the question: "Was Brennan the best coach available in the nation in 1954?" Was Brennan, IMHO, a great young man and a fine coach, the right choice? What about Vince Lombardi?

Expectations of any coach after Leahy, just like the post Rockne years, seemed to be that the Institution was so blessed that it might even be able to return to the seven years from 1887 to 1893 when there was no need to even pay for a coach. The student athletes coached themselves then, and the teams were always tough and they did quite well. Well, not exactly, but it makes one think. Just as in academics, if there is no work by the talented, there is no success.

Brennan at 26 was already a success!

Terry Brennan is an original native of Milwaukee, Wisconsin, where he was an outstanding multi-sport athlete at Marquette University High School, He went on to play halfback at Notre Dame from 1945 to 1948 for Frank Leahy, graduating in 1949.

After receiving his degree from Notre Dame, Brennan took a coaching slot at Mount Carmel High School in Chicago, where his team won three successive city championships. He came back to Notre Dame in 1953 as freshman football coach, and rumor has it to become the next head coach at Notre Dame. He did indeed succeed Frank Leahy as head coach the following year in 1954. His college coaching incubation period was way too short.

Every article about Brennan's hiring has this one question and Brennan's answer as a key part of the piece. When asked if he thought he was too young to be named head coach at the age of 25, Brennan replied, "Oh, I don't know. I'll be 26 in a few months."

As we will see in this chapter, Brennan got off to a fine start with a (9-1) campaign in 1954 with players that had been recruited and coached by Leahy. In 1955, the Irish lost just one more game than in 1954 and slipped to (8–2). Just as had occurred in Leahy's worst year ever when athletic scholarships were reduced, with Brennan in 1956, results suffered. However, Notre Dame officials did not have to argue with the personal power of Frank Leahy and so the young coach was forced to take whatever they gave in scholarships.

The ND administration was always interested in highlighting academics above athletics but it had always supported maintaining Notre Dame's football legacy. Until this year, other than one time in Leahy's time, when his record went to hades, there was never so broad a cut as in Brennan's scholarships. The 26-year old responded as an obedient employee. It was the hand he was dealt. He figured the Catholics would be fair.

Maybe Terry Brennan and Joe Kuharich after him were not such bad coaches? Just maybe???

NDNation's Rock report http://ndnation.com/archives/3722 offers a perspective on the scholarship issue dating back to Frank Leahy.

ND Nation's reports so far surely appear to be spot-on:

> *"In 1947 Notre Dame cut scholarships from 32 to 18 (Michigan and Ohio State had 45-50 scholarships to give) hobbling Leahy's great run and hastening his exit. [After Leahy's 4-4-1 1950 season, he got more scholarships and the team made a comeback]. That move was followed by questionable hires and rising academic standards. During Terry Brennan's era, Hunk Anderson said "You can't run this program with these numbers and I'll tell you what else, when the shit comes down, you guys will be the fall guys." Anderson actually organized a group of monogram winners to plead for more scholarships (Hesburgh turned him down.) To sum up quotes from "Talking Irish", and "Resurrection," Notre Dame's mediocrity seemed to come from a combination of poor coaching, low scholarships and a general lack of support.*
>
> *When Ara came to Notre Dame, the Irish were far behind in the scholarship arms race. It started with the neutering of Leahy and Notre Dame didn't wake up until Ara. When Parseghian came in he convinced Hesburgh to increase scholarships from 24 to 34. Still far behind the land grant schools, but that move gave Notre Dame a chance to build a program and, importantly, signaled that Notre Dame was serious about competing again. Parseghian continued to push the administration along, earning concessions where Brennan and Kuharich failed."*

Academics trumped Athletics at ND

What this meant was that Notre Dame had determined that either it could do well without scholarships or that it was OK if it did not do well so it could be recognized as more elite in academia.

The result for a fine coach such as Terry Brennan, was that he got stuck with an intolerable situation as without Leahy, nobody was fighting for the continued health of the football program. As a respectful young man, Brennan did what his elders and superiors told him to do and did not take them on as Leahy and as Parseghian after him would do.

There are many stories about talented players not coming to Notre Dame because of its de-emphasis of football and reemphasis of academics. People across the universe make decisions that benefit them, not somebody else. Therefore, many great players from across the nation, who would have come and played for Notre Dame, were forced to look for other opportunities for a free education. Why pay tuition at Notre Dame in a football program that no longer seemed to care to invest in winning, when a college education and a brighter football career someplace else was free?

On top of not having the proper cadre of replacement players for normal duty. Brennan's team were injury prone in 1956 and the coach was forced to play mostly sophomores. There were numerous player injuries and the lack of players resulted in a (2 – 8) record. This was the first losing season for Notre Dame since 1933 and it was the worst football season in the history of the school. Nobody said that it was not Terry Brennan's fault. Even students blamed Brennan. The ND community, not tuned into the impact of scholarship reductions felt that Brennan was being paid to win… period.

Despite Brennan's poor record there was a lone bright spot—Paul Hornung. The great Paul Hornung, the bad boy everybody seemed to love, who would go on to be a phenomenon for the Green Bay Packers, won the Heisman Trophy for Brennan and Notre Dame despite the 2-8 season. To this day, Hornung remains the only player ever to win the coveted Heisman award while playing for a team with a losing record.

Unfortunately, many fans and alumni were not prepared to look into why the personnel on the team could not play as well as the opposing teams. They were not into giving Brennan a second chance and they steadfastly called for his resignation, but the young coach, after this miserable 2-8 season, was unexpectedly retained.

It was tough not being able to replace able players who had been injured, but the movement by school administrators to put more emphasis on academics and less on athletics naturally led to the popular notion that Notre Dame had deemphasized football. This did nothing for the recruiting program.

In addition to less scholarships, players with talent who could have gotten an available Notre Dame scholarship had to deal with coaches from other teams using a recruitment message that Notre Dame was doing away with football to be a better academic school. Why compromise your football career on a wish? —was the message.

Brennan therefore was forced to do his best with players who were not as talented as most scholarship athletes. His total was reduced to 20 football scholarships per class, while Notre Dame was not willing to drop to Division II. The Irish continued to play tough schedules. Brennan worked hard and did surprisingly well.

Academics had always come first at Notre Dame, but for a few years after Leahy went 4-4-1, the prior coach had carte blanche to do what he wished until the Rev. Theodore Martin Hesburgh became president of the university. One of Hesburgh's first priorities as president was to reaffirm Notre Dame's position on academics.

Brennan's 1957 squad showed improvement and were nicknamed "Comeback Comets" after finishing (7–3). This team had some great moments such as a win W (23-21) comeback over Army and a monumental W (7-0) shutout of Oklahoma, snapping the Sooners' NCAA record 47-game winning streak. After ND loosened up on the scholarships, there was not enough time to rebuild. Seniors with experience are typically not in any coach's recruiting class. Nobody was out there lobbying for Terry Brennan, the kid who took a chance on Notre Dame.

Brennan's Irish posted a (6-4) record in 1958. This did not make the Notre Dame faithful happy and again the call came out to dismiss Brennan and it gained momentum. The administration fired the coach along with his entire staff in mid-December; Hugh Devore, who was a mainstay, was eventually retained.

There was another group of fans and alumni that saw firing Brennan as a big mistake by the Notre Dame administration, and they criticized Brennan's ouster. The coach's record was not really bad at (32-18), when the pundits examined the caliber of Notre Dame's opponents. Moving forward to 1958, Brennan was succeeded as Notre Dame's head coach by professional coach Joe Kuharich. Let's now take a very brief look at each of Brennan's seasons. See what you think. Nobody's perfect, even the most well-intentioned officials.

1954 Coach Terry Brennan Year 1

First year coach Terry Brennan guided the 1954 Notre Dame Fighting Irish football team to a well-played 9-1 season and a #4 national ranking. Their one loss was against rival Purdue L (14-27) in the battle for the Shillelagh Trophy. The Irish beat Michigan State at home W (20-19) to claim the Megaphone trophy and they beat USC at home W (23-17) to snag the Jeweled Shillelagh.

1955 Coach Terry Brennan Year 2

The 27-year old Coach, Terry Brennan brought the Irish to an 8-2 season in 1955, which gave them a # 9 ranking with AP and a #10 ranking in the Coaches poll.

1956 Coach Terry Brennan Year 3

Terry Brennan coached the 1956 Notre Dame Fighting Irish football team to its worst record of all time (2-8) as Notre Dame remained unranked for the season.

Paul Hornung

Hornung, who later had a great career with the Green Bay Packers was in his senior year in 1956. He carried the ball 94 times for 420 yards for an average of 4.5 yards per try. The versatile Hornung also completed 59 of 111 passes for a total offensive figure of 1,337 yards.

Hornung is the only Heisman winner to have ever played on a losing team. Hornung's path to the Heisman was filled with intrigue, surprise and adventure. Many pundits would suggest that his was the most controversial **Heisman Trophy Award** ever given, but nobody could deny his phenomenal athletic abilities.

Paul Horning Being Paul Hornung a great ND Heismann Winner --

Leahy had recruited Hurnung and beat Bear Bryant for his services. He took Hornung aside when he came to visit Notre Dame and calmly looked Hornung in the eye and told the young recruiting prospect that he thought "he could become the best football player in America if he came to Notre Dame." Hurnung signed up.

Hornung was the ideal football player. He was what they called "A triple threat." He could run, pass and KICK. When I was a kid I remember Hurnung also got a KICK out of life. "The lad" was a free spirit, very handsome, making it perfect for him to double as a playboy type with many off-field escapades well noted in what some call the sleepy hamlets of South Bend and Green Bay. Hornung had it all. He was personable and in fact dashing. He earned the nickname, the "Golden Boy!" Later in life he had some neck issues which limited his mobility.

Notre Dame's Press Agent, well-liked Charlie Callahan was continually lobbying for Hornung to be awarded the Heisman in his senior year. He was very convincing and very successful. The Golden Boy beat Johnny Majors by just 72 votes and he beat the great pass-catcher, Tommy McDonald, who came in a strong third.

Terry Brennan was Hornung's coach in his senior year, and surely Brennan claims Hornung as a product of his personal mentoring. However, for those who count things further back, Hornung counts as the fifth ND player to have been coached by Frank Leahy (freshman) to take away the Heisman. Leahy, I am convinced would have given this stat to Brennan but surely was not asked while in retirement.

Head coach Terry Brennan, and Heisman Winner Paul Hornung in his monogram sweater, with the Enterprise Football Medal.

1957 Coach Terry Brennan Year 4

The 1957 Notre Dame Fighting Irish football team coached by Terry Brennan had a much better year than in 1956. The team finished ranked # 9 in the coaches' poll and #10 in the AP with a 7-3 overall win/loss record.

Irish QB Bob Williams # 9 on ND's winning drive

The historical highlight of the season was on November 16. Terry Brennan's Fighting Irish marched into Oklahoma Memorial Stadium to play the proud Sooners, who were sporting a 47-game winning streak. At the time, this win streak was the record. Notre Dame's W (7–0) victory over Oklahoma snapped the Sooners' NCAA record 47-game winning streak.

A lot of forgiveness was given by Notre Dame Fans for the 1956 season after this great triumph. The win against Oklahoma was monumental. Victory was denied the Sooners that day by QB Bob Williams, Terry Brennan, and all of the Fighting Irish that afternoon at Owen Field.

"Quarterback Bobby Williams, [my cousin from Wilkes-Barre PA] played superbly. "You could have quarterback meetings forever," Brennan said. "But the kid's gotta go out there and do it. And he did it." The Irish reached first-and-goal at the OU 8-yard line, then finally faced fourth-and-goal at the three. Williams called the play, a sweep for Lynch. A field goal never entered Brennan's mind. "We wanted a touchdown," he said. Lynch gave them one, with an easy trot around right end, and with 3:50 left in the game, OU trailed." They lost!

THE DAILY OKLAHOMAN

IRISH SNIP OU STREAK AT 47

In the Nov. 16, 1957 photo on the prior page, Notre Dame head coach Terry Brennan is carried off Owen Field by Jim Just (44) and other players following their 7-0 win over Oklahoma in an NCAA college football game in Norman, Okla. Notre Dame's Ron Toth (43) and Jim Colosimo (41) also celebrate the final. That victory ended the Sooners' NCAA-record winning streak at 47 games and came just a season after the Sooners beat the Irish 40-0 in South Bend, still the most lopsided home loss in Notre Dame history.

1958 Coach Terry Brennan Year 5

For a Notre Dame fan, there is only one thing that is just a little worse than a (7-3) season. That of course is a (6-4) season. It's just a little worse. The 1958 Notre Dame Fighting Irish football team, coached by fifth-year coach Terry Brennan could not find that seventh win, and the Irish thus finished the season at 6-4. Notre Dame had just increased the number of scholarships but not in time for its 1958 season. Notre dame finished the season ranked # 18. Brennan had to take the fall. There would be no forgiveness.

Regardless of Joe Kuharich's prowess as a pro-football coach, I think with scholarships restored, Terry Brennan had learned how to field and coach college football players. I was only ten years old at the time so nobody asked me for advice and at the time, I could not have given it. I wanted ND to win… that was it!

After the end of this season, Terry Brennan and his whole coaching staff were fired and Joe Kuharich was appointed the new Notre Dame Head Coach. Coach Hugh Devore was eventually retained for Coach Kuharich as an assistant.

Let me end the Terry Brennan Era with two well-written, poignant articles that give different perspectives on Brannan's time at Notre Dame. This first article on Terry Brennan is from Notre Dame's Scholastic Magazine's January 1959 edition. The students saw Brennan's firing as a just outcome of not performing as promised:

> *It is certainly probable that sometime in the future Notre Dame will not be financially dependent on "big-time" college football, but it still is today. The income from Notre Dame's intercollegiate football program finances all the other sports at the University as*

far as I can ascertain. It is obvious then that a serious reduction in the income from football would result in the forced abandonment of the rest of Notre Dame's intercollegiate sports program.

There are many idealists both here at the University and outside it who feel that football, as well as all other sports, should be not the business it is now but purely an athletic outlet for the students. This column will not try to decide the merit or lack of it in this statement. It rather merely assumes as a basis the fact that Notre Dame at present needs "big business" football.

Inasmuch as football here is a business and necessarily so from a financial standpoint (whether this is the way it should be or not), those who have concerned themselves with the recent firing of Head Football Coach Terry Brennan must remember that Brennan had a job to do. Whether or not he should be retained by the University depends on how well it feels he is accomplishing his job.

Obviously, the five-man faculty board which recommended Brennan's release looked at his record and concluded that he had not done as well as he should have. What I mean by "as well" is this: He had not performed his job as a FOOTBALL COACH as well as he should have.

WRONG BASIS

This is one of the two points on which the newspapers around the country, in their practically unanimous denouncement of Brennan's release have been carried away by their own emotionalism. The newspapers have argued against Brennan's dismissal on the grounds of his character, personality, and integrity. I doubt that any of the backers of the dismissal base their arguments on the lack of these attributes in Brennan. The release was based on an evaluation of his ability' as a football coach, not on an evaluation of his character.

Just as the University would tend to release the head of any academic department if he were not measuring up to the University's high academic standards, it reserves the right to release the football coach for the same reason if the faculty board feels the situation warrants such action. While the football coach is more publicized than any head of an academic department here, he still must perform up to the expectations of his employer.

ACADEMIC EMPHASIS

The second and more poignant point on which the newspapers and magazines, although not as many, have taken what is in my mind an unreasonable stand is the diminution of emphasis on the academic. Some publications have concluded that the release of one football coach and the replacement of him by another leads inexorably to a drop in the academic emphasis and ideals at Notre Dame. Academic standards at the University need not drop because of the change in coaches.

Academic standards do not depend on how many games a football team wins but rather on the emphasis on the academic life of the students and the faculty. A desire to win football games is not incompatible with this emphasis.

Most of the newspapers and magazines that have expressed an opinion on this matter have brought up the fact that Brennan compiled a 32-18 record in his five years here. It is also true that he had a 6-4 record against major opposition in his last season.

Last year it was different. Newspapers have claimed that a 6-4 record against major opposition is creditable enough for any school; many schools would be more than satisfied with this record. It is significant that Notre Dame was satisfied apparently with Brennan's 2-8 record two years ago. Father Hesburgh endorsed him enthusiastically at that time.

Brennan was not released because he compiled a 6 & 4 record in itself. He was released because he compiled a 6-4 record when the faculty board felt he should have done better with the material he had. I feel the same way. —T.T.

*** **End of Scholastic article** ***

By the way, I disagree. Brennan, I believe would have been a great coach with the scholarships back and a little more age. He was just 30 years old in his last season for heaven's sake. Think about that. Many of our children today still don't have good jobs at age 30.

Before I release you all to read the second transition article that takes us past Brennan, through Kuharich, and on to Parseghian, permit me to add another postscript on the Terry Brennan Era? Here we go:

I was expecting, at about a 100% level, to find that Mr. Brennan had either become a successful head coach in another college football program or perhaps he had become a great pro football coach. In many ways, he was before my time so he was not a household name.

I did not know which to expect; but figured one or the other. I expected success for Brennan in football. Since he was before my time, I looked him up and I kept looking as what I expected to find in my research just was not showing up. I eventually tried the Notre Dame web site.

In his biography on http://www.und.com/sports/m-footbl/mtt/brennan_terry00.html, Notre Dame captured the fact that in 1959, Brennan ended his football coaching career and

"... became the player conditioning coach for the Cincinnati Reds in spring training. Eventually, he joined a Chicago investment banking firm."

That's all she wrote. Coaching at Notre Dame is like nothing else in the world. Terry Brennan stopped coaching for good after being fired by Notre Dame. It took me by surprise.

There is another great article about Terry Brennan available from the Sports Illustrated vault. If you are interested in a professional pundit's take on ND and Terry Brennan, feel free to take the link below.

SURRENDER AT NOTRE DAME

http://www.si.com/vault/1959/01/05/668468/surrender-at-notre-dame
By Leon Jaroff

Chapter 13 Coach Joseph Kuharich; Coach Hugh Devore: 1959-1963

Coach Kuharich # 21
Coach Devore # 19 (second time)

1959	Joe Kuharich	5–5
1960	Joe Kuharich	2–8
1961	Joe Kuharich	5–5
1962	Joe Kuharich	5–5
1963	Hugh Devore	2–7

The Desert Sun Newspaper reported the following on Dec. 22, 1958

Joe Kuharich New Coach at Notre Dame

Succeeds Brennan, Fired by Irish, as Gridiron Mentor
December 22, 1958; **SOUTH BEND. Ind. (UPI)**

"Joe Kuharich. head roach of the Washington Redskins of the National Football League and former Notre Dame guard, today was named football coach at Notre Dame, succeeding Terry Brennan. Kuharich's appointment was announced oy the Rev, Edmund P. Joyce, Notre Dame executive vice president, and chairman of the faculty Board in Control of Athletics. Release of Brennan, Notre Dame's coach for the past five years, was announced Sunday by university officials. Father Joyce said that Kuharich has been given a four-year contract. Since 1954, Kuharich has been coach of the Washington Redskins. The new Notre Dame mentor, who is a native of South Bend, actually began his coaching career at Notre Dame in 1938, the year of his graduation, when he served as an assistant freshman coach while taking graduate studies."

1959 Coach Joe Kuharich Year 1

Joe Kuharich took over the Notre Dame Fighting Irish football team in 1959 from Terry Brennan when Brennan was able to achieve just six wins. It is always difficult for a new coach to come to a program and start with great results. Kuharich would also find this true.

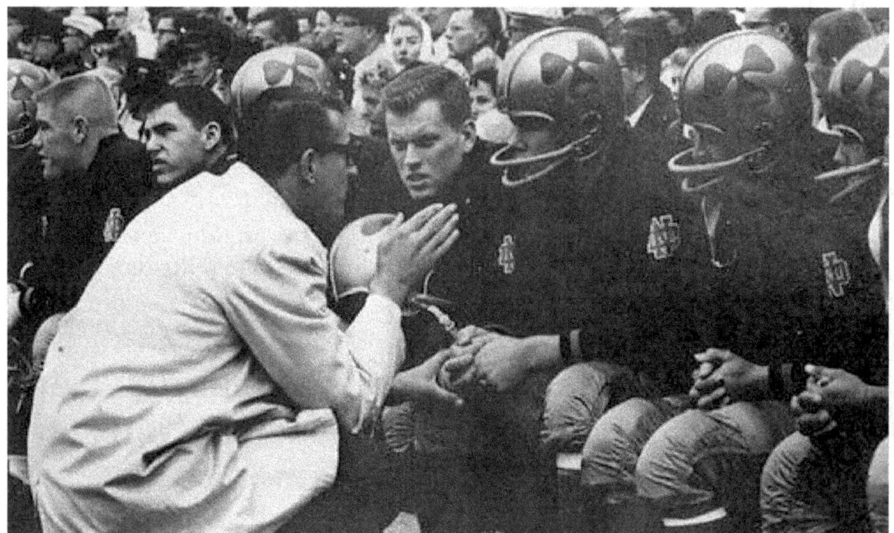

Coach Kuharich made his mark at Notre Dame with the addition of the green shamrock to the gold helmet. The Irish opened the '59 season with the standard all gold shell, facing off against North Carolina and Purdue in their first two games. When they took the field against Cal on October 10th, they unveiled the green shamrock design. However, the decal was placed upon each side of the helmet from a perspective that made it appear as if an airplane propeller was facing the observer, a most unique design! Some thought that the decal was placed upside down but it was merely an attempt by the Kuharich's staff to help jolt the program into a new era.

In his first year Kuharich's Fighting Irish finished 5-5. With a four-year contract in his possession. Coach Kuharich knew he would be able to eventually prove himself to Notre Dame fans.

1960 Coach Joe Kuharich Year 2

The 1960 Notre Dame Fighting Irish football team, coached by Joe Kuharich equaled the season and post-season misery index of Terry Brennan's 2-8 1956 team that many fans think set the stage for Kuharich to be replaced. He was only in year 2 but the murmurs persisted.

The Irish started off their 1960 season sandwich with a nice slice of bread against California at home with a W (21-7) victory. Then, something went wrong. No matter how well Notre Dame played and no matter how close the games were, for eight straight games Notre Dame could not scrounge out one victory for luck or money. There were many close games in these eight and none went the luck of the Irish. The meat of the sandwich was the eight losses in a row.

1961 Coach Joe Kuharich Year 3

The 1961 Notre Dame Fighting Irish football team were coached by Joe Kuharich in his third year as head coach. Coach Kuharich's team struggled in 1960 at 2-8 but came back this year to a 5-5 record and like all ND coaches more would be expected in the future.

Kuharich had two fine co-captains, Norb Roy, and Nick Buoniconti, who had a major claim to fame for years in the NFL.

Darry Lamonica set to pass

Kuharich had matched his first 5-5 season when all was said and done. Many fans were talking about Terry Brennan having been ousted after a 6-4 season. How long would Joe Kuharich last if he did not turn around the team in his fourth year as coach? South Bend Tribune sports editor Joe Doyle in 1961, wrote of Kuharich's third year:

"It is hard to believe the same football team played the various parts of the schedule. One moment the Notre Dame team of 1961 seemed to be an eager, hustling squad that believed it could lick any opponent. At other times, it was indifferent, lethargic and unable to cope with anything out of the ordinary on offense or defense."

1962 Coach Joe Kuharich Year 4

The 1962 Notre Dame Fighting Irish football team again was coached by four-time head coach Joe Kuharich. Darryl Lamonica was Notre Dame's star quarterback but even with Lamonica, the record was another 5-5. Other eventual pro players such as Ed Hoerster and John Slafkosky also played their hearts out on the University of Notre Dame's 1962 college football team.

Nobody thought Notre Dame was laying down and everybody thought Coach Kuharich, who had been a professional coach with the Washington Redskins was doing his best. Yet, the team could not get more than five wins for the fourth time.

Those who think that talent was the problem in the Kuharich era are looking in the wrong place. It was not academics, or any other non-reason including the perception that the university had de-emphasized football under University President Rev. Theodore Hesburgh C.S.C. That too was not the issue this year.

Notre Dame still had lots and lots of interest from great players, and great players were already on the ND roster. Roger Staubach has let it known that he dreamed of going to Notre Dame.

Great players selected & not selected

Somehow a lot of the greats with such dreams were not selected as they were deemed not talented enough to play football at ND. Of course, we all know that in the Kuharich years, an untalented quarterback named Roger Staubach won the Heisman at Navy instead of at Notre Dame in 1963. He then went on to become one of the biggest star pro football players of all time.

Notre Dame players included some future NFL greats such as linemen Paul Costa and Jim Snowden. Kuharich liked these mooses playing in his "Elephant Backfield." Besides Staubach who never got to play for Kuharich, he had several great future NFL stars on his team and a few other big names. You all have heard of quarterback Daryle Lamonica, linebackers Nick Buoniconti and Myron Pottios and of course tackle, Joe Carollo… and there were others.

Parseghian studied Notre Dame

Ara Parseghian eventually took over the reins after Hugh Devore. Parseghian knew how to beat Notre Dame by watching Kuharich as a coach. Northwestern enjoyed playing ND as their coach (Ara Parseghian at the time) always did his homework.

Ara Parseghian, from playing ND, knew how Notre Dame played. This is not a negative aspersion on the ND players or the coach. But, somehow Notre Dame was a gimme win for Northwestern even though they were limited in talent.

When Coach Parseghian and his staff from Northwestern arrived in 1964, they came with some first impressions of the players and their attitudes about playing top level football. They recall the impressions in words such as: "Geez, we never had personnel as talented as this at Northwestern" – even though the Wildcats were 4-0 against the Irish during the Kuharich years (1959-62).

The problem according to flies on the wall in the ND locker room was that during the period of Northwestern's dominance, the Irish talent was either out of position and / or lacking direction. Ara Parseghian as ND coach gave the Irish troops a pep talk early in his tenure before the 1964 season. He told the team that they were not a disciplined team – that when he was at Northwestern he could count on a lot of Notre Dame Penalties, and that those penalties would help shape the outcome of the game.

Notre Dame players concluded that they did not have to wait for spring practice to begin learning how to play for this coach because just listening to coach Parseghian in his once over, they realized that things were about to change.

Joe knew

Joe Kuharich, a good guy for sure but not necessarily a good college football coach, knew he had not done the job for the University and he voluntarily stepped down after his third 5-5 season. He was succeeded with interim coach Hugh Devore in his second stint as an interim coach. (Leahy 1945).

The irony is that Joe Kuharich never achieved any of the fine season marks as Terry Brennan, including Brennan's last season at 6-4 record, which was "so bad," the young Brennan, barely thirty years of age with five-years head coaching experience at Notre Dame was fired.

Notre Dame had finally learned that it was not predestination but fine, determined talented coaching that brings victories, despite how good the players may be. Unfortunately, after extended victory seasons by immortal coaches, the Irish Brass would be forced to learn the lesson several more times before future a potential future immortal, Brian Kelly came to town.

1963 Coach Hugh Devore Year 1 of Second Run

The Press was not as kind to Joe Kuharich as the administration of Notre Dame:

Four Horsemen in 1963

From 1959 to 1962, Kuharich had become the first and only coach at Notre Dame to compile a losing career record. His 17 victories against 23 defeats are still a record. Kent Baer who filled in for Ty Willingham in 2004 for one game and lost it may technically have the worst record of 0-1, but if I made the rules, as a fill-in for one game after the season, he would not be included.

1963 some games with Hugh Devore

Devore had put a lot of heart back into the Irish team during his season at the helm. Although Notre Dame began the season by losing two games-- they played very tough teams bravely and with spirit and the scores were very close. For example, a powerful Wisconsin team beat Notre Dame in the home season opener, L (9-14), and then Purdue scored a victory L (6-7) at Purdue when an Irish two-point conversion try for the win, failed.

The Irish looked pretty good. Then ND played two games at home in which they upset a tough Southern California team W (17-14) and then clobbered UCLA W (29-12). They looked so good, it was as if the Irish were back and Devore had the spirit of Rockne and Leahy helping him drive the team to victory.

At (2-2), the prospects of a good season seemed achievable for the remainder of the season. ND had devastated UCLA and beat their big nemesis Southern Cal. After just four games, it did not appear that Notre Dame was about to be pushed around by anybody.

Hugh Devore, who had been on campus for a long time and was as familiar as a relic on campus as the Golden Dome itself, would become very hard to demote in favor of a "permanent" coach if he kept directing ND to victories. The plight of an interim coach is that the interim is interim.

The new coach had been mentoring the freshman squad until spring 1962 when he reassumed the head coaching job. As you may recall from this book, Devore was head coach for one year during World War II in 1945 the year before Frank Leahy came back from the Navy. He had a 7-2-1 record that year.

When Joe Kuharich resigned at the end of his contract, Father Theodore M. Hesburgh, Notre Dame's president, announced Devore's appointment. He liked Devore. The interim nature of the appointment, however, displeased ND alumni. They wanted Devore to either be appointed the coach or not appointed but they were not happy about the iffy-ness. Some were concerned that Devore would not invest in the job as an interim coach.

Devore took to the head coaching job, however, like he was permanent party. They say he stood a little straighter, walked a little more briskly and his already gravel voice grew even huskier. "We've got too many French poodles around here," he said to the squad at a workout one day. "What we need are some mad dogs." That's a coach who means business.

Devore made some position changes to help the team. Fullback Joe Farrell went to halfback. End Jim Kelly, the fine pass receiver, became a defensive halfback for a while. The Coach also instructed his quarterbacks not to throw so much to Kelly, who caught 41 passes in the prior year, because he did not want the team or opponents to become "Kelly conscious." In the end, he said, "the ideas all have to be your own."

Unfortunately for Hugh Devore, things got really tough. First of all there was the assassination of President John F. Kennedy which caused a national lament and among other things, the cancellation of the Iowa game. The Irish won no more games that season.

Despite the 2–7 record for the year, Hugh Devore was still loved by all members of the Fighting Irish Community. He was their beloved, personable Devore, affectionately known as "Hughie."

The following year, after the permanent coach was hired, Hugh Devore was presented with a game ball after Notre Dame's victory over Stanford. The 1964 new head coach, Ara Parseghian praised Devore for making his job that much easier. Hugh Devore was 9-9-1 as a head coach. His not-too shabby football record was well exceeded by his record as a human being.

Wrap-Up of the Kuharich Era

My earlier observation as a football layman and great fan of Notre Dame and Notre Dame Football still stands. To remind the reader briefly, that observation is that Rockne and Leahy are exceptions to all endeavors and all achievements in all areas of life.

They were both unique and special and great people. Rockne and Leahy in fact spoiled the Notre Dame faithful into believing that it was Notre Dame itself as the guiding force rather than the brute will of these two fine coaches that made the difference at the University of Our Lady. Dismissing a great coach such as Terry Brennan, who was a consistent winner, gives us all a clue about how predestined Notre Dame at the time, believed its hallowed program had become.

Chapter 14 Coach Ara Parseghian 1964-1974

Coach # 22
Two National Championships 1966 & 1973

Rockne, Leahy, Parseghian, All Time Greats—National Championships

1964	Ara Parseghian	9–1
1965	Ara Parseghian	7–2–1
1966	Ara Parseghian	9–0–1 *
1967	Ara Parseghian	8–2
1968	Ara Parseghian	7–2–1
1969	Ara Parseghian	8–2–1
1970	Ara Parseghian	10–1
1971	Ara Parseghian	8–2
1972	Ara Parseghian	8–3
1973	Ara Parseghian	11–0 *
1974	Ara Parseghian	10–2

Introduction to the Ara Parseghian Era

Ara Parseghian, just like Frank Leahy and Knute Rockne before him was an inspirational person. The story goes that like these two "immortals," Parseghian could make it stop snowing or stop raining if he chose to do so.

There were times many Irish fans chanted to stop the snow or stop the rain and magically, they got their wish. Ara Parseghian could take what would have been a lousy team if coached by anybody else and turn it into a dynasty. And, for many, he often did stop the rain and the snow. They'll swear to it!

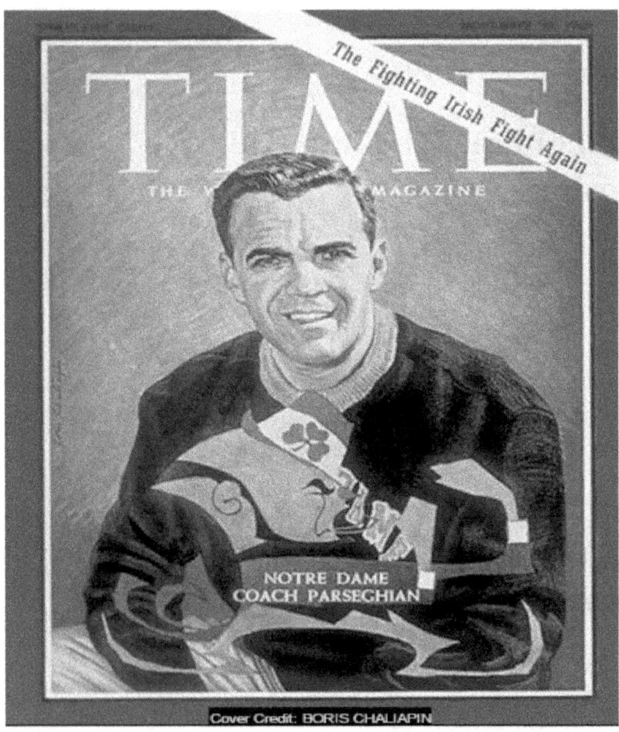

I recall sitting with my dad on Saturdays as a sixteen-year old senior in High School in 1964 and later when I attended King's College, a Notre Dame founded school in Wilkes-Barre PA.

We watched many a game together and we loved Ara Parseghian as the coach. As Roman Catholics, we were surprised he got to be the coach but we were ever thankful for it. After all, he was one of God's creatures just like us. God surely shined his great light on Ara Parseghian and most of the light went right on through to the Notre Dame Football Team.

As we enter the Ara era in this book about Notre Dame coaches, I have collected some very nice historical pieces which relate the Ara Parseghian story at Notre Dame. Here is the first, which is from the Daily Illini, a student newspaper from the University of Illinois. They capture the essence of the negotiations to bring him on-board and the results.

THE DAILY ILLINI

The independent student newspaper at the University of Illinois since 1871

These pieces capture the essence of what happened in the negotiations between Notre Dame and Ara Parseghian, then coach of Northwestern. The Illini paper also got in some stuff about Alex Agase, Parseghian's replacement at Northwestern

From Daily Illini, 18 December 1963

Ara Named Irish Mentor

Ex-Illini Agase New NU Pilot

SOUTH BEND, Ind.

After nearly 36 hours of confusion and speculation, Ara Parseghian was named head football coach at the University of Notre Dame Tuesday and minutes later Alex Agase was appointed his successor at Northwestern University.

Parseghian's appointment was announced here by the Rev. Edmund P. Joyce, executive vice president of Notre Dame. Agase's appointment was announced in Evanston by Northwestern Athletic Director Stu Holcomb. Agase had been head line coach of the Wildcats under Parseghian.

The rapid-fire sequence began with a statement by Father Joyce that Parseghian was in as mentor of the Irish. Only Monday, the fiery, 40-year-old Parseghian had walked out of a meeting with Father Joyce concerning a four-year contract with the Irish. Since Parseghian's walkout, speculation ran rife as to the real reason for the apparent break between the Wildcat head coach and Notre Dame. There still is no immediate answer to the question.

There still was no immediate answer except that Notre Dame did see fit in the face of what could amount to national embarrassment, to keep the door open for Parseghian.

The following statement was released by Father Joyce:

The slight difficulty which arose Monday morning has been resolved. Ara Parseghian will immediately assume the position of head football coach at the University of Notre Dame and will be resident at the university following the East-West Shrine game in San Francisco.

As we said before, we are delighted to have Mr. Parseghian as our head football coach and we look forward to a successful football program under his direction. Simultaneously at his home in Wilmette, Ill., Parseghian made the same announcement given to the press by Father Joyce and said:

"I regret the embarrassment caused Notre Dame by the brief delay. I'm looking forward eagerly to directing football fortune of the Irish. He said: I will immediately assume the position of head football coach at Notre Dame and will be a resident of Notre Dame after the East-West Shrine game.

A native of Evanston, Agase began his athletic career as a guard at Evanston Junior High School. He slipped away from Northwestern and went on to All America fame at Illinois and also at Purdue, where he was a Marine trainee, in 1943, after serving as a lieutenant in the Pacific, where he was wounded in the Okinawa campaign and earned the Purple Heart and Bronze Star, Agase returned to Illinois to lead the Illini to the 1946 Big Ten championship and a 1947 Rose Bowl victory over UCLA.

Agase is one of five children. Two of his brothers also earned letters at Illinois, Lou Agase played football at Illinois and was on the 1946 Big Ten championship team.

Another brother, Herb Agase was a star left-handed pitcher for Illinois in the late 1940's. Alex Agase played with the Chicago Rockets in the defunct All-America Professional Conference, and with the Cleveland Browns for four years before ending his professional career with the Baltimore Colts in 1953. He entered the college coaching ranks as line coach at Iowa State in 1954. Two years later he came to Northwestern as line coach and No. 1 assistant under Parseghian.

We thank NDNATION for permission to use this article to help introduce Ara Parseghian. It is posted on their site: http://ndnation.com/archives/3930

Hardnose

by SEE

(The Rock Report) – Sports Illustrated described Parseghian thusly, "Ara is an impatient, determined man, convinced he can return Notre Dame to a position of dominance in college football, and this he undoubtedly will do one day – but not in 1964."
...

Nicknamed hardnose at Miami by none other than the legendary Paul Brown, Parseghian has lived his life with a passion and conviction that led him to stick his hard nose and square chin into tough situations and create change through force of will and stalwart determination.

Ara simply wouldn't accept mediocrity for himself or his teams and never let conventional thought dictate his success. In fact, Ara Parseghian may never have become a legend at all at Notre Dame if he didn't take matters into his own hands.

Just to get into the running for the position, Ara had to overcome two hurdles. One, Ara didn't go to Notre Dame and to that point in time, Notre Dame had a history of only hiring Notre Dame Alums for the head coaching role. Two, Notre Dame had an unwritten rule that it did not "poach" coaches and Ara was the coach of Northwestern. [The third rule about having to be a Catholic with eight kids was just a rumor.]

Knowing this, Ara made the first move. He called Father Joyce, and inquired first to see if ND was looking for a new coach (that Hugh Devore was just an interim coach.) Father Joyce confirmed that he wasn't stealing another man's job, Ara made it clear to Father Joyce that he was not going back to Northwestern.

But the question about a non-alumnus, no less an Armenian-Protestant non-alumnus, coaching at Notre Dame wasn't answered clearly and Ara left the conversation doubting that Notre Dame would break tradition. Parseghian deemed the conversation, "a little chilly" to his wife and made plans to interview at Miami.

The Miami down south.

While on his way to Florida, at a layover in St. Louis, Ara called home to see if Notre Dame had returned his call.... they had and wanted to meet with him. Ara ditched the Hurricanes and jumped back on a plane, this one was headed to Chicago.

Still, the marriage almost didn't happen. Ara was eventually offered the job verbally, but he didn't feel comfortable with a verbal agreement that didn't have dollars attached to it and after flirting with Northwestern again, finally hammered out a deal with Father Joyce.

After that, things moved quickly.

When Ara spoke to the team, according to Resurrection, he held up his fist "Just look at my fist" he said, "When I make a fist, it's strong and you can't tear it apart. As long as there's unity, there's strength." He went on for over an hour mesmerizing a team that had stumbled through a decade of mediocrity.

By the time he was done, Tony Carey said he was ready to run through a brick wall for him.

And Ara returned the favor. Upon learning that Nick Rassas didn't have a scholarship, Ara called father Joyce and got him one. When he learned, Carey might be eligible for medical-year, he picked up the phone and called father Joyce again, securing an extra year.

Ara could relate to the players, because he had it in his blood. One of his great disappointments was an injury that kept him on the sidelines in the pros for much of his "career."

His playing career over, he channeled that passion into Miami of Ohio, where he became head coach, and compiled a 39-6-1 record. Ara was in the crucible period at the cradle of coaches.

Then, on to Northwestern where after one magical season and many other "good for Northwestern seasons," Northwestern grew tired of Ara constantly pushing for more and told him his contract wouldn't be renewed. Tired of fighting a battle with scholarships tied behind his back, Ara was determined to move on.

When he arrived at Notre Dame he brought order quickly to a program that had fallen into disorder.

Parseghian immediately started fixing what was broken, bringing process and precision where previously there was dysfunction and indecision. He kicked players off the team for rules violations and enforced discipline while motivating players in a way they'd never seen before. In summing up his impact, Jim Dent noted that "more than anything, he was a master organizer" and that Notre Dame's staff operated like a "finely tuned military unit."

Ara brought that same precision to the roster. When Ara evaluated the team, he found players in the wrong positions all over the field. When at Northwestern, Ara befuddled Kuharich, whose "elephant backfield," made Notre Dame easy to defend. Parseghian, who'd had small and fast teams that passed all over the field (for the day) with Tommy Myers at Northwestern, promptly moved the entire elephant backfield to the defensive line at Notre Dame.

Perhaps his biggest position move was really a position elevation. John Huarte, 4th or 5th on the depth chart, threw gorgeous spirals all over the practice field and Ara was intrigued. But after years of what Huarte viewed as unfair treatment by prior coaches, he was stricken with confidence problems. Ara would mold him into a Heisman winner. [He brought back Huarte's confidence in himself.]

Huarte had gone through some rough times, but Ara shared his own experiences at Northwestern and noted how he battled through them. He turned to Huarte and said, "I think your time has come."

The same was true for Notre Dame.

Happy Birthday, Hardnose.

I'd love to hear other stories from Ara's Era if you have them

1964 Coach Ara Parseghian Year 1

After enduring a losing composite record after the Frank Leahy years, Notre Dame Head Coach Ara Parseghian, the new coach, immediately put fight back into the Irish and put the Fighting Irish back on the map. It was the beginning of the Parseghian Era in 1964, the coach's first season at the helm.

This 1964 Notre Dame Fighting Irish football team was nothing short of remarkable. Many sports pundits suggest that without some questionable officiating in their final game against Southern California, the Irish would have been undefeated and untied in the coach's first year, and would have been the consensus National Champions. All it takes is a will!

http://bluegraysky.blogspot.com/2005/05/call-him-hardnose.html

"The spirit might be willing, but it takes a powerful amount of flesh to make a football winner—and the most optimistic experts did not figure Notre Dame for much this year [1964]. The school hadn't had a winning season in five years; 22 out of 38 lettermen had graduated from the prior year's squad that lost seven of its nine games. Parseghian rebuilt the team as though he were running a fire sale."

John Huarte

What would have or might have is not the 1964 Notre Dame story. Parseghian would have his time to win championships for Notre Dame. The 1964 Notre Dame story is that Ara Parseghian, fresh from turning in a terrific job at Northwestern, came to Notre Dame and took a team that barely broke 500 and with mostly the same players, including quarterback John Huarte, turned them into a #3 consensus ranking team and clearly one of the best, if not the best in college football.

Inspirational stores such as these make Notre Dame watchers become Notre Dame lovers and Notre Dame faithful and fans.

During this season, a great player who benefitted from the one-on-one mentoring of a great coach and great person, John Huarte, a quarterback who re-learned the word "can" instead of "can't" from his new coach, became the sixth Notre Dame player to win the **Heisman Trophy**. Bravo Irish! Bravo John Huarte; Bravo Coach Parseghian. Huarte's talents had gone unrecognized by Joe Kuharich and Hugh Devore.

By season end, Huarte had become a household name in sports. He kept throwing touchdown passes to another ND great from California, Jack Snow, who incidentally had also been overlooked by the previous coaching regimes. With Parseghian, Notre Dame had become a football power again.

John Huarte got his Heisman by being a great player. His Heisman Trophy victory, however, went down in history as one of the biggest upsets for the award. Huarte missed much of his sophomore season due to injury and he had not played enough for Coach Kuharich as a junior to win a monogram (Letter). Yet, he was brilliant as a senior. The Passes between Huarte and Snow are legendary. (60 passes for 1,114 yards and a record nine touchdowns). Moreover, Snow was not Huarte's only receiver.

Ara Parseghian threw out the Joe Kuharich book on the team, its procedures and its players and John Huarte was the greatest beneficiary. Parseghian used his own cranium and took ND from a 2-7 team in '63 into a 9-1 squad with John Huarte leading the charge. Moreover, Parseghian and Huarte were within minutes of the national title.

With the Fighting Irish ranked a consensus # 1, the opponent was the resilient and very tough USC Trojans, a team who enjoyed beating Notre Dame as much as living.

Off to the LA Coliseum, the Irish played a fine game against USC and the officials. After a last-minute field goal, the Irish had to go back to South Bend with a loss L (17-20). It was a great season. It was an unexpectedly great season.

Parseghian took what arguably was Joe Kuharich's 5-5 team and made it work. It would be the first of many great seasons with a brand new fired-up great man and great coach, Ara Parseghian. Watching Notre Dame games with my dad became a lot more fun, when Notre Dame began to excel. Notre Dame all of a sudden believed it could win.

1965 Coach Ara Parseghian Year 2

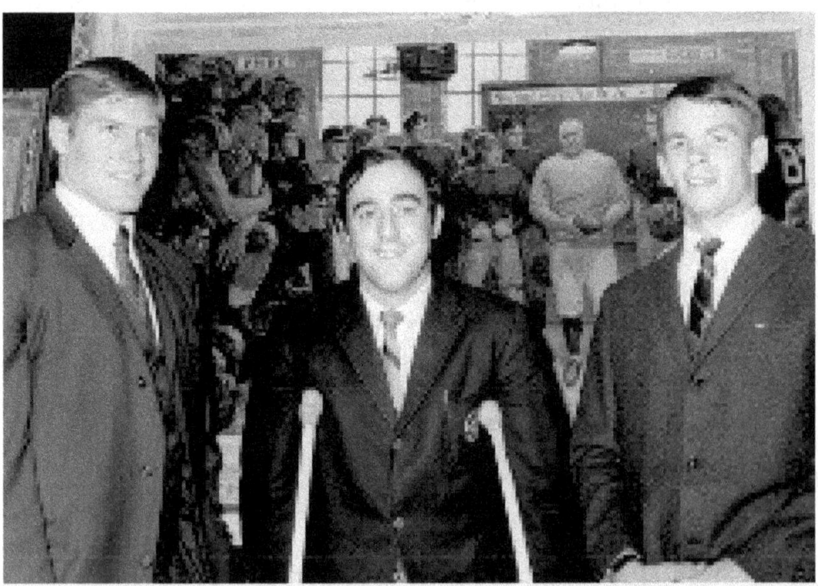

Left to right, tackle Georgie Kunz, quarterback Terry Hanratty and wide receiver Jim Seymour led the 1965 recruiting class

The 1965 edition of the Notre Dame Fighting Irish football in the second year of the Parseghian Era were voted # 8 in the coach's poll and # 9 in the AP poll against every other college team in America. Notre Dame was clearly back on the map. When ND showed up or a team had to play in South Bend, they did not come ready to lose.

They played to win. They were aware of the Notre Dame tradition and its hall of fame coaches from the past. They had a sense that there was another Hall of Fame coach inspiring new National Championship teams in a new era and they were ready to try their darndest to get a win against Notre Dame.

Consequently, the Fighting Irish needed all the fight it had to squeeze out wins against the best teams in America, who wanted more than anything to take a win from Notre Dame. The Irish finished 1965 with a season record of (7-2-1.) and a top ten finish in the rankings.

1966 Coach Ara Parseghian Year 3

In his third year as head coach of Notre Dame, Ara Parseghian brought a National Championship to Notre dame for the first time since Frank Leahy's teams in the 1940's. The 1966 Notre Dame Fighting Irish football team ended the 1966 season undefeated with nine wins and one tie away at Michigan State.

The Fighting Irish earned a consensus title after beating No. 10 Oklahoma W 38–0 in Norman, tying unbeaten and No. 2 Michigan State T 10–10, and ending the season defeating No. 10 USC, W (51–0), in the LA Coliseum. The 1966 squad became the eighth Irish team to win the national title and the first under Parseghian. The Irish outscored its opponents 362–38.

The 10–10 tie between The Spartans and the Irish remains one of the controversial games of college football, and is considered today to be one of the great "games of the century."

This game had its controversies

For nearly 50 years, Parseghian has defended his end-of-the-game strategy, which left many fans feeling disappointed at the game not having some sort of resolution. A 10-10 tie even without Terry Hanratty was tough to take with an undefeated season on the line.

Michigan State fans and other Notre Dame detractors called Parseghian a coward, and college football expert Dan Jenkins, leading off his article for Sports Illustrated, said that Parseghian chose to "Tie one for the Gipper."

In that same article, Parseghian was quoted as saying, "We'd fought hard to come back and tie it up. After all that, I didn't want to risk giving it to them cheap. They get reckless and it could cost them the game. I wasn't going to do a jackass thing like that at this point."

The tie resulted in 9–0–1 seasons for both Michigan State and Notre Dame. The final AP and Coaches' polls put the Irish and Spartans at #1 and #2, ranking both teams above the undefeated, and two time defending national champion 11–0–0 Alabama. Both schools shared the MacArthur Bowl.

1967 Coach Ara Parseghian Year 4

The 1967 Notre Dame Fighting Irish football team was coached by Ara Parseghian in his fourth year. The Irish finished 8-2 and were # 4 in the coaches' poll and # 5 in the AP poll. The season started a little rocky and after the first four games, the Irish were unranked with a record of 2-2.

1968 Coach Ara Parseghian Year 5

The 1968 Notre Dame Fighting Irish football team under Coach Ara Parseghian had another fine year. Notre Dame consistently played the best teams in the nation and 1968 was no exception. The Irish record was (7-2-1).

1969 Coach Ara Parseghian Year 6

The 1969 Notre Dame Fighting Irish football team was coached by Ara Parseghian. The Fighting Irish finished the regular season with eight wins, one loss, and one tie.

1970 Coach Ara Parseghian Year 7

The 1970 Notre Dame Fighting Irish football team was coached by Ara Parseghian. The squad played to a 10-1 record and finished # 5 in the coach's poll and # 2 in the AP poll. If you could take Purdue and USC off the ND schedule in the Parseghian years, the Irish would have had three or four more national championships.

Again in 1970, the only blemish on the Fighting Irish record was a season finale against unranked USC at USC in which the Irish lost L

(28-38). Not having an especially good year with a 5-4 record, John McKay's 1970 Trojans were ready for the Fighting Irish and they played their hearts out to gain the victory.

1971 Coach Ara Parseghian Year 8

The 1971 Notre Dame Fighting Irish football team was coached for the eighth year by Ara Parseghian. Notre Dame finished the season with an 8-2 record and were #15 in the coaches' poll and # 13 in the AP.

1972 Coach Ara Parseghian Year 9

The 1972 Notre Dame Fighting Irish football team was coached by Ara Parseghian. Notre Dame finished the regular season with an 8-2 record and were #12 in the coaches' poll and # 14 in the AP. The Fighting Irish were invited to the Orange Bowl against Nebraska and the Irish had a tough time in defeat L (6-40)

1973 Coach Ara Parseghian Year 10

The 1973 Notre Dame Fighting Irish football team was the tenth season coached by Ara Parseghian. Parseghian's squad ended the season undefeated with 11 wins and no losses, winning the national championship. The Fighting Irish won the title the hard way. They earned it!

First of all, they defeated the previously unbeaten and No. 1 ranked Alabama Crimson Tide in the Sugar Bowl by a score of W (24–23). The 1973 squad therefore became the ninth Irish team to win the national title and the second team under Parseghian to win this coveted recognition.

Stranger things have happened but despite Notre Dame finishing No. 1 in the AP Poll to claim the AP national title, they were not awarded the Coaches' title. The Coaches voted before the bowl season and selected Alabama as the # 1 team in the country.

Like most of Parseghian's teams in his ten years, the 1973 Fighting Irish were hardened and tough. His second national title team was led by its relentless rushing attack. Fullback Wayne Bullock topped the list with 750 yards; followed by halfback Art Best, who gained 700 yards, halfback Eric Penick with 586 yards and quarterback Tom Clements clocked in with his own 360 yards. This unit made up one of the fastest Irish backfields of all time. Penick and Best both ran the 100-yard dash in under 10 seconds.

1973 Sugar Bowl

Notre Dame accepted the Sugar Bowl bid, which set the stage for a real national championship game. Alabama was awarded the UPI title before the bowl season, but it was Notre Dame that had won the championship head to head against Alabama on the field, (24-23) in a nail-biting thriller that saw six lead changes.

Alabama's Paul W. (Bear) Bryant and Notre Dame's Ara Parseghian meet on the field of Tulane Stadium prior to the Sugar Bowl on Dec. 31, 1973. On Dec. 31, 1973, two of college football's most fabled programs met for the first time on the gridiron with nothing less at stake than the national championship. As the kickoff approached the Alabama Crimson was ranked No. 1 in the country, the Notre Dame Fighting Irish were No. 3 and both were undefeated. Anticipation was at a fever pitch and, as the game unfolded, absolutely warranted.

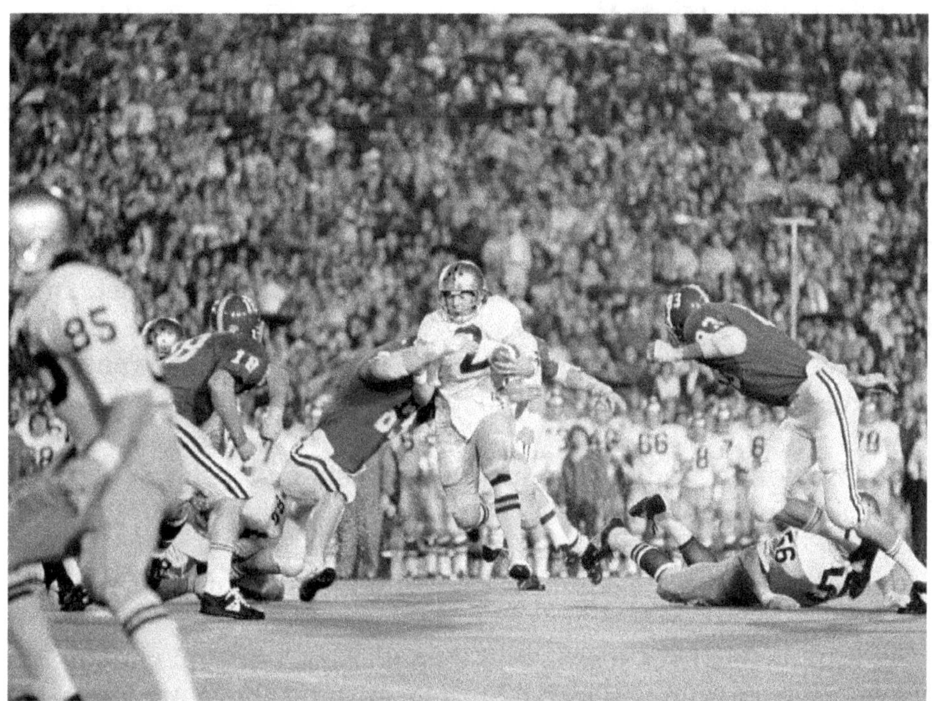

The result: Notre Dame beats Alabama, 24-23, for the 1973 national title. What happened? Both had perfect records, and the Tide came in No. 1 and the Irish No. 3 (No. 2 Oklahoma was on probation); this was the first meeting in history between the teams, and it took place on New Year's Eve. Alabama scored a TD to take a 23-21 lead early in the fourth quarter but missed the extra point. Notre Dame's Bob Thomas kicked a 19-yard field goal with 10:34 left to give the Irish a 24-23 lead. Late in the game, Alabama downed a punt at Notre Dame's 1. On third-and-8 from the 3 and with little more than two minutes left, Irish backup TE Robin Weber basically was left uncovered because of a blown coverage and hauled in a 37-yard reception from Miller-Digby Award recipient: # 2 Tom Clements, Notre Dame quarterback, to seal the win and the No. 1 ranking.

Notre Dame jumped to a 6-0 in front of 85,161 excited fans at Tulane Stadium in New Orleans. However, Alabama quickly answered with a Randy Billingsley 6-yard touchdown run. After Notre Dame's Al Hunter scored on a crowd dazzling 93-yard kick-off return, Alabama scored 10 straight points. In the fourth quarter, three turnovers occurred in 90 seconds, with Alabama getting the best of the action.

The Crimson Tide capitalized on a halfback pass from Mike Stock to quarterback Richard Todd for a 25-yard touchdown to take a slim 23-21 lead, but they missed the crucial extra point. Notre Dame responded and fought its way down the field with Tom Clements driving the Irish 79 yards in 11 plays. This set up a potential field goal on a clutch 15-yard pass to tight end Dave Casper. Irish kicker Bob Thomas kicked the field goal to give Notre Dame a slim victory W (24-23) and the AP national title.

1974 Coach Ara Parseghian Year 11

The 1974 Notre Dame Fighting Irish football team was the 11th season coached by Ara Parseghian It would be Coach Parseghian's final season as Notre Dame Head Coach. As all Parseghian seasons, this 1974 season was also a great one. I recall in my mid-twenties in 1974 missing Ara as soon as his departure was announced.

There is a lot of good fortune in winning a championship. There is a lot of skill and good fortune to win two great championships, especially in the Parseghian era as all football teams were toughening up and the competition was nothing to sneeze at.

Let's look at this 1974 season and then go back a bit and wrap up the Parseghian era, as much as it pains me. Writing about Ara Parseghian has been a real treat for me. It was fun the first time living it, and fun again as I relived it in this chapter. I hope reading this chapter has given you the same good feeling.

All my life – at least the part that remembers Notre Dame games, I hated it when ND was playing either Purdue or Southern Cal (USC). No matter how good the Fighting Irish were, there were always blips on the radar whenever ND was having an excellent season and were playing Purdue or USC. The Boilermakers and the Trojans were always better teams when they faced the Irish.

If it were not for these two teams, Notre Dame would have had many more national championship seasons and the mystery and the hard-fought battles extend even to today.

This particular year that we are examining, 1974 was typical. The prior year, 1973 was atypical. The Fifth Dimension used to sing about the moon being in the seventh house and Jupiter being aligned with Mars. That always needed to happen along with God's favor for the Irish to have an undefeated season no matter how good the coach or the team might be.

Either God or Lucifer placed USC and Purdue on this earth as more cuss words were yelled at TV screens in my day from Irish fans when these two teams played the Fighting Irish of Notre Dame.

In 1974, there was no alignment and there was no seventh house and as so many times before Purdue L (20-34) and USC L (24-55) both beat Notre Dame in the midst of what could have been an undefeated season.

Ara Parseghian must have felt the same frustration as all Notre Dame Fans. Whatever Purdue or USC ate before the games had to be the determining factor. Maybe sometimes, but I really don't think so, they played harder than Notre Dame. I don't think so; but they were always highly motivated to beat the Notre Dame Fighting Irish.

In 1974, the Irish were #4 in the coaches' poll and #6 in the AP. Their regular season record was 9-2 and they won the Orange Bowl again against Alabama (13-11).

The end of the Ara era

Ara Parseghian quit coaching all teams after the 1974 season for "health reasons." He began a broadcasting career calling college football games for ABC and CBS.

He also dedicated himself to medical causes later in life after his daughter was diagnosed with multiple sclerosis and three of his grandchildren died of a rare genetic disease.

This great coach was inducted into the College Football Hall of Fame as a coach in 1980. His career coaching record is 170–58–6. 1974 was his last season as Notre Dame Coach. Like Rockne and Leahy, this great coach made his mark and was missed from his first day of retirement. Thank you for a great job, Coach!

Thankfully, Mr. Parseghian is still around and still attending Notre Dame games. It is reported that he and Coach Brian Kelly have a great relationship. Long live Ara Parseghian, one of the great ones in life.

Chapter 15 Coach Dan Devine 1975-1980

Coach # 23
One National Championship -- 1977

Rockne, Leahy, Parseghian, Devine—Four Greats—National Championships

1975	Dan Devine	8–3
1976	Dan Devine	9–3
1977	Dan Devine	11–1*
1978	Dan Devine	9–3
1979	Dan Devine	7–4
1980	Dan Devine	9–2–1

Introduction to the Dan Devine era

When Ara Parseghian called it quits after the 1974 season, Notre Dame was forced into what seemed to many to be a common situation for the Irish—having to replace another legend. Like other not-too-shabby coaches before and after him, Dan Devine, a great coach—the only Notre Dame coach who in just six seasons brought home a national championship—stepped into this unenviable situation.

Father Hesburgh and Father Joyce had tasked Dan Devine with taking over the football program. He had been head coach of the Green Bay Packers for three years at the time, but his heart was always in college football.

Before Green Bay, he was head coach at both Arizona State and Missouri. At ASU he compiled a nice 27-3-1 record, including an undefeated season in 1957. He then moved on to Mizzou where his success continued, including one undefeated season (1960) and four top 10 finishes in the AP Poll (1960. Devine was a great college coach. He was so good that in 1963, he was almost offered the Notre Dame job after the 1963 season and right before Ara Parseghian accepted the position.

Maybe, just maybe that would have been OK, but few would ever replace Ara Parseghian with anybody else, ever—under any conditions.

Notre Dame fans were not particularly pleased at the choice of Devine. Then again, many alums questioned the appointment of a protestant non-alum as the head coach when Parseghian, was chosen. Parseghian had it lots easier than Devine, however, as he was not replacing a living legend.

So, to net it out, Devine was not a popular choice among many ND fans but nobody could have been. Besides Devine himself, the Irish administration had already tried its luck with a pro-football level coach, Joe Kuharich, and fans and alum were still stinging from that experience.

Rumors are always part of football. At the time, a big rumor was that Don Shula was going to leave Miami to coach at Notre Dame. There was another devastating rumor that nobody would be able to withstand. That rumor said that Ara Parseghian was merely taking a one-year leave of absence, and like Hugh Devore, two-time Interim coach, the Irish were just looking for somebody to fill the bill temporarily.

Moreover, though a great college coach, Dan Devine had some setbacks in the pros and was fresh off an unsuccessful stint as Green Bay head coach. So, most good memories of his past college accomplishments had faded. Nonetheless, he was always a fine college football coach but few could compare him to Ara Parseghian when it came to charisma and presence.

Scholastic January 1976 – re 1975 Football

The game stories themselves reflect the season Notre Dame football went through. Dan Devine inherited a fine team from Parseghian, yet rumors, injuries, NCAA rules and the like gave the Irish an 8-3 season. The point that many fail to realize is that we could have gone 6-5 if the breaks hadn't fallen our way. 8-3 is a very good record for any college team. But at Notre Dame, that record is a very mediocre one. Perhaps we have our standards misplaced or something, but everyone expects a winner at Notre Dame. Everyone wants a perennial championship team. But that doesn't always happen. We all make mistakes. We all ought to be thankful that no one was seriously hurt this season. But many don't care about that—they only want the team to go 11-0. We must reshape our priorities to understand that there is never going to be a perfect Notre Dame football team.

Notre Dame means so much more than a football game: only 11 guys can be on the field at once. What about the other 90 or so that never play in each game? Do they just sit around their rooms each day and bang heads at three o'clock? It is one of the greatest feelings in the world to realize your own capabilities; we all know that. And yet it is just as rewarding to see an athlete realize that he may never play here, and go out and work for a decent education. It takes something special to realize that the free education may mean everything for him, and it is only a few athletes that ever realize that.

Football itself at Notre Dame seems to change at Notre Dame whenever a legend, one of the immortals' time ends and a mere mortal such as Dan Devine must take over. I reached to Notre Dame's Student magazine, the Scholastic to find an article that showed the new attitude on campus. See piece on prior page.

Though Parseghian had not died like Rockne did ever so tragically, the Notre Dame faithful and the scribes at the Student Newspaper seem to have identified at the time, a major disturbance in the "FORCE." I don't know how else to say it. The predestination of an immortal taking Notre Dame to an undefeated season again seems to be in the front of this thinking, but, additionally, something morose seems to have overtaken the campus at this time.

One notable change after Parseghian is that the Football issue of Scholastic came out in January instead of December. Maybe it is because of bowl games.

1975 Coach Dan Devine Year 1

The 1975 Notre Dame Fighting Irish football team was coached by Dan Devine in his first year. Devine had taken over for the retired Ara Parseghian, and he had mostly a Parseghian selected team to work with in 1975.

Devine led the Irish into its first "Holy War." The Holy War is an American rivalry between the Boston College Eagles and University of Notre Dame Fighting Irish. In 1975 it became a new nonconference rivalry in college football. Unfortunately, for the Irish, in years to come, BC would add itself to the list which includes USC and Purdue as major ND championship spoilers, I regret to say.

Why Holy War?

Its name comes from the fact that both teams are run by orders of priests. The Eagles are directed by the Society of Jesus (Jesuits) and the Fighting Irish are directed by the Congregation of Holy Cross

(CSC). They represent the only two Catholic universities in the United States which still compete in the Football Bowl Subdivision of the National Collegiate Athletic Association. As we know, this is the highest level of competition in American college football.

On September 15, 1915, in a rare Monday night college football game, Notre Dame squared off against Boston College at Schaefer Stadium in Foxboro Massachusetts in the first of the Holy Wars. Notre Dame won the game W (17-3) before 61,501.

For its final game of the regular season, Notre Dame defeated Miami W (32-9) on November 22 before an attendance of just 24,944 in Orange Bowl Stadium. It was not a bowl game. The Irish team, not particularly liking its record chose not to attend a bowl game in 1975.

1976 Coach Dan Devine Year 1

Dan Devine was the University of Notre Dame Head Football Coach in 1976. From Irish standards, his first year had not gone well, though when compared to regular mortal men, it was not too bad at all. His squad lost three games in 1975 and did not go to a bowl game. Bowl games are a dime a dozen today but in 1975, there were only 11 bowl games.

Dan Devine's mission to painlessly replace the legendary Ara Paraseghian had gotten off to a fine start but the naysayers were calling it a slow start and they believed something needed to change. When ND faithful cannot find a reason to cheer for the team, they have sometimes in the past taken out their misery by cheering for the removal of the coach.

Often, I am among the typical fannage. Not this time with Dan Devine. The 1976 Notre Dame Football team won one additional game over 1975 and it looked like there would be even better things ahead. But, there were still three losses!

Things that end well do not always begin well and so it went for Notre Dame in 1976. The team was ranked #11 and played ninth ranked Pitt in the home opener during the Tony Dorsett years. Dorsett was on his way to a Heisman Trophy season. It was expected that the Pitt Offense would be formidable but worse than that, the Pitt Defense was stubborn and it dominated the game. Dorsett ran all over the Irish defense in the second half and Pitt won the game L (10-31). Pitt eventually won the National Championship. Pitt was not the same old Pitt as in the Ara era.

Notre Dame's Quarterback Rick Slager was inexperienced. Meanwhile Joe Montana was sitting on the bench. The following year of course, Joe Montana took over the duties. For the world as seen by Dan Devine in 1976 though, the Coach had to make do with what he had while his fledgling team's talent grew in experience.

1977 Coach Dan Devine Year 3

The 1977 Notre Dame Fighting Irish football team was coached by Dan Devine in his third year as head coach This Notre Dame football team was ranked third in the country to start the season. Its veteran defense was again expected to do well with returning Outland Trophy winner Ross Browner at defensive end.

Willie Fry was on the other end and Luther Bradley was the Irish key defensive back. The position coach in the secondary was the late Jim Johnson, a great defensive coach. Johnson was at the beginning of a career that would see him become the renowned defensive coordinator for the Philadelphia Eagles' best teams in the early 2000s.

Ole Miss Rebels player L.Q. Smith scores a touchdown v ND in 1977

This was a great season but it did have a major burp in the second game against Ole Miss. Devine brought the Irish to 10-1 regular season and a win in the Cotton Bowl Classic against Texas W (38-10). The 1977 squad became the tenth Irish team to win the national title and were led by All-Americans Ken McAfee, Ross Browner, Luther Bradley, and Bob Golic. Junior Joe Montana, a future Pro Football Hall of Fame member, was the starting quarterback on this team.

Third year coach Dan Devine expected great things from his talent-rich Notre Dame team after a well-played 9-3 season and 20-9 Gator Bowl win over Penn State the previous year. The team needed experience and they got it and in 1977 they were ready for big things.

The offense was playing poorly as junior quarterback Rusty Lisch, who started the first three games for Devine was struggling, and then he got hurt. Second-stringer Gary Forsythe got the chance against Purdue and Notre Dame fell behind 24-14. Devine was not pleased and looked to the bench and found another junior waiting to play. The new QB was their third-stringer—a kid named Joe Montana.

Montana becomes a Dan Devine star

Joe Montana had played well in some relief work as a freshman in 1975, then he missed the 1976 season with a shoulder injury. Montana proved his mettle at Notre Dame and in pro-football. Before immediately was up, he had led the Irish back to a win away over the Boilermakers W (31-24). He then led consecutive wins over Michigan State at home W (16-6) and Army away W (24-0). Those wins set the stage for a mid-October date with fifth-ranked USC, a team with the gift of having the Irish's number. Doing well against USC would bring relevance back to the ND program.

The 1977 Notre Dame-USC game has a special place in Fighting Irish lore. The Blue and Gold team was not going to wear blue and gold. When Notre Dame returned to their lockers after the pre-game warmups, to get their "Devine" pep talk, there was something different there. It was in their lockers already. The Irish saw something—Kelly green jerseys. On this day, Kelly green would replace the traditional dark navy customarily worn. It electrified the team and when they came running out of the tunnel again, the crowd went berserk.

As simple as the change to green jerseys may have been, it gave the Fighting Irish a huge emotional lift and there was no question about the outcome of the game from the moment the Irish took the field. They pummeled USC (49-19).

Led by Montana and tight end Ken McAfee, a third-place Heisman candidate, Notre Dame would finish its season with five straight wins to finish. Their 10-1 record was amazing considering the slow start. There was still one more challenge. On November 12, at Clemson a tough Tigers team took a lead and had Notre Dame down by double-digits. Montana put his helmet back on and began to lead the Irish back to victory.

Joe Montana was able to add another early chapter to his comeback legend. He got it done when it counted and led the Irish back to a win W (21-17) against Clemson.

A Buried Montana Sneaks Ball In for Game Winner at Clemson

Notre Dame concluded the season ranked #5 in the country and got an invitation to play #1 Texas in the Cotton Bowl.

On the way to the Cotton Bowl after USC, ND stopped Navy at home W (43-10), and then the next week crushed Georgia Tech W (69-14). After Clemson, it was Air Force at home W (49-0), and Miami at Miami W (48-10).

The Cotton Bowl was played on Sunday January 2 since New Year's Day was Saturday on the "long" football weekend. Few thought that a Notre Dame New Year's Day run to a national title was likely, but it was theoretically possible. ND had a fine season with the one burp being Ole Miss.

At the time, four teams were ahead of Notre Dame in the rankings—in addition to Texas, there was Oklahoma, Michigan and Alabama—all were in separate bowl games, so the Irish could hope to pull off a miraculous turnaround. It would be as easy to bring about as a completed "Hail Mary" pass for a touchdown. But then again. Notre Dame was named after Mary, the mother of Jesus, so all things were possible.

In 1977, there were no BCS champions and the bowl games were the end of the season. The AP and the UPI determined the champions and there were times that they did not even wait until the bowl games to make their decrees. So, without a BCS, in 1977, it was possible for the national championship to be determined on New Year's Day or even January 2 if it was a Sunday game.

On this January 2, a Sunday, playing against Texas, it was well known that the Cowboys from Texas had won the NFC championship the day before so the Texans were hoping for a two-for weekend. It sure would be nice for them if UT added a nice national championship to the Texas picture.

The Longhorns had an exceptional runner who had just won the Heisman Trophy, notably Earl Campbell. He was a powerful runner with some of the biggest muscular thighs ever seen on a back. Campbell had a great big NFL career ahead of him.

The good news for Notre Dame in the game was that its defense was able to prevent Earl Campbell from getting it going. Texas helped things by turning the ball over time and again. The Longhorns got the fans going by scoring first for a 3-0 lead, Notre Dame had stopped their advance for a touchdown. Joe Montana, along with running backs Jerome Heavens, Vagas Ferguson and Ken McAfee kept scoring after that. The final score was W 38-10, well worthy of a national championship, but it was not assured as other teams were also in the hunt.

Other than Alabama, who handily had beaten a 9-2 Ohio State team in the Sugar Bowl, all other teams seemed to eventually lose their place in the championship line. Michigan was upset by four-loss Washington and quarterback Warren Moon in the Rose Bowl. The heavily favored Sooners were an almost sure bid for the national championship title if they were able to defeat Arkansas.

Oklahoma found Arkansas weakened when Razorbacks coach Lou Holtz suspended three players for disciplinary reasons prior to the game. Yet, somehow, the Razorbacks were not going to lie down.

Despite not having his key players, who had scored more than 75% of the season's points playing in the game, Hogs coach Lou Holtz made his first mark on South Bend history even before he arrived to coach the 1986 season. Holtz's Arkansas smoked OU 31-6 and it was then down to Notre Dame or Alabama for the national championship. The pundits would have to decide.

The pundits were chatting that it would have been an ideal time for a plus-one format after the bowls, because the Irish and Tide both appeared to be deserving of championship status. Alabama had played a consistently tougher schedule and their September loss to Nebraska was infinitely more defensible than Notre Dame's defeat at Ole Miss.

But the Tide had mostly close games that were nothing like the ND blowouts. Alabama had no great runaways like the wins—shall I say the catastrophes—Notre Dame had hung on USC and Texas, beating two highly regarded opponents by a combined 58 points.

The Voters do like "trophy wins" over a consistently steady long haul. In the end, the fact that Notre Dame had in fact buried the consensus #1 team in a bowl game only heightened the Notre Dame case. And, so the Fighting Irish won the national championship, and just like Parseghian before him and Holtz after him, Devine had done it in his third year. Congratulations Coach Devine.

Notre Dame Quarterback Joe Montana attempts a pass during the January 2, 1978 Cotton Bowl against Texas

1978 Coach Dan Devine Year 4

The 1978 Notre Dame Fighting Irish football team was coached by Dan Devine. His squad went 8-3 in the regular season and Notre Dame Also won the Cotton Bowl against Houston (35-34), ending the season at 9-3.

Joe Montana was at quarterback for his senior year and the Irish were ranked #5 to begin the season. Losing two at home was a less than stellar start to the season.

Montana did not make All-American. Chuck Fusina QB for Penn State got those honors and Fusina also was # 2 in Heisman voting. Fusina had led Penn State to an undefeated regular season in 1978. Nonetheless, Montana remained the foremost author of comebacks.

In the season finale at USC, the Irish fell behind 24-6. Montana put himself into comeback gear and led a fourth-quarter rally that put

ND ahead 25-24. The win appeared to be in the books when USC quarterback Paul McDonald was sacked and fumbled on the final possession. But a Pac-10 official ruled that McDonald had his arm going forward and the pass was ruled as incomplete. Soon, USC was in field goal range and a perfect kick brought them the game L (25-27). This was the first of two straight games that USC would win with help from officiating that was—at best—shaky.

As for Notre Dame, they were still #10 in the country and were preparing for the Cotton Bowl against Houston to be played in Dallas.

Cotton Bowl in Houston

Forever known as the "Chicken Soup Game" because of frigid temperatures, heavy winds and a frozen Irish quarterback, Notre Dame trailed 34-12 in the fourth quarter at Austin, Texas.

With quarterback Joe Montana battling the flu and back in the locker room trying to fight off hypothermia, hopes looked bleak for the # 10 Irish to come back against the No. 9 Cougars.

It was so cold and wet at game time that Montana suffered from a hypothermia attack and could not function. Notre Dame's star quarterback was kept in the locker room for safety purposes, eating hot chicken soup while covered with blankets. He was not expected to play at all.

The rescue efforts to make Montana OK were more than successful as he actually recovered before the end of the game. But, by this time, the Irish were well behind 34-12. Montana emerged from the locker room and excited the ND crowd by being back in the game with just 7:37 to play. The comeback kid was on the field. The adrenalin overcame the cold.

Tony Belden started the comeback for Notre Dame by blocking a punt that Steve Cichy returned for a touchdown. Montana converted the two-point play. The score was then 34-20. Notre Dame got the ball back and Montana led a 61-yard touchdown drive and gained another two-point conversion and suddenly it was 34-28 and there was still 4:15 to play. The comeback kid was at it again.

Notre Dame got the ball back, but Montana fumbled on the Houston 20 with 1:50 left. It looked like fate had caught up with the Irish and even chicken soup could not pull this game from the nether world.

The Cougars, however, with great ND defense soon were faced with 4th-and-1, and decided to go for it on their own 29-yard line. Facing a heavy wind, this was a defensible decision—they weren't going to get more than 10-15 net yards on a punt in these conditions. The Irish defense did not give an inch.

Notre Dame's quarterback Joe Montana shown during the 1979 Cotton Bowl. Montana led Irish to a final second win. The team was coached by Dan Devine.

A still-warm Joe Montana led the team to the eight-yard line with six seconds to play. His first pass to Kris Haines in the left corner of the end zone was incomplete. Because he released so quickly, there was at least another second on the clock.

Devine and Montana went back to the same play, and this time Montana hit Haines. The final score was W 35-34. The comeback kid had brought Notre Dame back again for a victory. If it were today, somebody would have figured out how to take Montana's injury season and give the senior a fifth year. But, then again, Joe Montana's big opportunities were about to present themselves in the NFL.

This great player, who had been on the bench his first two seasons at Notre Dame under Joe Kuharich, would go on to win four Super Bowl rings with the San Francisco 49ers. Pundits at the time who wrote about the Irish after Montana noted that Notre Dame didn't have quite that many great moments in its future after Montana moved on.

However, all of the future ND moments would add to the lore. Together, a storied school and a legendary quarterback made the 1978 Notre Dame football season one to remember. Lou Holtz, the great one would be called on in a few years to add zip once again to Notre Dame. Dan Devine was already putting on a good show for the Irish.

1979 Coach Dan Devine Year 5

The 1979 Notre Dame Fighting Irish football team was coached by Dan Devine in his fifth season. Notre Dame finished with a regular season record of 6-4 and with its Bowl victory in Japan against Miami (40-15), overall the Irish finished the season at 7-4.

1980 Coach Dan Devine Year 6

The 1980 Notre Dame Fighting Irish football team was coached by Dan Devine in his sixth and last season. As was customary, all home games were played at Notre Dame Stadium in South Bend, Indiana.

Classified as an EPIC game, The Notre Dame 1980 writing team wrote this about the ND v Michigan game:

1980 V MICHIGAN

In one of the greatest late-game see-saw affairs on this list, No. 8 Notre Dame and No. 14 Michigan swapped the lead three times in the second half before the smallest and most unlikely of heroes emerged with the game-winning play under the most difficult circumstances.

Pinned at his own 20-yard line with only 40 seconds remaining -- all while working against a steady 15 mph wind and trailing 27-26 -- Irish head coach Dan Devine *benched his starting quarterback and called on confident big-armed freshman, Blair Kiel, to lead the final drive.*

A couple of clutch passes -- and the help of a fortuitous 32-yard pass interference call -- helped Kiel move his team to Michigan's 34-yard line with only 0:04 remaining on the clock to set up Irish kicker Harry Oliver's impossible 51-yard field goal attempt for the win.

"I just remember thinking this wind is very strong and half-thinking, `I don't have a chance at making this thing,'" the late Oliver would recount in a 2004 interview with Irish Sports Report.

Call it luck of the Irish, or a just a well-timed weather break, legend has it the winds calmed just long enough for the 5-11, 185-pound Oliver to boot the kick and clear the crossbar by inches as the clock expired, delivering arguably the most memorable field goal in Notre Dame history for a 29-27 Irish win.

I love these stories. This was a big game. Here is just a bit more about the game:

The home team jumped out to a 14-0 lead, but then fell behind 21-14. After coming back to a 26-21 lead, Notre Dame allowed a late Michigan touchdown and the score was 27-26. The game was not over and the comeback kid had graduated two years before in 1978.

This would not be the last test that the Irish defense would have before the year was out, but their showing against the Wolverines was one that would appear in the W column. ND had a new gutsy quarterback John Wangler, who was hurt yet who played on what appeared to be one leg because of a prior injury. He would help the Irish make the difference.

Notre Dame had a good kicker Harry Oliver waiting to be needed. Wangler moved the ball into Michigan territory and lined up for a last-gasp 51-yard field goal into the wind. Oliver stunned everyone by knocking this difficult field goal through the uprights and it sent the home crowd into a frenzy. Despite the win, W (29-27), Notre Dame remained at # 8 in the polling.

1980 Cover Michigan V Notre Dame Devine's last Season

Wrap-up article on Dan Devine

This is the closing of the Dan Devine era. This Washington Post article describes the ups and downs of Dan' Devine as a college coach and as the coach of Notre Dame. God bless Dan Devine RIP, who passed away at the age of 77 on May 9, 2002. He was a great college coach in my book. This is the link. I have provided excerpts below so that we can see the conundrum of Dan Devine & Notre Dame. He was a successful coach with a fine record.

https://www.washingtonpost.com/archive/sports/1980/11/12/dan-devine-38/aaa07da9-0865-41ca-85e1-4cfa5f0a906e/

Article Title: Dan Devine &

by John Feinstein, Washington Post

Consider the record: Four bowl bids in six years, one national championship achieved, a second being worked on. A record of 7-0-1 this year and a six-season mark of 51-14-1. A winning percentage of almost .800. In return, the coach is being run out of town.

The coach is Dan Devine and the school is Notre Dame, and that should at least partly explain the situation. Since the day, he arrived in 1974 to succeed Ara Parseghian, Devine has not been able to escape the shadow.

Parseghian was emotional and easy to identify with; Devine is low key and distant. Parseghian was colorful and glib; Devine is colorless and often fumbles for words. Parseghian took a 2-7 loser and won immediately; Devine took a winner and won slightly less.

The alumni have never accepted him, many of the players have made fun of him and the press, at times, has ravaged him.

This is a story about the second-winningest active college football coach in America. It is also a story about a man whose superb record has not been enough to quiet his critics. Finally, it is a story about a man whose consistent ability to win baffles many of his closest associates.

...

It is the fifth week of the 1975 season. The record is 3-1. The Irish are being whipped by North Carolina, 14-0, when quarterback Rick Slager is hurt. Devine looks around and sees Joe Montana. Last-string quarterback under Parseghian, elevated to fourth string by Devine. Ignoring quarterbacks two and three, Devine sends in Montana.

To this day, Devine cannot explain why. "Just a feeling," he says. Led by Montana, the Irish come back in the fourth quarter and win, 21-14.

...

This is a man with a 171-54-9 record. In 22 years as a college coach he has had one losing season. He has had two perfect seasons and won a national championship with an 11-1 team three years ago, His teams have always had a flair for the dramatic comeback, the most memorable in the 1979 Cotton Bowl when the Irish trailed Houston, 34-12, with 7:30 to play and won, 35-34, on the game's final play.

"You would have to have been stupid to think we were going to win that one," Devine says today. "I knew we were going to win."

He has won almost every coaching award in collegiate football. From a distance, this is clearly a major success story. Move in closer and the vision blurs.

"If Coach Devine wanted to please all the people who complain about him he could do it," defensive end Scott Zettek said. "But he's a coach, not a used car salesman. He doesn't have to sell himself. I'd rather play for him than someone like Digger (Phelps, the Irish basketball coach) who is always being all things to all people."

Joyce acknowledges Devine's non-acceptance but says he can't understand it.
...
"I don't have any regrets," Devine says. "No reason to. If some people say I haven't received the credit I'm due, that's nice, but I've always been taught you don't receive your just rewards in this life anyway."

He is asked two last questions. Why is his image so mixed? Why is he an enigma to so many?

"I could explain it to you," he replied, the brown eyes dancing. "But I won't."

Dan Devine, a fine man and a fine coach, **R.I.P.**

Chapter 16 Coach Gerry Faust 1981-1985

Coach # 24

Tough road for Faust

1981	Gerry Faust	5–6
1982	Gerry Faust	6–4–1
1983	Gerry Faust	7–5
1984	Gerry Faust	7–5
1985	Gerry Faust	5–6

Article from the Washington Post on Faust's appointment

The best introduction to the Gerry Faust years at Notre Dame would be to display the hype as it was in 1980 for Gerry Faust, when he was sought after to be the coach of the University of Notre Dame football team. He was hired to succeed retiring coach Dan Devine. Here it is:

Notre Dame Picks Faust, Ohio High School Coach

November 25, 1980

Reprinted from the Washington Post with thanks.

Gerry Faust, who guided Cincinnati Moeller High School to national prominence during the past 18 years, was named Notre Dame football coach today, succeeding Dan Devine.

Notre Dame President Rev. Theodore Hesburgh made the announcement of the appointment of Faust, whose teams have compiled a 174-17-2 record since 1963. They also have won 70 of their last 71 games.

Edmund P. Joyce, executive vice president, said Faust was chosen because of his record on the high school level.

"We feel quite strongly that Gerry Faust is the perfect individual to carry on the great tradition associated with athletics at the University of Notre Dame," Joyce said. "I don't know of anyone acquainted with Gerry who doesn't have the greatest respect and admiration for him and his accomplishments."

Faust's teams have won five of the last six Ohio Class 3A championships, including the latest one on Sunday when his Crusader team finished a 13-0 season by defeating Massillon, 30-7.

"I'm extremely pleased and tremendously honored to have been chosen to come to Notre Dame," said Faust, 45, whose teams have sent 250 players into the college ranks.

"I said several years ago the only job other than the one at Moeller in which I would be interested in would be at Notre Dame and I meant that sincerely."

Faust, whose team had a 33-game winning streak, explained why he decided to leave Moeller to take the Notre Dame job.

"I am a strong believer in tradition and discipline in educating your people," said the Dayton University graduate. "I don't believe there is a university in the country that combines those two items along with academic and athletic excellence better than Notre Dame does."

Devine announced his resignation before the start of the season, citing personal reasons, including the health of his wife.

The Irish, currently ranked No. 2 in the nation, are 9-0-1 on the season, giving Devine a 53-14-1 mark entering the regular-season finale at Southern California Dec. 6.

Notre Dame also has a shot at the national championship with a date against top-ranked Georgia Jan. 1 at the Sugar Bowl.

"We felt that whoever took over at Notre Dame," Devine explained, "they would be inheriting a veteran squad. This is a great bunch of young men and we know that the transition will be that much easier."

Faust will become the 24th head coach in the history of the tradition-rich Midwest independent dating back to 1894.

At Moeller, Faust has been turning out college-looking teams for years at Cincinnati Moeller High.

Faust's high school team never looked more collegiate than on Sunday. Some of Faust's players suspected then that their coach was Notre Dame-bound.

"We dedicated this game to Coach Faust because it might have been his last game at Moeller," fullback Mark Brooks said immediately after Sunday's game.

Gerry Faust was a great high school coach. It is easy to see with the credentials noted in this introductory article how the Notre Dame Brass would see in Faust both a great coach and a great man. Perhaps he was the perfect coach to take Notre Dame to another championship, but it probably was not this year, and it probably was not without more college experience.

All of us learned a lot through Gerry Faust's experience. High School and College Football players need different coaching styles. Many high school coaches become great college coaches either by mentoring with a great head college coach or by moving to a small college and learning the ropes while advancing through the ranks. Too bad Gerry Faust could not have worked with Dan Devine or Ara Parseghian for a year or five before becoming the big mahoff for the Irish. The spirit is willing…

1981 Coach Gerry Faust Year 1

The 1981 Notre Dame Fighting Irish football team was coached by Gerry Faust in his first year as head football coach. The 1981 offense scored 232 points, while the defense allowed 160 points. Despite Dan Devine's feeling that he had left his successor a solid team, it was Notre Dame's first losing season (5-6) in 18 years. There were no bowl offers and no rankings. b

It was not a good start for Coach Faust who coached his first college football game at Notre Dame on September 12, 1981.

Former Notre Dame Football Coach Gerry Faust stands on the sidelines in South Bend, Ind. during the 1983 season. (AP Photo/Joe Raymond)

1982 Coach Gerry Faust Year 2

The 1982 Notre Dame Fighting Irish football team was coached by Gerry Faust in his second year as head football coach. Faust was no longer in awe of Division I coaching and teams and he did better plotting how to become victorious against them. Notre Dame's record was 6-4-1. The team was unranked throughout the season, and it was not invited to play in a bowl game.

Notre Dame was a much better team in 1982 under Gerry Faust than they were in his first season. They were beating good teams.

But, the reality of life is that ND success and history was tough to live up to every season. There were no big stars in Faust's lineup that he had recruited or that had come from Dan Devine.

The fans and alum were picking on Faust and they were nailing players as well. Junior quarterback Blair Kiel, a starter since his freshman year with Devine was criticized by fans and alumni for an unproductive, conservative and predictable Irish offense. It was tough for any kid to survive such attacks.

Even though the Irish were beating teams, this QB was taking it on the chin simply because he was no Joe Montana. But, how many Joe Montana's are there. Ask Joe M. With 13 field goals in 13 attempts, kicker Mike Johnson was personally responsible for two of the three victories and the tie. The fans and alumni should have been buying him big dinners every night.

On the other side of the ball, Notre Dame sported a really tough defense. The Irish ranked fifth in total defense, permitting 232.9 yards per game, second against the rush at 56.4 yards per game and allowing less than two yards per carry, and hadn't permitted two touchdowns to any team. That takes coaching. There are two sides to the game of football.

The Notre Dame losses this season all were close. There were no blow-outs. Coach Faust could have used a little guidance from Rockne, Leahy, or Dan Devine. He was just a little green from making the transition from HS to college. The season could have been much different. It appeared that the team was ready and they were inspired by the coaching but in close calls, a little more experience would have helped.

1983 Coach Gerry Faust Year 3

The 1983 Notre Dame Fighting Irish football team was the third season for head coach Gerry Faust. Notre Dame's big 1983 moment was that it had made it to the Liberty Bowl where they faced Boston College and the Eagle's prized quarterback Doug Flutie.

It was an ND football season that in many ways was non-descript.

1983 Liberty Bowl – ND 19, BC 18

It was BC's first bowl game in 40 years. The Eagles were 9-2 on the season, ranked # 13 in the country and had really captured the imagination of the Boston area behind the play of junior QB Doug Flutie. Notre Dame had been struggling. The Irish limped into the game unranked at just 6-5, after opening the season at #5. Gerry Faust and Blair Kiel, the ND leaders were both having tough years.

ND v BC in Liberty Bowl. Head to Head Play

BC got a 6-0 lead quickly on a 63-yd drive. Flutie hit Brennan for the score. The Irish came right back and it was 7-6 after Alan Pinkett took it in from the 1 followed by the game's only successful extra point.

In Q2, Kiel hit Alvin Miller for a 13-yard TD to put the Irish up 13-6. ND scored again on its next possession for a lead of 19-6. Flutie tossed a nice 42-yarder one to Bob Biestek setting up a 28-yard reception by Gerard Phelan 28 for another Flutie TD. After two-point attempt failed, the half ended with ND up 19-12.

Nobody got anywhere in the second half until Flutie mustered up a sustained drive which ended in a 3-yard TD pass to TE Scott Grossman. ND was still up 19-18 after Flutie's pass for the conversion was batted away.

BC had one last chance with 1:08 remaining. They got the ball to the ND 35 but the Irish held on for the one point win W (19-18). The kicking game was clearly critical and it served to be the margin of victory for Notre Dame.

1984 Coach Gerry Faust Year 4

The 1984 Notre Dame Fighting Irish football team was coached by Gerry Faust in his fourth season. The Fighting Irish were 7-5 and finished # 17.

1985 Coach Gerry Faust Year 5

The 1985 Notre Dame Fighting Irish football team was coached by Gerry Faust in his fifth and final season with Notre Dame. This was the second losing Season (5-6) with Coach Faust and Irish fans were getting restless with the lack of what seemed to be long-term solid play.

1985: Faust's Last Season

Farewell to Gerry Faust. May God, bless you as you are a good man. Here is a closing article to summarize the Faust years as written by the New York Times:

http://www.nytimes.com/1985/11/27/sports/embattled-faust-resigns-as-coach-of-notre-dame.html

EMBATTLED FAUST RESIGNS AS COACH OF NOTRE DAME
From the New York Times
Published: November 27, 1985
SOUTH BEND, Ind., Nov. 26—

Gerry Faust, who resigned earlier today after five troubled years, took the blame tonight for Notre Dame's lackluster football performance and said his decision will allow the university to move quickly to find a new coach.

"If you're going to put the blame somewhere, put it on the coach," Faust said during a news conference. "That's where it ought to be. We got started on the wrong foot five years ago, and never did bail out of the thing."

Faust, 50 years old, has a 30-26-1 record at Notre Dame, including a 5-6 [Counts Miami game] mark this season after consecutive defeats by top-ranked Penn State and Louisiana State the last two weeks. Those two defeats made him the Irish coach with the most losses. Joe Kuharich is next, with 23 losses from 1959 to 1962. With only 17 victories, Kuharich is the only Notre Dame coach with a losing record.

"Bottom line is, you've got to win on the field," Faust said. "That's what you play the game for."

Face Miami Saturday

The Fighting Irish have one game left, against powerful Miami Saturday in the Orange Bowl.

Faust's resignation at the beginning of a weekly news conference earlier today came as a shock. "It's best for me to resign now and give the university an opportunity to get another coach before recruiting starts next week," Faust said. "It's best for the university, best for me, best for my family."

Faust said he would consider a coaching offer from another Division I-A school, but he has received none so far. "I'm going to sit back for a couple of weeks and hope I get some calls, maybe in the business world, the coaching world, and evaluate things and go from there," he said.

Faust said he would hold his Notre Dame years in special regard, whether or not he continues in coaching. "I don't regret any of the years at Notre Dame," he said. "If I knew what the results would be there after that five-year period, the tough times and the good times, I'd do it again."

Speculation on Successor

Faust's decision sparked speculation on a possible successor.

Gene Corrigan, the athletic director, denied a rumor that Coach Lou Holtz of Minnesota had already been offered the job. Holtz, whose son attends Notre Dame, recently said he wouldn't leave Minnesota for any coaching job except that at Notre Dame. Holtz said earlier today he had not been contacted by Notre Dame about the job.

Corrigan said a successor might be chosen by Monday.
In addition to Holtz, coaches whose names have been mentioned as possible successors include George Welsh of Virginia, Bobby Ross of Maryland, Terry Donahue of U.C.L.A. and Dick Vermeil, former coach at U.C.L.A. and of the Philadelphia Eagles.

Donahue, however, issued a statement saying any speculation on his behalf is unfounded. "I have never been in contact with anyone from Notre Dame," he said.

Followed Dan Devine

Faust succeeded Dan Devine as Notre Dame's 24th head coach on Nov. 24, 1980.

Faust stepped into that pressure-packed atmosphere directly from Moeller High School in Cincinnati.

Faust struggled through seasons of 5-6 in 1981, 6-4-1 in 1982, 7-5 in 1983 and 7-5 in 1984. Instead of the Cotton and Sugar bowls, Notre Dame backed into the Liberty and Aloha bowls the last two seasons.

The Rev. Theodore M. Hesburgh, university president, accepted Faust's resignation "with genuine regret."

Faust said he first thought about resigning after last Saturday's 10-7 loss to Louisiana State. "You're always high when you win and low when you lose," he said, "and I didn't want to make a decision then."

----Report Says Irish in Contact MINNEAPOLIS (AP) - While Lou Holtz, the Minnesota coach, continued to deny that he has been offered a job as head coach at Notre Dame, The Minneapolis Star and Tribune, citing unnamed sources, said the job has been offered to him.

Quoting the Minnesota athletic director, Paul Giel, the newspaper said Holtz had talked within the last two days to Gene Corrigan, Notre Dame's athletic director.

"Lou told me that Corrigan had called him," said Giel, adding that Holtz asked if Corrigan "has to get permission from me to talk about the Notre Dame job. I said it was fine, that no permission was necessary."

The newspaper said Holtz met tonight with Giel, University President Ken Keller and Frank Wilderson, vice president for student affairs. Holtz could not be reached for comment, but Keller said Holtz has not reached a decision on Minnesota's latest contract offer.

"He's going to have to make a decision," Keller said. "If we don't succeed, it's not for wanting of trying."

"I came here two years ago, with certain feelings," Holtz told a news conference that had been called to discuss the Gophers' Dec. 21 Independence Bowl trip. "But right now, I don't know what my feelings are."

For several days, Holtz declined to discuss news reports concerning his candidacy for the Notre Dame job.

Holtz disclosed that when he first signed his five-year contract at Minnesota two years ago, he insisted on a clause that would free him from his obligation if he were ever offered the Notre Dame job.

End of New York Times Article

Post Script: November 30, 1985. The Gerry Faust era ends at Miami with a loss L (7-58).

Chapter 17 Coach Lou Holtz 1986-1996

Coach # 25
National Championship 1988

Rockne, Leahy, Parseghian, Devine, Holtz—Five Greats—with National Championships

1986	Lou Holtz	5–6
1987	Lou Holtz	8–4
1988	Lou Holtz	12–0*
1989	Lou Holtz	12–1
1990	Lou Holtz	9–3
1991	Lou Holtz	10–3
1992	Lou Holtz	10–1–1
1993	Lou Holtz	11–1
1994	Lou Holtz	6–5–1
1995	Lou Holtz	9–3
1996	Lou Holtz	8–3

As you can see by his record, Lou Holtz is one of the best coaches ever at Notre Dame. He is one of the elite. He fits in well with the Notre Dame immortals as he is one.

The best way to introduce the Lou Holtz era is to see what the pundits were writing about Coach Holtz when he got the job in 1985 for the 1986 season. This Chicago Tribune Article by Reporters Skip Myslenski and Phil Hersh gets us right where we want to be to start off the next eleven years of Great Moments in Notre Dame Football. We have all now arrived in the Lou Holtz era of Notre Dame.

Please enjoy this wonderful piece introducing Lou Holtz. It was published on November 28, 1985 right after Holtz got the ND coaching job. Our thanks to the Chicago Tribune for permission to include this article: Enjoy!

http://articles.chicagotribune.com/1985-11-28/sports/8503220538_1_football-coach-arkansas-and-minnesota-minnesota-coach-lou-holtz

From The Chicago Tribune

Notre Dame Picks Holtz

Minnesota Coach Couldn`t Pass Up Opportunity

November 28, 1985
By Skip Myslenski and Phil Hersh.

Minnesota coach Lou Holtz was named the new football coach at Notre Dame Wednesday just 30 hours after the surprise resignation of Gerry Faust.

Holtz, who leaves Minnesota after two years of leading that program back to respectability, was officially unveiled at a late afternoon press conference *in Notre Dame, Ind.*

"There isn`t a job in the country that I`d leave Minnesota for--with the possible exception of Notre Dame," Holtz said last Sunday. "I`d be less than honest if I didn`t say that I`d have to seriously consider a chance to coach at Notre Dame if it was ever offered to me. I`ve always had a warm spot in my heart for Notre Dame."

Holtz, who rebuilt programs at North Carolina State and Arkansas before he refurbished Minnesota, takes over the Irish with 16 years of head coaching experience in college and a lifetime record of 116-65-5. His 1985 Golden Gophers, who face Clemson in the Independence Bowl on Dec. 21, had a surprising 6-5 record that included narrow losses to national powers Oklahoma and Ohio State.

"What he did in two years at Minnesota was a miracle. I guess that`s one reason they call him a magician," said CBS college football commentator Pat Haden. "He`s a very good coach, a very good fundamental coach, and I think he`s always played well in big games.

I think he`s a coach who`s always gotten the most out of his players. The last two places he`s been, Arkansas and Minnesota, didn`t have the best athletes in their conferences by a long shot, but he managed to play very, very well and get into some major bowls. I think it will be interesting to see what he gets out of better players. He`s going to have better athletes than he ever had before."

Added Northwestern coach Dennis Green: "He gets the most out of his talent. He`s one of those guys who has the ability to maximize the talents of the guys he has."

Concluded Haden: ``He has always wanted to go there, he has a son there, so it makes sense. One thing makes it an interesting choice--people say he didn`t handle the pressure well in New York (during his one season as head coach of the Jets). But he`s glib, and he has a great reputation for integrity. To my knowledge, his programs have never been in trouble. He cares about his kids. He`s the perfect guy for Notre Dame."

The same was said of Gerry Faust when Notre Dame plucked him from Cincinnati`s Moeller High School and named him as its football coach five years ago. He was glib and honest and caring during his stay at the school,* *yet his college coaching inexperience often showed and his teams` performances never matched expectations.

That failing prompted speculation on his future to begin even before the start of the 1984 season, which would be Faust`s last under the five-year deal he signed when hired. As his team struggled, rumors that his contract would not be renewed grew rampant, yet his announcement Tuesday surprised even university officials, who did not learn of his decision until that morning.

Athletic director Gene Corrigan, whom Faust informed just moments before entering a press conference and announcing his resignation publicly, responded to the news by saying "unquestioned integrity" would be the paramount quality he would look for in a new coach. He added: "We need someone who is experienced at this level and has been a success at this level."

Corrigan, the first Notre Dame athletic director in 30 years to have a say in the selection of the school`s football coach, said he did not begin contacting possible replacement until after he learned of Faust`s decision on Tuesday. But he must have had his choice in mind, for later that same day Minnesota athletic director Paul Giel told the Minneapolis Star and Tribune:

"Lou told me that Corrigan had called him and asked if he (Corrigan) has to get permission from me to talk about the Notre Dame job. I said it was fine, that no permission was necessary."

That was true because Holtz`s contract with Minnesota contained an escape clause that would release him from the deal if Notre Dame offered him a job. Yet Giel, university president Ken Keller and Frank Wilderson, the school`s vice president for school affairs, met with Holtz Tuesday afternoon to try and lure him into staying. "He`s going to have to make a decision," Keller said later. "If we don`t succeed (in keeping him), it`s not for want of trying." "I came to Minnesota two years ago with certain feelings, "Holtz himself said at a news conference to discuss the Independence Bowl. "But right now, I don`t know what my feelings are."

But by Wednesday morning, his feelings were settled and he was on his way from Minneapolis to Notre Dame for the press conference that would announce his selection. Back at Minnesota, the sign marking his parking space outside his office building was already removed, and his secretary was busy cleaning out his closets and packing his belongings.

1986 Coach Lou Holtz Year 1

The 1986 Notre Dame Fighting Irish football team was coached by Lou Holtz. It was clearly a rebuilding year for Coach Holtz. Notre Dame produced a 5-6 record under first-year coach Holtz. Despite the poor record, the moxie that Notre Dame showed all season long, even in defeat, lifted the spirits of the fans as we all knew that Notre Dame was in for something good.

With an average of 5 points as the margin separating the Fighting Irish from victory in its six defeats, Irish fans knew that with just a little tweaking, Notre Dame would soon be back to the Devine, Parseghian, Leahy, and Rockne days.

Sports

A Breath Of Fresh Air

By Larry Burke

Notre Dame Dropped Its Opener To No. 3 Michigan,
But A Solid Irish Performance Proved
That Lou Holtz Had Put The Fight Back In The Irish

Brown (81) and Green (24) combined for 24 carries and 122 yards on the ground.

Michigan 24; Notre Dame 23

The Fighting Irish always have a tough schedule. Notre Dame's big games in 1986 began with a one point loss against #3 ranked Michigan in the home opener L (23-24).

1987 Coach Lou Holtz Year 2

The 1987 Notre Dame Fighting Irish football team was coached by Lou Holtz in his second year as Notre Dame Head Coach. Tony Rice became the starting quarterback for Notre Dame following an injury to Terry Andrysiak. Rice would become one of the Notre Dame stars that few fans would ever forget.

This year, Tim Brown would end ND's 23 year Heisman drought (John Huarte) as he would pick up the sixth **Heisman Trophy** for Notre Dame. The Irish would finish the season 8-4 and they earned a berth to the Cotton Bowl Classic for the first time since the 1978 season. But, unfortunately, the Irish lost L (10-35) in the Bowl game against Texas A & M. Nobody denied that it was the best season since Dan Devine had retired.

SOUTH BEND, IN- NOVEMBER 1987: Tim Brown #81 of the Notre Dame Fighting Irish carries the ball during a game against the Navy Midshipmen in November 1987 in South Bend, Indiana.

When ND played Navy, it was not even close. Still at home and holding the #9 position nationally against Navy, the Irish dominated W (56-13).

One of the big reality tests for Holtz's Irish was on the schedule for Notre Dame Stadium. The # 10 ranked Alabama's Crimson Tide was ready to make its mark in South Bend against the # 7 ranked Notre Dame. Notre Dame won W (37-6).

1988Coach Lou Holtz Year 3

The 1988 Notre Dame Fighting Irish football team was coached by Lou Holtz in his third year. This magical and mythical Holtz-led ND squad ended the season with 12 wins and no losses and no ties, winning the national championship. In other words, the Fighting Irish were unbeaten and they were good enough to convince all the Notre Dame haters in the world that they were worthy of being voted the # 1 team in the country.

The Fighting Irish had nothing handed to it, nor had it ever. The Irish won the title by defeating the previously unbeaten and No. 3 ranked West Virginia Mountaineers in the Sunkist Fiesta Bowl in Tempe, Arizona by a score of a 34-21. This powerful 1988 squad, one of 11 national title squads for the Irish, and a squad coached by the eternally great Lou Holtz, is considered to be one of the best undefeated teams in the history of college football.

The Irish always had tough schedules and that is why some of us think that they missed out on a few past titles. This time, there was no choice. Notre Dame had beaten teams, which had finished the season ranked #2, #4, #5, and #7 in the AP Poll. How about that?

They also won 10 of 12 games by double digits. This phenomenal 1988 squad may best be remembered for its 31-30 upset of No. 1 ranked Miami, when Miami was at its best in Miami. It was Coach Jimmy Johnson's last year of his dynasty. Johnson had built a powerhouse that won and won and won and won. Notre Dame ended Johnson's and Miami's 36-game regular season winning streak. According to Irish fans, it was Notre Dame's landmark 31-30 win over top-rated Miami in 1988 in a game that keynoted that Irish national championship season.

The notion of "*Catholics vs. Convicts*" came from an ND student who put it on a t-shirt. The students liked it and he made money printing many more shirts. They sold like hotcakes during the buildup for the Top 5 showdown.

The teams really did not like each other and it seemed there was no love lost between the coaches. There was a pre-game fight between the two teams outside of the entrance tunnel lead credence to the slogan on the shirts. Both teams—players and coaches—wanted the victory badly. The fans seemed to want it even more.

The game has gone down as one of the most memorable in all of college football. Other than their loss to Notre Dame in South Bend, Miami would have been undefeated as they literally ripped through all of their other opponents. Miami and Jimmy Johnson, a coach people loved to hate, and many still do, did not have what it took in 1988. Notre Dame beat the Hurricanes and that is that.

This game has gone down in history as Good v. Evil. It was the Midwestern choirboys vs. South Beach renegades. It was the Catholics v. Convicts. It was ND V UM: Football at its best and worst.

Miami was #1 and Notre Dame #4 (5 wins, 0 losses) when they met in South Bend on Oct.15. Miami was the defending national champion. They came in with a 36-game regular season winning streak. The Irish, led by Tony Rice, held a 31–21 lead in the third quarter, but the Hurricanes rallied to within 31–30 on a touchdown with 45 seconds left in the game. The Canes went for the two-point conversion and missed. ND won the game W (31-30)

1989 Coach Lou Holtz Year 4

The 1989 Notre Dame Fighting Irish football team was the fourth ND squad coached by Lou Holtz. The Irish played its home games at Notre Dame Stadium in South Bend, Indiana. This was the perfect follow-up season to a National Championship year, except for one thing—# 7 Miami L (10-27), a team that finished the season 11-1. Jimmy Johnson, the long-time Miami Coach stepped down unnoticed in 1988 to coach Dallas as the new 1989 Hurricanes coach Dennis Erickson did not miss a single beat.

The Hurricanes had lost to Bobby Bowden's #9 ranked Florida State Seminoles (10-24) earlier in the season. After winning the Notre Dame game, Miami beat Alabama in the Sugar Bowl (33-25). They got the nod for #1 national ranking in both polls over Notre Dame because of the head to head win. Notre Dame was 11-1 in the regular season and won the Orange Bowl W (21-6) against Colorado for an overall 12-1 record. ND was #2 in the AP poll for their 12-1 record but the coaches poll picked Bowden's '10-2 'Noles as #2 and ND as #3 because Bowden's team had beaten Dennis Erickson's 'Canes during the regular season.

Notre Dame began the season early having been invited as National Champion to play in the kickoff classic against Virginia at Giants Stadium before 77,323 fans. Notre Dame had its championship form and dominated the game W (36-13). The rest is history. It was a "coulda-been" season.

1990 Coach Lou Holtz Year 5

The 1990 Notre Dame Fighting Irish football team was coached by Lou Holtz in his fifth season with the Irish.

After the season, Notre Dame at (9-2), were invited to play (10-1-1) Colorado, the #1 ranked team in the Country at the time in the Orange Bowl. It was a game with little offense. Both defenses were strong but Colorado had just a little bit more in them than the Irish as they beat Notre Dame L (9-10) bringing Notre Dame's season record down to 9-3 and the Irish ranking to #6. Another year with title hopes unmet but a fine year by anybody's standards.

1991 Coach Lou Holtz Year 6

The 1991 Notre Dame Fighting Irish football team was coached by Lou Holtz in his sixth year as head coach. In 1991, the National Broadcasting Company (NBC) signed an agreement with Notre Dame to televise all games exclusively.

In 1991 with Lou Holtz at the helm, there was no concern about interest in the Notre Dame program. Notre Dame had another banner year but with a record of 10-3, the Irish came up short again in its attempt for a second Holtz championship. At season end, the Fighting Irish finished #12 in the coaches' poll and #13 in the AP.

1992 Coach Lou Holtz Year 7

The 1992 Notre Dame Fighting Irish football team was coached by Lou Holtz in his seventh year as head coach. Notre Dame had a nice-looking squad ready to go and they were ranked # 3 in the preseason polls. There was always hope for another championship. Rick Mirer was quarterback and he also served as captain of the fighting Irish.

During the season, #22 Penn State came to South Bend and played a really close match W (17-16). Here is a recap of the PSU game known as The Snow Bowl:

The Snow Bowl

In this 1992 season, ND had just won the Holy War v BC and now Penn State was coming to Notre Dame. The Irish were ranked # 8 and Paterno's PSU was at # 22. The series was going on hiatus after this game and nobody knew when the next game might be. Penn State had won eight of the last eleven games and held a slight edge in the series 8-7-1. The word on campus was that the Irish had this game circled all season long, wanting a big victory on Senior Day. As you can see from the picture it was snowing and to some this is still known as "The Snow Bowl."

Snow Bowl – 1992 Encounter between Penn State and Notre Dame

The score was knotted at half-time, 6-6. The weather had improved by the second-half kickoff and the Irish D came up with a big stop. Notre Dame took 9-6 lead before Penn State drove to the goal line.

The Irish knew they needed a monumental goal-line stand to keep the game on the Irish side.

They rallied behind captain Demetrius DeBose, and executed what some have called a picturesque goal line stand. This forced the Nittany Lions to kick a field goal. As the teams prepared to play the fourth quarter, the score was still tied at 9-9.

Penn State scored another touchdown and Notre Dame had some time on the clock but not much. They had to get a TD to tie or go ahead. There was 4:16 left in the game. As the Irish advanced the clock was ticking. Now behind 16-9 with fourth down at the three-yard line, Notre Dame called judiciously called time out with twenty-five seconds remaining.

Coach Holtz called a play normally reserved for two point conversions and that had never been used in a game before. Rick Mirer checked to his last option and told Jerome Bettis to go out. The "Bus" caught the touchdown pass in the middle of the end zone. Notre Dame then trailed 16-15. Under Holtz's leadership, the Irish were already once booed at home after a tie so it was clear that they needed to put the game on the line and go for two.

In what looked like a broken play, Mirer rolled to his right and Brooks mirrored him in the end zone. Brooks caught his third collegiate pass for the two points. The gutsy two-point conversion was successful. Notre Dame led 17-16 and withstood three Penn State passes after the kickoff before time expired. At the end of this game, the seniors had gotten their victory and the series was then tied 8-8-1.

"It was kind of weird because [Holtz] basically came up with a play on the fly," said Brooks, who only had two previous career pass receptions. "And we never even thought twice about going out and executing it."

The teams met again in 2006 at Notre Dame and 2007 in Beaver Stadium. Both teams won their home games and the series remains tied 9-9-1.

1993 Coach Lou Holtz Year 8

The 1993 Notre Dame Fighting Irish football team was coached by Lou Holtz in his eighth year. Paul Failla and Kevin McDougal shared the QB duties. Backup Failla got time when McDougal hurt his shoulder. The season went so well that it surely looked like Lou Holtz was about to get his second national title at Notre Dame. Just two points and a Holy War later and things looked different.

On November 13, Notre Dame played Florida State in a late-season matchup of "unbeatens." The winner of this game, at Notre Dame Stadium in South Bend, Indiana, was certain to play #3 Nebraska (which would then move up to #2) in the Orange Bowl for the National Championship. What could stop that eventuality?

Let's look at the write-up from EPIC ND games to see a nice story about this game and then I may offer my few additional words:

1993 FLORIDA STATE V NOTRE DAME

Still the last time Notre Dame was featured in a No. 1 vs. No. 2 matchup, the second-ranked Irish hosted top-ranked Florida State at Notre Dame Stadium for the fourth installment of the "Game of the Century."

This one lived up to the hype, though through most of the game that didn't appear to be the case.

The Irish looked in control with a seemingly comfortable 31-17 lead in the fourth quarter. Florida State responded when quarterback Charlie Ward, the eventual Heisman Trophy winner that season, got a fortuitous bounce off a Notre Dame defender on a 4th-and-20 pass that went for a Seminole touchdown that pulled FSU within 31-24.

After the Irish went three and out, Florida State had one last chance to tie or win. In just three plays, Ward moved the Seminoles to the Notre Dame 14-yard line with three seconds remaining.

On the game's final play, Ward rolled to his left, looked and threw to the end zone where Notre Dame cornerback Shawn Wooden batted the pass down to preserve the win and move the Irish to No. 1 in the polls the following week.

The celebration was so jubilant after the pass break-up, Wooden had his knee severely injured when a teammate jumped on his back.

"It was kind of a great moment at the time," recalled Wooden, who can laugh about the moment now. "But it was also one of those times, I was kind of like, `Uh, yeah.'"

When ND and Florida State met that day, the game had been hyped by many as the "Game of the Century". This much-acclaimed clash between #1 and #2 did not fail to live up to expectations. With Notre Dame ahead by a touchdown and Florida State driving, hoping for a tie, or two to win. Irish defensive back Shawn Wooden batted down a Charlie Ward pass in the end zone with three seconds left to play. Notre Dame won the battle W (31-24).

Nothing but a holy war

Boston College was ranked # 12 when the next week, the Eagles came roaring to Notre Dame Stadium for the continuation of the Holy Wars. It was one of the best games of the year. The Notre Dame offense piled up 427 yards of offense, scored 5 touchdowns, including 22 points in the last 11 minutes. Yet, the game would forever be remembered on Boston College's last drive as their kicker David Gordon hit a 41-yard field goal as time expired to win it L (39-41), ending Notre Dame's bid for a national title.

ND was #2 in the AP poll for their 12-1 record but the coaches poll picked Bowden's ' 10-2 'Noles as #2 and ND as #3 because Bowden's team had beaten Dennis Erickson's 'Canes during the regular season. Notre Dame fans are probably still upset about being kept out of the 1993 national championship game despite having beaten FSU. You bet we are. So is ND Quarterback Kevin McDougal.

On Nov. 24, 2000, Scott Merkin wrote a special to the Chicago Tribune that captures Notre Dame fans' sentiments on the game and on the voting snow-job. Here is an excerpt:

"One 42-yard field goal by a little-known left-footed kicker from Boston College prevented Kevin McDougal from leading Notre Dame to the 1993 national championship. One kick and some questionable pre-BCS voting that put Florida State ahead of Notre Dame in the final polls. "If we beat Florida State, like we did, and Boston College beat us, it just means Florida State should have been behind both of us in the voting," McDougal explained. "I still think we should have won the..."

1994 Coach Lou Holtz Year 9

The 1994 Notre Dame Fighting Irish football team was coached by Lou Holtz in his ninth year. Ron Powlus was the ND Quarterback. This year brought the worst record for Coach Holtz since his first season. The Irish were unranked at 6-5-1 and struggled all year. A 6-4-1 Notre Dame qualified for the Fiesta Bowl and played Colorado. The Buffaloes dominated L (24-41). ND finished 6-5-1.

1995 Coach Lou Holtz Year 10

The Notre Dame Fighting Irish football team with its ten-year coach Lou Holtz played its 1995 home games at Notre Dame Stadium in South Bend, Indiana. The team compiled a 9-3 record and finished # 13 in the coaches' poll and # 11 in the AP.

Northwestern coach Gary Barnett and Notre Dame coach Lou Holtz shake hands after Northwestern's upset win on Sept. 2, 1995 n South Bend. (Phil Greer / Chicago Tribune)

The #9 Fighting Irish were invited to the Orange Bowl to play Florida State. The Seminoles won the close game L (26-31).

1996 Coach Lou Holtz Year 11

The 1996 Fighting Irish football team was coached by Lou Holtz in his eleventh and final year as Notre Dame Head football coach. Notre Dame began a new tradition of periodically engaging in a football match outside the United States. This year, the Fighting Irish participated in the Emerald Isle Classic. It was played on November 2 In Ireland, and Notre Dame beat Navy by a score of 54-27. Both Notre Dame and the US Navy enjoyed the experience.

Lou Holtz resigns as ND Football Coach

On Monday, November 18, 1996, Lou Holtz met with his team and gave them the news first of his decision to leave Notre Dame and pursue coaching opportunities elsewhere. In much the same way that he could not explain his feelings about the Golden Gophers two years after leaving Minnesota, Holtz had a tough time explaining why he was leaving Notre Dame.

He knew it was time to go, and so he made the decision. Lou Holtz coveted the Notre Dame Job for much of his adult life. He got the job, did very well in the job, and simply believed it was time to go. For the rest of us at the time, there were a lot of unanswered questions. For Lou Holtz, he knew it was his time to move on, even though he may not have been able to give anybody else a hint about his future or show relief after such a difficult decision.

At a press conference, he noted that he first contemplated leaving the job nine months earlier. His rationale for the timing on the Monday after the Pitt game before playing 2-7 Rutgers was that he wanted the kids to have a coach, and so his early announcement gave the ND administration more time to find a replacement.

Holtz said: "You have no idea how proud I have been to hear, 'He's the coach at Notre Dame,' " he said. "That's something you just can't buy."

"Whenever Coach Holtz comes in and doesn't look happy, it's not going to be good news," said Bert Berry, a senior linebacker. "We could just tell from the way he came in -- 'Oh, no, Coach is leaving.' What a shame for the University of Notre Dame."

In this book, I have tried to find an appropriate article that coincides with the arrival and/or departure of an important Notre Dame historical figure. This November 20, 1996 piece written by Mike Jensen of the Philadelphia Inquirer does a nice job of putting Holtz tenure and his departure in perspective as we sign off from the Lou Holtz coaching era in this book. Enjoy:

http://articles.philly.com/1996-11-20/sports/25649667_1_lou-holtz-emmett-mosley-job-in-college-football

Headline: **Lou Holtz Resigns As Coach Of The Irish He Has 99 Victories At Notre Dame, Six Away From Knute Rockne's All-time School Record.**

By Mike Jensen, INQUIRER STAFF WRITER
This article contains information from the Associated Press
POSTED: NOVEMBER 20, 1996

> *To the end, Lou Holtz wanted to show that he was in control. He began yesterday's nationally televised news conference with an injury report about flanker Emmett Mosley's eye. Then he took 10 minutes' worth of questions about Notre Dame's next opponent, 2-7 Rutgers.*
>
> *Only then did he get around to announcing his resignation from the most prestigious job in college football.*
>
> *"I have no desire to be the all-time winningest coach at Notre Dame," said Holtz, who has won 99 games in 11 seasons as coach of the Irish and is six wins away from tying the school record. "That record belongs to Knute Rockne. I didn't come here to become a legend, but merely to coach Notre Dame."*
>
> *Everybody at Notre Dame has insisted that the decision to leave belonged solely to Holtz, 59, who led the Irish to the 1988 national championship. But there also was a feeling around campus that maybe this was the time for Holtz to go, and he certainly was capable of picking up that vibe. The*

administrators who had hired Holtz and remain close to him all had left the school, replaced by a group with no ties to him.

"You say, `Wait a minute, has this thing run its course?' "' said John Dockery, an NBC analyst who works as a sideline reporter for Notre Dame games. "I think Lou saw it that way."'

While insisting "there is absolutely nothing"' to rumors that he may become the next coach of the Minnesota Vikings, Holtz also said: "If I do retire, it will because I couldn't find a job. . . . If I feel the way I do today, then I will want to coach."

As for his successor, Holtz said, "I hope it is one of my able assistants."' Speculation in South Bend continues to center on Northwestern coach Gary Barnett and Irish defensive coordinator Bob Davie.

If Barnett hadn't signed a 12-year contract last year with a buyout that would cost "a fortune," according to Northwestern athletic director Rick Taylor, he would be the clear-cut favorite. At Notre Dame, "they're not used to writing checks, they're used to getting checks,"' NBC's Dockery said.

Yesterday, Barnett confirmed that he has been contacted by Notre Dame Officials. He issued a statement saying, "Once I have had time to fully consider my options, I will let them know whether I wish to be considered for the job."

The other leading candidate, Davie, has the support of many Irish players, but his lack of head-coaching experience is very much a factor.

Yesterday, Holtz choked up several times during his 75-minute news conference. He had returned a hug from a cameraman on his way into the room.

"I felt this would be the end of my life," Holtz said, referring to his coaching tenure at Notre Dame. "It's hard for me to even think of coaching anywhere else."

Junior cornerback Allen Rossum said there were a lot of bowed heads as Holtz told players on Monday of his plans.

"That makes me sad,"' Holtz said of the reaction. "I expected indifference. What I got was a strong reaction, an emotional reaction. That's my main concern right now."

There are rumors that Skip Holtz, Lou Holtz's son and the coach at the University of Connecticut, may be up for the vacant job at the University of Minnesota, where Lou Holtz coached before going to Notre Dame. Skip Holtz also is rumored to be a possibility for a coordinator's job with the Vikings if his father ends up there, though Lou Holtz could meet some resistance... .

...

Lou Holtz insisted that he wanted to get the announcement of his leaving out of the way now, with two weeks left in the regular season, so Notre Dame could hire a new coach before the crucial December recruiting period.

"The worst thing is to bring players in without having a football coach,"' Holtz said.

Some people wonder if Holtz isn't already banking on returning to Minneapolis as coach of the Vikings. One of the Vikings' owners, Wheelock Whitney, was quoted in Saturday's St. Paul Pioneer Press as saying he believes that there is "no finer football coach or human being"' than Holtz. Another Vikings owner, Jaye Dyer, is a close friend of Holtz's who received a lucky penny from Holtz after the Vikings won their first three games this season. Dyer wore the penny around his neck.

Final look at Lou Holtz's last season- 1996

The Lou Holtz era at Notre Dame had begun in 1986 and the Master Coach's last team in 1996 would be Holtz's last hurrah on the lovely and sprawling ND campus. Though things looked good preseason, the year 1996 would be up-and-down. The biggest down occurred late season when the rug was ripped out at the very end.

1995 was not a bad football year but it was not a great one for Notre Dame—a team looking to win a championship once again. The Fighting Irish did win nine games and they claimed an Orange Bowl berth. The 1995 season's first disappointment was an upset loss at the hands of Northwestern L (15-17) but the Irish did make the Orange Bowl. They played well in the Orange Bowl but lost to Florida State in a game the Irish should have had tucked away. Unfortunately, with the Fighting Irish holding a 26-14 lead in the Fourth Quarter, Florida State rallied to score 17 late points (just 12 minutes to go), beating Notre Dame 31-26.

Notre Dame students love Lou Holtz!

In their Football wrap-up, the Student Magazine, Scholastic had some very nice words for Coach Holtz. They clearly loved him and knew they would miss him. He is one of the great ones. This was not missed on anybody from Notre Dame.

FROM THE EDITORS of SCHOLASTIC
Lasting Memories

It wasn't supposed to end this way. It should have been different. It should have been better. Lou Holtz - both the man and the legacy - deserved better. Where are the classic Hollywood endings when you want them the most? Why couldn't we see Holtz, drenched from icy Gatorade, carried off the Los Angeles Memorial Coliseum turf on the shoulders of his players?

Why weren't we entitled to a battle of wits between two giants of the sport - Holtz and Paterno - in the Fiesta Bowl on New Year's Day? Why does the lingering image of the Notre Dame coaching pantheon's newest member have to be one of a man sitting at the USC press conference looking utterly defeated and sounding even worse: "I feel like somebody reached into my stomach and pulled out my guts. I've never felt this low."

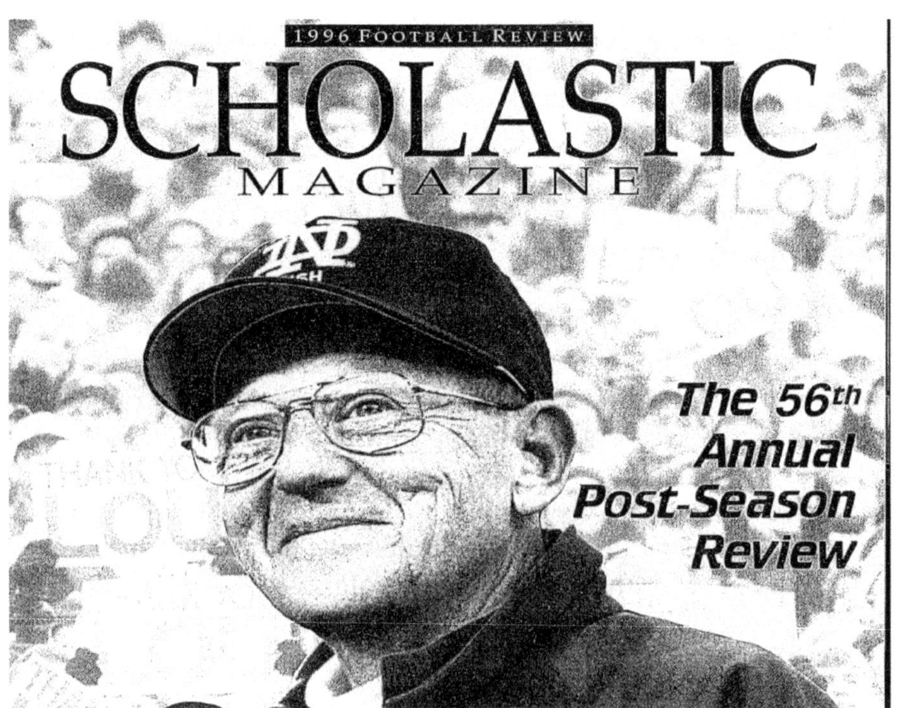

It doesn't. For every Holtz quote that makes you want to cry, there are 10 that leave you smiling or laughing out loud. Don't remember the beaten-down Holtz after the USC game. Remember the Holtz who spoke from the heart following the romp of Rutgers, the one beaming with so much pride he looked ready to burst. Remember the Holtz who made your emotions well up at every pep rally, the man who got you so juiced you thought you could take on the next day's opponent yourself. Above all, remember the Holtz who gave every ounce of his being to Notre Dame for 11 years. It shouldn't be hard.

Notre Dame's Student Magazine – Scholastic pays tribute to Coach Holtz in 1996

Take the same approach with the departing players. Clearly they didn't accomplish all they hoped for at Notre Dame, all that they expected after the dreamlike 1993 season. But each player had his proverbial 15 minutes of fame. There's Robert Farmer, who battled injuries and frustration for his first three years to emerge as a senior with 660 yards (an eye-catching 8.5 yards per carry) and eight touchdowns, including the game-breaking score against Boston College. There's Lyron Cobbins, who couldn't match his impressive 1995 numbers but made the critical interception against Texas to spur the Irish comeback. There's Kevin Carretta, pegged as a career walk-on, who fought and battled until he earned a scholarship and this year became the team's special teams' ace.

In the end, the 1996 season - the past three years, for that matter - will not go down in Irish lore. But certain moments inevitably will. Jim Sanson's kick to beat the Longhorns' will. The three second-quarter punt returns against Pittsburgh will, And Lou Holtz's heartfelt words after the Rutgers game will. Remember those moments.

God bless Lou Holtz, forever.

Dear Lord, please keep him and his supporting family healthy!

Chapter 18 Coach Bob Davie 1997–2001

Bob Davie Coach # 26
George O'Leary Coach # 27

Served as Holtz Defensive Whiz

1997	Bob Davie	7–6
1998	Bob Davie	9–3
1999	Bob Davie	5–7
2000	Bob Davie	9–3
2001	Bob Davie	5–6
2001	George O'Leary	0–0

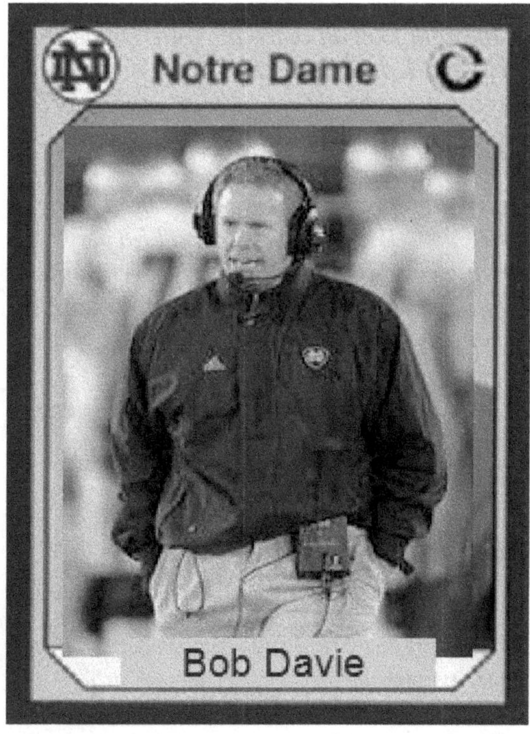

In 1994, Lou Holtz asked Bob Davie to come to Notre Dame to serve as Defensive Coordinator. Davie did nothing less than a great job. Under Davie, the defense improved so much that in 1996, the team set a school record for number of sacks and allowed the lowest total yardage of any Notre Dame team since 1980.

Holtz liked Davie and when in September 1995, Holtz had surgery and missed one game, he asked Davie to be the interim head coach. Under Davie, Notre Dame beat Vanderbilt, 41–0. Technically, if he had never become head coach, Bob Davie would have been the only undefeated and untied coach who ever won a game as head coach for Notre Dame.

This article by Mike Penner from the LA Times, captures the flurry and the hype about Bob Davie becoming Irish head coach, replacing one of the immortals, Lou Holtz.

The Chosen One

New Coach Bob Davie Is Confident Notre Dame Made the Correct Call

November 28, 1996
MIKE PENNER
TIMES STAFF WRITER

"Among the dozens of letters, phone messages and faxes stacked in a box inside Bob Davie's office at Notre Dame is a note from an old colleague at Texas A&M.

"Congratulations," Bob Toledo wrote Davie. "Your life is about to change."

Davie, anointed last weekend as the 26th football coach at Notre Dame and keeper of everything hallowed, holy and Knute, suspects Toledo might be right, and hopes to get a free minute soon to be able to sit back and see for himself.

"We were talking in the locker room after practice about what's been going on here the past few weeks," Davie says. "We've been to Ireland [to play Navy]. We get back from Ireland and go to Boston College, right when the Boston College scandal is breaking. Then we play Pittsburgh and we start to hear reports about Coach Holtz contemplating retirement.

"Then Coach Holtz resigns and I'm given the job the day before the Rutgers game--I had it then, but I couldn't tell anybody--and now we have to get ready for USC."

The overflowing box in Davie's office is one reminder of the gold-and-navy tsunami cresting over his head in his last days as defensive coordinator.

So too is the green leprechaun's hat worn last Sunday by the preacher at the Pittsburgh church that Davie's parents attend.

"My parents," Davie reports with an amused chuckle, "have kind of become media celebrities back home."

Davie, 42, is the first Notre Dame assistant to be promoted to head coach since, well, the year he was born. In 1954, assistant Terry Brennan was named to succeed the legendary Frank Leahy. Brennan lasted five years, went 32-18, and won no national championships. At Notre Dame, this was regarded as a failed experiment and the notion of promoting from within was shelved.

Now, after Ara Parseghian, Dan Devine, Gerry Faust and Lou Holtz, comes Davie, a collegiate assistant coach for 20 years and a head coach for none. He got the job after Northwestern's Gary Barnett chose to ignore the calling when it came--and after Notre Dame figured out that if it didn't hire Davie, Maryland or Boston College or Purdue most likely would.

Toledo, who worked with Davie on R.C. Slocum's staff at Texas A&M before moving to UCLA, calls Davie's hiring by Notre Dame "an interesting marriage.

"You know, he's never been a head coach before. Like anything else you do for the first time, there's going to be trial and error. When you're an assistant, you think you've got all the answers. Then you become a head coach and find out it's not quite the same. You've got to stumble a little bit before you start running.

"That's not to say he can't do it. But Notre Dame is a very difficult job. You're talking about the Subway Alums and all that. Bob loves to coach. As an assistant, that's all you do--coach. As a head coach, you spend less time coaching and more time talking to alumni."

Of course, many of the Subway Alums are saying much the same thing, when they aren't muttering about how Barnett got away or why the Irish didn't go harder after Bobby Ross.

To them, Davie offers this succinct counterpoint:

"I am totally confident that I am the best person for this job."

Despite the lack of previous head coaching experience?

"I coached at places, high-profile places, where I was delegated a lot of jobs," said Davie, who was assistant head coach at Tulane and Texas A&M.

"You can be head coach at a lot of places, but that doesn't necessarily prepare you for being the head coach at Notre Dame. My three years at Notre Dame matured me in a lot of ways. You watch Coach Holtz, day in and day out, and you learn about the mental toughness it takes to do this job. . . .

"In a lot of ways, I'm more prepared for this job than anyone they could have brought in from the outside. Notre Dame is different. It's not for everyone. It takes time to understand what Notre Dame's all about."

Davie got a taste last September when Holtz had spinal surgery to remove a bulging neck disk. Holtz appointed Davie interim coach and handed him the game plan for the game against Vanderbilt.

Notre Dame won, 41-0, and afterward Davie left the field on the shoulders of his players.

"It was really unique," Davie said. "I walked in Monday morning to meet with the coaching staff at 5:30 and Lou walks in and announces he has to have back surgery. Right away you're thinking he might be out for the season. That's serious surgery.

"By 10 a.m. I was sitting in a press conference and thinking I might be head coach at Notre Dame the rest of the season. It's something you've never prepared for. But as I did it, I found out I do enjoy being a head coach."

Holtz missed only one game. Davie had taken care of the shop. The dome didn't melt. More than that, Davie tacked together some credentials Rockne couldn't match: unbeaten and unscored upon as Notre Dame head coach.

Average margin of victory: 41 points.

"That's why I wasn't sure at first to take the job," Davie says, laughing. "I wanted to keep that intact--'the only coach with an undefeated record in Notre Dame history.' "

Now, let's take a look at Bob Davie's time as head coach of the University of Notre Dame:

1997 Coach Bob Davie Year 1

The 1997 Notre Dame Fighting Irish football team was coached by Bob Davie in his first season. Since Davie had been part of Holtz's team as defensive coordinator, despite there being a new coach, the Irish had high expectations. The team was ranked eleventh in the pre-season polls.

Fifth-year senior quarterback Ron Powlus was back at QB and Autry Denson, Tony Driver, and Joey Goodspeed were back at running backs. Besides these mainstays, Joey Getherall, Bobby Brown, and Malcolm Johnson were back at the wide receiver positions and on defense, cornerback Allen Rossum was back and in good health. The team looked so good that there were a number of pundits who thought that the Irish were good enough to finish in the top-10.

1998 Coach Bob Davie Year 2

The 1998 Notre Dame Fighting Irish football team was coached by Bob Davie in his second season. This year's record was 9-2 in the regular season and Notre Dame lost to Georgia Tech in the Gator Bowl. The Irish finished 9-3, and #22 in the Nation. Notre Dame started the season with some inertia and confidence from the last five regular season games of 1997 going down in the win column. Things looked promising.

1999 Coach Bob Davie Year 3

The 1999 Notre Dame Fighting Irish football team was coached by Bob Davie in his third season as head coach. This year's record was

5-7 in the regular season and Notre Dame was not invited to a Bowl game and the Irish were unranked in both polls.

2000 Coach Bob Davie Year 4

The 2000 Notre Dame Fighting Irish football team was coached by Bob Davie in his fourth season as head coach. This year's record was a very respectable 9-2 in the regular season and Notre Dame was invited to the BCS Fiesta Bowl to play Oregon State. Notre Dame had a much better year than in 1999. With the Fiesta Bowl loss, the team finished the season at 9-3, ranked # 16 in the coaches' poll and 15 in the AP.

After losing ten players good enough to play in the NFL, Notre Dame had some rebuilding to do. With its 5-7 record from 1999, many were amazed that the team had such talent. This year, the Irish began the season playing four ranked teams in a row, including the team expected by the pundits to win the national championship—Nebraska.

2001 Coach Bob Davie Year 5

The 2001 Notre Dame Fighting Irish football team was coached by Bob Davie in his fifth season as head coach. Davie had just signed a five-year extension to his contract and after the 9-3 season in 2000, despite the bowl blowout, Notre Dame had great expectations of the team but they were not realized.

After being 9-3, and slipping to 5-6, there was some obvious inconsistency with the team. At the end of the 2001 season, there were no bowl offers and ND was unranked.

By December 1, the regular season was to have been completed. Instead, Notre Dame traveled to Purdue to play the game delayed by the 9-11 attack. The Irish won W (24-15). The Irish defense secured the win. With a 5–6 record, nobody asked ND to play in post-season bowls but there were a lot of questions being asked inside Notre Dame.

Would the Notre Dame administration keep the status quo? Davie had just re-upped his contract for five more years. The answer arrived the next day. Bob Davie was fired on December 2, 2001. No coach was named as his successor.

Here is what LA Times writer Chris Dufresne saw when Davie and his whole staff were fired by Notre Dame's AD, Kevin White on December 2, 2001.
http://articles.latimes.com/2001/dec/03/sports/sp-10906

Davie Fired by Irish

College football: Notre Dame Coach let go after 5-6 season. No timetable set to hire successor.

December 03, 200
CHRIS DUFRESNE
TIMES STAFF WRITER

> *"Bob Davie won his first and last game as Notre Dame coach, but not enough in between to keep his job at a school that has always gauged success in football with a different measuring stick.*
>
> *Less than 24 hours after Notre Dame defeated Purdue to finish the season 5-6, Athletic Director Kevin White fired Davie and his staff Sunday and announced a search for a successor.*
>
> *"We are a place that's won 11 national championships," White said Sunday. "Can we win a 12th? I believe we can."*
>
> *The Irish have not won a national title since 1988.*
>
> *Davie's firing had been long anticipated. In five seasons, he looked, acted and sounded like an Irish coach but finished with a 35-25 record that more closely reflected Gerry Faust's five-year record of 30-26 than the legendary runs of Knute Rockne, Frank Leahy and Ara Parseghian.*
>
> *When Davie replaced Lou Holtz as Irish coach in 1997, Parseghian offered the new coach some advice.*

"There are a lot of things to worry about," Parseghian told Davie, "but worry about one thing, and that's winning."

Davie didn't win enough. He went 7-6 his first year, 9-3 his second, 5-7 his third, 9-3 his fourth and 5-6 in his last.

Under Davie, Notre Dame did not produce a first-round NFL draft choice or win a bowl game, losing in the Independence, Gator and Fiesta bowls. "I am in no way bitter," Davie said. "No way will I have a chip on my shoulder as I leave Notre Dame. I am not the least bit embarrassed. In fact, I'll walk out of here with my head held high and am really proud of what we have done."

After Notre Dame went 9-2 during last year's regular season, White extended Davie's contract through the 2005 season.

Only days later, however, Oregon State embarrassed Notre Dame in the Fiesta Bowl, 41-9.

Davie then boasted that his 2001 squad would be his most talented, but the Irish opened this season with a listless loss at Nebraska that led to the first 0-3 start in school history.

White said he thought he made the right decision at the time in extending Davie's contract.

"A year ago at this time, I believed that we had turned the corner under Bob, and that we were prepared to reclaim our traditional standing among the nation's elite college programs," White said.

"Today, I can no longer say that."

White said the contract extension was a "misread on my part."

White also fired Davie's staff, but indicated they could stay on through the upcoming recruiting season.

Davie's fate probably was sealed Sept. 29 after Notre Dame dropped to 1-4 with a 24-3 loss at Texas A&M.

,,,

The most prominent name mentioned has been Oakland Raider Coach Jon Gruden, who grew up mesmerized with Notre Dame during a period when his father was an assistant coach under Dan Devine.

Asked about the opening Sunday after the Raiders' overtime loss to Arizona, Gruden said: "I haven't had any conversations with anyone. I like where I am a lot. We're going to finish the job."

Recently, however, over the objections of the Raiders, Gruden gushed openly of his love for Notre Dame in an interview with South Bend Tribune columnist David Hough.

There are potential hang-ups to any Gruden hiring, though, foremost being that the Raiders' season could run into early February if they reach the Super Bowl.

...

Post Script on Bob Davie

Everybody knew when Lou Holtz recommended Bob Davie for the job of head coach at ND when Holtz stepped down, that Bob Davie was a good man. In his early forties at the time, Davie had not necessarily had the time to get gritty and tough enough to consistently win at Notre Dame.

Ara Parseghian had offered 100% accurate advice when Davie took the job: *"Worry about one thing, and that's winning."* Davie did not win consistently at Notre Dame and he lost the job because of that one pesky requirement—*winning*.

Nonetheless in his life, Bob Davie was never a bad coach and never was a bad man. He always had integrity and he still does. I am happy to report that after a number of successful years as an ESPN analyst, Bob Davie is still a fine man and he is doing some fine coaching today at New Mexico.

On December 17, 2015, the New York Times hosted a nice article about Davie. Here is an excerpt to serve as the post script for ND Coach Bob Davie:

"When Bob Davie became New Mexico's coach in 2011, he said bluntly that he would make no promises. The Lobos had lost 35 of their last 38 games, and the previous coach had been fired after a slew of embarrassing off-the-field problems.

Davie said only that he would seek to "stabilize this program."

Four years after taking over the embattled football program, and 14 years since being ousted as Notre Dame's head coach, Davie, 61, has the Lobos playing in their first bowl game in nearly a decade. New Mexico (7-5) will meet Arizona (6-6) in the New Mexico Bowl on Saturday after a surprisingly solid season in which the Lobos shocked Boise State and Air Force, the Mountain West's Mountain Division champion."

Nice Going Bob. We wish you well!

George O'Leary 2001 Five Days

On December 9, 2001, Notre Dame hired George O'Leary away from Georgia Tech. to replace Bob Davie. However, New Hampshire Union Leader reporter Jim Fennell, while he was researching for a piece about a "local boy done good!" story on O'Leary, uncovered misrepresentations in O'Leary's resume. These were severe enough that they had influenced the administration's decision to hire him.

The resulting media scandal embarrassed Notre Dame officials, and tainted O'Leary. The coach resigned five days later, before coaching a single practice, recruiting a single player, or hiring a single assistant coach. Yet, he is credited as a Notre Dame head coach in this book and others. George O'Leary's tenure is the shortest of any head coach in FBS history. He would go on to become the head football coach at UCF.

Chapter 19 Coach Tyrone Willingham 2002 – 2004

Willingham Coach # 28
Baer Coach #29

Willingham had great credentials

2002	Tyrone Willingham	10–3
2003	Tyrone Willingham	5–7
2004	Tyrone Willingham	6–5
2004	Kent Baer	0–1

ESPN has given us a proper introduction to Tyrone Willingham as the new Notre Dame Coach. We thank ESPN for its permission to use this piece. Willingham had negotiated a six-year contract to coach the Fighting Irish.

The article which begins on the next page is written by the Associated Press and presented by ESPN Sports. Our sincere thanks for permitting this reprint:

http://assets.espn.go.com/ncf/news/2001/1231/1303561.html

We find it fitting to begin and end many of the ND coach's stories with a nice perspective from the pundits. Enjoy:

Willingham accepts 6-year deal to coach Irish

Associated Press

Monday, December 31
Updated: January 1, 11:47 PM ET
SOUTH BEND, Ind. –

> *"Tyrone Willingham pledged to return Notre Dame to the championship levels of its storied past when he was introduced as the new Irish coach on Tuesday.*
>
> *Tyrone Willingham*
>
> *Tyrone Willingham left no doubt that he intends to return Notre Dame to national championship contention as new coach of the Irish.*
>
> *Willingham, 44-36-1 in seven seasons at Stanford, signed a six-year contract with Notre Dame on Monday and said he believed it was a great opportunity for a football coach.*
>
> *"I am excited, I am eager to begin the work, not just of the football program, but of this university," said Willingham, the first black head coach at Notre Dame in any sport.*
>
> *Willingham gets a guaranteed contract with a base salary of about $1.5 million per year with bonuses that could increase the yearly total to $2 million. Notre Dame associate athletics director John Heisler declined to discuss the financial figures.*
>
> *It is believed Willingham's deal would make him only the third coach to earn at least $2 million annually, joining Florida's Steve Spurrier ($2.1 million) and Oklahoma's Bob Stoops ($2 million).*
>
> ...
>
> *The news of Willingham's hiring drew praise from prominent black leaders.*
>
> *"It's a victory for fairness and equal opportunity to succeed or fail," said the Rev. Jesse Jackson, who previously urged Notre Dame to*

consider black candidates. "To even the field for athletes, you have to be willing to even the field for coaches."

Players said they were happy with the hiring.

"With all the things that have gone on the past few weeks, I think they've looked him over pretty close and I think he'll be a good choice," cornerback Vontez Duff said.

While Willingham's winning percentage of 54.9 percent is worse than Davie's 58.3 percent (35-25), Stanford doesn't have the storied history of the Irish. Notre Dame coaches historically have done better than at their previous stops.

Ara Parseghian was 36-35-1 in eight seasons at Northwestern. Dan Devine was 25-28-4 in four seasons with the Green Bay Packers, including 6-8 his last year. Both won national championships at Notre Dame.

...

Though Stanford had a winning record in just one of four seasons from 1997-00, Willingham maintained his status as one of college football's best organizers and managers. He led the Cardinal to a Pac-10 title and the Rose Bowl in 1999, and never lost a game against rival California in seven seasons.

2002 Coach Tyrone Willingham Year 1

The 2002 Notre Dame Fighting Irish football team was coached by Tyrone Willingham in his first year as head coach. The Fighting Irish were ranked #17 in the coaches' poll and #17 in the AP with a 10-3 record. Not too—too bad! Willingham's Irish were invited to the 2003 Gator Bowl in Alltel Stadium.

After Bob Davie's 5-6 2001 season, Notre Dame was looking for good news and Tyrone Willingham was delivering that good news for the Irish almost every week all season long. Notre Dame had green t-shirts printed with "Return to Glory." The Kelly family of Wilkes-Barre, PA proudly wore those T-shirts. They were classics.

ND *Return to Glory* T-shirt decal in Willingham's time

The 2002 season became known as a "Return to Glory" for the Irish. You can see the phrase in the T-shirt image above. On November 23, 2002, my two best buddies—Dennis Grimes & Gerry Rodski and

I, were in the stands for the Rutgers game and I wore my commemorative t-shirt over protective clothing. I picked it up at the ND Bookstore the prior day.

2003 Gator Bowl

The Irish had won 10 games but had messed up late in the season instead of earlier. Consequently, Notre Dame was not invited to a BCS bowl game. Instead, the team accepted a bid to play North Carolina State in the Gator Bowl. Though it was better than Joe Smith's Happy Bowl at a high school stadium in Wilkes-Barre, PA, it was not something for which ND was hoping.

Quarterback Pat Dillingham #9 of the Notre Dame Fighting Irish prepares to hand-off the ball against the North Carolina State University Wolfpack in the Toyota Gator Bowl at Alltel Stadium on January 1, 2003 in Jacksonville.

The Irish played the bowl game tentatively, not as tough as expected, as if they were outmatched both on offense and defense. The Wolfpack won the game solidly L (6-28), giving the Irish its sixth consecutive bowl loss. Despite the three losses at the end of the season, the Irish salvaged a top-20 ranking at # 17 in both the Associated Press (AP) and Coaches' Polls.

2003 Coach Tyrone Willingham Year 2

The 2003 Notre Dame Fighting Irish football team was coached by Tyrone Willingham in his second year as ND Head Football Coach. Despite great expectations, Notre Dame had a less than sterling season. For ND faithful; it was startling but not sterling. The Irish finished the season unranked at 5–7 and failed to become bowl eligible. Few actually know what had happened between a successful season and a less than mediocre effort.

Notre Dame Fans simply do not like losses and unless there is a real reason that is understandable, and it is not an eternal notion, there will be grumblings.

ND fans like one thing a lot worse than losses—***losing streaks***. This particular season was punctuated by a pair of three-game losing streaks. Besides losing close games, ND fans hate blowouts. This particular season featured ugly blowout losses against Michigan, USC, and Florida State. Ugh!

2004 Coach Tyrone Willingham Year 3
2004 Coach Kent Baer – Insight Bowl Game

The 2004 Notre Dame Fighting Irish football team was coached by Tyrone Willingham in his third season. Notre Dame finished the regular season 6-5 under Willingham. The only good part of the record was that it was above the .500 mark. At 6-5, with all of the new bowl games added to post-season college play, teams in 2004 needed to win just six games to be invited to a post-season game.

Hoping to claim another win for the "Gipper," Willingham's Notre Dame accepted an invitation with its six-win qualification, to the Insight Bowl. Tyrone Willingham would not get to coach this bowl game. He was released at the end of the 2004 season before playing the bowl game. Assistant Coach / Defensive Coordinator Kent Baer, a good guy—never expecting to have to do the University a favor—was asked to coach the Irish in its bowl game appearance. He agreed because he is a good guy.

Many Irish followers and fans and many pundits had their share of doubts after 2003 as to how this season might begin and end. First of all, 2003 had not been a banner year. Secondly, Julius Jones, fourth-leading rusher in ND history had graduated. Coach Willingham hoped to replace Jones with a talented recruiting class. However, Willingham struggled in his second full year of recruiting. His new class was ranked 30th in the nation

Willingham was losing on the field and then again in the recruit locker room. Despite signing highly sought after recruit Darius Walker, the 17 man Willington class included only three four-star recruits and no five stars. The football stars in the nation look first to institutions that can make them stars.

New Coach Kent Baer

In a move highly criticized by those who believe football should be played with flags in back pockets and each team should be granted the opportunity for as many as ten apologies for seemingly aggressive plays, Notre Dame decided that it needed a new head coach. Tyrone Willingham had proven to be a great man but not as great a football coach.

The Insight Bowl

Two days USC trounced the Irish 45-14, ND fired a great guy, Tyrone Willingham, whose major fault was that he did not bring wins into the football program as quickly as he had promised. Defensive coordinator, Kent

Baer, led the Irish after the firing to prepare the team for the Insight Bowl. Many at Notre Dame hoped that Baer would "win one for Ty." Even another great guy like Kent Baer could not make this particular 2004 Notre Dame Team work well enough to win its last bowl game

The Oregon State Beavers, like every other team that plays Notre Dame, were highly inspired to win. They picked up a lead brought about by four touchdown passes from Derek Anderson. They beat the Irish to give ND its seventh consecutive bowl loss. Notre Dame ended 2004 with a 6–6 record and when the season was completed, they were coach-less.

Summary on Tyrone Willingham

Like a number of great guys and great coaches before and after Willingham—those who paid his salary after giving a look, right or wrong—decided to give it up and get somebody else. He was not the first and he will not be the last and it had nothing to do with what he looks like.

Nonetheless, I decided that I would take my closing article from a source that could offer a proper close with a slant that is both pro-American and pro-minority. For me and for all of my relatives and friends, whiteness or blackness was not the issue at Notre Dame regarding Tyrone Willingham.

Notre Dame was not conducting a social experiment. Willingham was not a bad coach and would have killed it perhaps in a few more years at Notre Dame. Who knows? I think Notre Dame gives both white and black guys the same opportunity—win or plan to find another job! Parseghian said it to Bob Davie. Win! That idea is not about to change as long as there are Notre Dame fans and alumni.

The university simply tries to hire the best coach possible for a team that many think ought to always be the best team. I thought Willingham was a great choice, just like I liked Bob Davie when he was appointed. In both cases; nobody asked me. Here is a great perspective: Here is the piece from
http://diverseeducation.com/article/4186/
It is signed non-descriptively **by *Mostly Black Issues***

Chapter 20 Coach Charlie Weis 2005-2009

Coach # 30

Weiss early on was treated like a god

2005 Charlie Weis 9–3
2006 Charlie Weis 10–3
2007 Charlie Weis 3–9
2008 Charlie Weis 7–6
2009 Charlie Weis 6–6

New coach had great credentials

Notre Dame is always excited when the University takes a not-so-productive coach and replaces him. The new guy is always going to save the program and every now and then, he actually does.

After Tyrone Willingham produced two poorly played seasons in a row, his time had passed at Notre Dame, and when Notre Dame started looking, they forgot that their best coaches were former head coaches. Nonetheless, when they hired Charlie Weiss, he was the brains of the New England Patriots' offense and despite the difference in jobs between being a strategist and a coach, Weiss got the nod at Notre Dame because the Patriots were doing so well, and perhaps because Bill Belichick does not hire anything other than the best.

Weis served as offensive coordinator under head coach Bill Belichick from 2000 through 2004, and he did some commendable work. He installed what is known as the Erhardt-Perkins offensive system, and assisted the Patriots in three Super Bowl victories—(XXXVI, XXXVIII, XXXIX).

Therefore, anybody who hired Charlie Weiss, knew they would not be hiring a *johnny-come-lately*. Yet, other than a one year stint as head coach at a high school before his pro career, Charlie Weis never had full control of all the marbles for a football team. From his record at Notre Dame, it apparently would have served him better if he had more field coaching experience at a college level. Here is an introductory article I selected from the Washington Post. You and I would more than likely have been pleased to hire Charlie Weiss in 2005 after reading this:

http://www.washingtonpost.com/wp-dyn/articles/A58013-2004Dec11.html?referrer=email

Patriots' Weis to Coach Notre Dame

By Mark Schlabach
Washington Post Staff Writer
Sunday, December 12, 2004

> *"New England Patriots offensive coordinator Charlie Weis agreed to become football coach at Notre Dame and will receive a six-year contract that will pay him nearly $2 million annually, a source close to the search said last night. Weis becomes the first Notre Dame alumnus to coach the Fighting Irish since Hugh Devore in 1963.*
>
> *Notre Dame, which fired coach Tyrone Willingham on Nov. 30 after three seasons, is expected to announce Weis's hiring at a Monday news conference in South Bend, Ind. The Patriots play the Cincinnati Bengals today in Foxboro, Mass.*
>
> *Willingham's controversial dismissal left only two black head coaches -- Karl Dorrell at UCLA and Sylvester Croom at Mississippi State -- among the 117 at the Division I-A level.*
>
> *Weis, 48, who is white, has worked the past 15 years as an NFL assistant, spending the past five seasons as the Patriots' offensive coordinator. He is credited with the development of quarterback Tom Brady, a sixth-round draft choice who has led the team to two Super Bowl victories. Weis, who hasn't coached in college since 1989, has won three Super Bowl rings -- one with the New York Giants and two with the Patriots.*

A Notre Dame committee of trustees and boosters, which voted to fire Willingham over the objections of the Rev. Edward "Monk" Malloy, the school's outgoing president, and Athletics Director Kevin White, met again yesterday. The committee chose to begin negotiations with Weis after selecting him over former Fighting Irish quarterback Tom Clements, now offensive coordinator of the Buffalo Bills, and Washington Redskins defensive coordinator Greg Blache, a former defensive back at Notre Dame.

Clements was informed yesterday morning that he wouldn't be hired by Notre Dame; associates of Blache said he withdrew his name from the search.

Blache -- who declined to comment through a Redskins spokesman -- was initially considered a long-shot candidate. However, he interviewed extremely well during a meeting with school officials early this past week. Redskins Vice President Vinny Cerrato, Notre Dame's recruiting coordinator from 1986 to 1990, played a role in the interview, according to one source who requested anonymity.

Two days after firing Willingham, White and incoming Notre Dame president John Jenkins flew to Salt Lake City to interview Utah Coach Urban Meyer, who had already begun contract negotiations with Florida. On Dec. 3, Meyer signed a seven-year contract to replace Gators Coach Ron Zook, who was fired in October. The Irish also contacted Detroit Lions Coach Steve Mariucci, Denver Broncos Coach Mike Shanahan and Iowa's Kirk Ferentz about replacing Willingham, but they all indicated they weren't interested.

Weis, who nearly died two years ago from complications of gastro-intestinal surgery, is expected to finish the season with the Patriots, the defending Super Bowl champions, who are 11-1 going into today's game. If the Patriots advance to their third Super Bowl in four years, their season wouldn't end until Feb. 7 -- one day after both Super Bowl XXXIX in Jacksonville and college football's national signing day.

Weis was expected to leave the Patriots after this season even if he didn't accept the Notre Dame job. He is in the final year of his contract with the team and was upset that the Patriots didn't extend his deal before this season. Weis is paid about $500,000 per year—about half of what other top NFL coordinators are being paid. He also has grown increasingly frustrated about his inability to land an NFL head-coaching job despite the Patriots' success. NFL sources said he would have been hired as coach of the Buffalo Bills after *last season, but the Bills were unwilling to wait until after the Super Bowl to interview him.*

Staff writers Nunyo Demasio and Mark Maske contributed to this report.

2005 Coach Charlie Weis Year 1

The 2005 Notre Dame Fighting Irish football team was coached by Charlie Weis in his first year as head coach. Weis's Irish, after a dismal (6-6) 2004 season, took Tyrone Willingham's team and played a fine season in 2005, finishing at 9 wins and 3 losses. They capped off the season with a post-season invitation and acceptance to the Fiesta Bowl and a # 9 ranking in the nation.

At 6-6 in 2004, Notre Dame hired Charlie Weiss from the New England Patriots. Weis, former offensive coordinator with the Patriots is a ND grad. This made Weis the first Notre Dame alumnus to coach the team since 1963.

One of his first tasks was to create a coaching staff. Charlie Weis looked for experienced coaches that would be able to make the team competitive. Notre Dame was thrilled with having Mr. Weis on board at Notre Dame after his hiring.

Always seeming to add the kiss of death to a new coach by extolling his excellence prematurely, when the first Weis season was just half-over, concerned that Weis might jump ship if he did not see a lifetime appointment, and being so tickled to have a new coach doing so well with the team, Notre Dame officials offered Mr. Weis a major extension on his contract. Weis got an offer from Notre Dame that neither he nor any person with a sound mind could refuse.

It took most by surprise. Notre Dame Football Coach Charlie Weis completed just seven games to earn a new contract. Notre Dame was non-apologetic: Athletic director Kevin White offered: "In a very short period of time, Charlie has clearly and impressively demonstrated the ability to take the Notre Dame program where we all want it to go."

The new 10-year deal was worth $30 to $40 million, and made Weis the highest paid coach in college football. Some saw the extension as controversial, as Weis' record was 5-2 at the time while Willingham started his first season with an 8-0 record.

First Games

On September 3, at Pittsburgh, the Irish played its first game of the season against the No. 23 ranked Pittsburgh Panthers, led by first-year head coach Dave Wannstedt. Tyler Palko was the Pitt QB. The game started with a quick Palko TD pass to Greg Lee. Brady Quinn then came in and threw a 51-yard touchdown pass to Darius Walker. The Irish led 35-13 at halftime. There was much less scoring. In the second-half. The Irish won the game W (42-21), and jumped to 23rd in the national rankings.

Next game was at Michigan, who had a new coach, Lloyd Carr. The #3 Wolverines had not lost a home game to anybody since 2002. ND had not won at Michigan since 1993. Quinn quickly led the Irish with a number of successful passes and touchdowns to Rhema McNight and Jeff Samardzija. Darious Walker went through big holes in the defense. ND had a 14-3 halftime lead before Zbikowski returned a punt to the Michigan 33-yard line before the third quarter closed. Then, at the beginning of 4Q, D.J. Fitzpatrick kicked a 43-yard field goal. Score was 17-3.

Chad Henne, Michigan QB then threw a 26-yard touchdown pass to Mario Manningham, bringing the score to 17-10. With two minutes remaining, Michigan failed to score. Charlie Weis became the first Notre Dame Coach since Knute Rockne to win his first two games on the road. The Irish were then ranked #12 in the nation.

2006 Coach Charlie Weis Year 2

The 2006 Notre Dame Fighting Irish football team was coached by Charlie Weis in his second year as head coach. After a nice 9-3 start in his first season, Weis brought in a #19 finish with ten wins and three losses in 2005. The ND regular season record of 10-2 was enough for the Notre Dame Fighting Irish to be invited to the Sugar Bowl.

Five offensive starters, three defensive starters, and placekicker D.J. Fitzpatrick went to the NFL after the 2005 season. Many key Irish returned such as quarterback Brady Quinn, wide receiver Jeff Samardzija, running back Darius Walker, and safety Tom Zbikowski. The Irish were given a lot of pre-season hype about being possible national championship contenders. Weis still had god-like status at Notre Dame.

Charlie Weis had a great recruiting year in 2006 with 28 recruits. It was a top ten ranked recruiting class, included three five star recruits on offense and 14 four star recruits with eight on offense and six on defense. Things were looking good for the future.

Air Force, Army, & USC

When Notre Dame traveled to Air Force on November 11, the team was ranked #9. Less than a minute into the game Brady Quinn proved just why he was one of the top QBs in College Football, and he didn't stop there. That's how the rest of the game went and Notre Dame won W (39-17).

ND wearing their splashy green jerseys against Army

Army came into South Bend to play #6 ranked Notre Dame in the Irish's final home game for the team's senior class. The Irish wore their special green jerseys. ND won handily W (41-9)

The season finale for Notre Dame with a trip to the LA Coliseum is often a close call, no matter who wins. This year, USC was ranked # 3 and Notre Dame came in at # 6. The Irish were suffering from a four-game losing streak to the Trojans. After their epic 2005 game, the Irish were hopeful that they could end this losing streak. The Trojans, however, knew that with a win they would still be in the national title hunt.

Marching Band on the field at the Los Angeles Memorial Coliseum got the crowd going at the start of the 2006 #3 USC vs. #6 ranked Notre Dame football game

After Notre Dame's first drive stalled, QB John David Booty led the Trojans on a 61-yard drive ending with a 9-yard TD pass to Dwayne Jarrett. The Irish punted and the Trojans returned it to the Irish 26, Booty got another touchdown on a pass to Jarrett and the Trojans were ahead 14-0. On the ensuing Irish drive, the Irish scored 3. The half ended with the Trojans leading 21-10.

The Trojans began the fourth quarter moving effectively and settled for a 32-yard field goal by Mario Danelo. The Irish were held and punted. Then, Booty threw a 43-yard touchdown pass to Dwayne Jarrett, giving USC a 37-17 lead. Quinn then took the Irish 78-yards and threw a 2-yard touchdown pass to Jeff Samardzija to lower the Irish deficit to 13 points. The onside kick failed. USC scored again and the Irish lost L (24-44). Notre Dame finished the regular season 10-2.

2007 Coach Charlie Weis Year 3

The 2007 Notre Dame Fighting Irish football team was coached by Charlie Weis in his third year as head coach. Notre Dame opened the season with five losses without a win. It was the team's worst opening prior to 2007 (0–3). The Irish would go on to compile the worst record in team history (3-9)

Their nine-loss season was also a school record. Few expected such a season as for two years with Brady Quinn as a starter, Weis' team played well most of the time if we choose to ignore the bowl losses. How could this happen?

Alumni were not pleased for sure but Weiss had just renewed a ten-year contract. It would cost Notre Dame a ton if there was an abrupt termination of the contract. But, this season was nothing less than terrible and most were blaming Weis for the trouble.

Freshman quarterback Jimmy Clausen was brought off the bench into action as Notre Dame started the season upside down. He played in 10 games for the Irish, starting nine of them, and the young QB finished with 1,254 yards, seven touchdowns and six interceptions. Though Weis noted he expected a fine 2008 from Clausen, other than his word, the win/loss stats were not an indicator of greatness to come.

2008 Coach Charlie Weis Year 4

The 2008 Notre Dame Fighting Irish football team's head football coach was Charlie Weis. This was Weis's fourth season as Notre Dame's head coach. He entered the season with a 22–15 record, coming off a 3–9 season after having posted back-to-back BCS level seasons in his first two years. In 2008, the Irish had to show some life after the 3-9 finish. No Irish coach had ever been fired mid-season.

The team started 4–1, but hit some tough times and completed the regular season 6-6. This included an unexpected loss to a struggling Syracuse team. The records being broken by the Irish were not good records. For example, this was the first time that Notre Dame had fallen to an eight-loss team. The combined 15 losses from 2007–08 was the most losses for any two-year span.

Even in this, year four of an extended contract, 2007 had been so tough on fans and alumni they there was rampant speculation that the university might fire Weis. When the Irish finished the season, the administration announced that Charlie Weiss would remain as head coach in 2009.

The Irish ended the 2008 season on a positive note. They had lost nine bowl games in a row. This year, they beat Hawaii W (49–21) in the Hawaii Bowl.

While doing this, the Irish scored its highest point total of the season, its highest point total ever in a bowl game, and it broke 8 other bowl records.

The bowl win also helped Notre Dame to a 7–6 final record, its 102nd winning season in 120 years of football. Every ND fan hoped the bad days were over. One might have concluded that God wanted Charlie to have a few more chances. It was premature to start thinking, "Sorry, Charlie!"

After the dismal 3-9 2007 season, there were few fans with high hopes for 2008. Many were apprehensive about what 2008 would actually bring. Surprisingly, things did not start off too bad.

The Irish finished the regular season at 6-6 and thus qualified for a minor bowl game—the Hawaii Bowl.

The Hawaii Bowl

Notre Dame soundly beat Hawaii 49–21 in its first bowl victory since the Irish defeated Texas A&M in the 1994 Cotton Bowl Classic to end the 1993 season.

In 2008, Irish quarterback Jimmy Clausen broke loose and with that breakout, he broke school bowl game records by passing for 401 yards and five touchdowns. Clausen was on the money. His 84.6% completion rate was the second-best completion percentage for any player ever in any bowl game in NCAA history.

Wide receiver Golden Tate was golden as usual. He also set Irish bowl records by catching three touchdowns and passes for 177 yards. Both players were honored as co-MVPs of the game.

2009 Coach Charlie Weis Year 5

The 2009 Notre Dame Fighting Irish football team was coached by Charlie Weis who had entered his fifth season as head coach. This season for Weis had an asterisk in the beginning. The ND Administration knew things were not copacetic but they also knew they could become OK with a great season.

So, they hoped that the coach, Charlie Weis would help the team recover from the last two bad years. Weis had unexpectedly become an underachiever. It was hoped by many ND faithful that he would finally blossom as a college coach. With two bad years behind him, Charlie Weis surely knew there was an "or else," attached to everybody's well wishes for his improvement.

The implied demand to Weis was that after five years and two years of really bad results, the Notre Dame administration expected their team would be in position to compete for a BCS Bowl berth. It was that simple. Ara Parseghian knew that winning was the secret to ND Head Coach Job Retention and so did Charlie Weis.

After all, that's why Mr. Weis had agreed to the deal when the university broke long-time salary records at the time he was hired and again when his contract was extended. This was not Catholic Charities operating at Notre Dame University; it was pay for performance. That was the deal.

When two entities engage in an arrangement in which both have a stake, such as marriage, both must bring something of reasonably equal value to the table. Notre Dame had paid the agreed upon salary for four years and were paying it again for the fifth year while its marriage partner in this case had been failing in his part of the covenant. Notre Dame Officials, to begin the 2009 season, did not need help from the alumni or from fans to remind Coach Weis what his part of the deal was. It was clear. Win!

The season

Weis's team began 2009 at 4-2, with close losses to Michigan on September 12 L (34-38), and USC on October 12 L (27-34)

The ND season ended miserably after the fun victory after Purdue with four straight losses, including a second loss in three years to Navy L (21-23). Losses were recorded also at Pittsburgh L (22-27); Connecticut at home L (30-33) in double OT; and a close call at Stanford L (38-45).

Even Starkist couldn't stop this "Sorry Charlie!"

Weis took the medicine he knew was coming as he was summarily fired as head coach the Monday after the Stanford loss at the end of the season. Notre Dame was embarrassed that 6-6 was the best it could do with so much talent and so much invested.

Though the Irish team was bowl eligible with 6 wins, nobody felt like playing a consolation bowl game. Rather than play in a loser's version of a winner's bowl, Notre Dame used its energy to move its program forward.

Athletic director Jack Swarbrick hired Cincinnati head coach Brian Kelly after a 10-day coaching search. It just happens that I have the very same first and last name as Coach Kelly. Like most other real Irish fans, I am very pleased that the "the real Brian Kelly" is the head coach at Notre Dame. One day when we get to talk, and after a few gifts of books that I have written, we will know each other; but not now and that is OK!

Weis's last season with the Irish was unremarkable. My personal glimpse of the coach on the field in the Boston College game the year before had told me that it was all over for ND if Weis were retained indefinitely as the coach. If I were a great football analyst, I could deduce what was wrong with Charley Weis as a coach. I have some thoughts that I would prefer not to share. I wish Coach Weis the best and sure hope he has a fruitful life.

After the season, Notre Dame Athletic Director Jack Swarbrick, when asked about what his biggest disappointment had been that season, took a long pause, then said, "The Navy outcome." He was not ready to evaluate the football season until season's end, but he knew that "Up until the Navy game we were in the BCS conversation." The Navy game, however, was the first of the tragic season-ending four-game losing skid.

Swartbrick fired Weis as head coach the Monday after the Stanford loss. At the same time, he announced that wide receiver coach Rob Lanello would take charge of football operations, including recruiting, *until Brian Kelly was names head coach.*

As I like to do in this book, in order to close out major positive or negative coaching eras, I searched for an appropriate piece to end the Charley Weis era, and this chapter. Most Notre Dame fans could have written an appropriate piece about Charlie as he had represented a lot of hope and then some results and hope; more hope, and then mental anguish. Chicago news outlets normally have a way of getting to the core of the matter so I selected this piece:

http://chicago.suntimes.com/news/7/71/805420/charlie-weis-fired-at-notre-dame-in-shortest-coaching-death-watch-ever

Charlie Weis fired at Notre Dame in shortest coaching death watch ever

WRITTEN BY CHICAGO SUN-TIMES WIRE POSTED: 11/30/2009, 01:23PM

> *The New York Daily News reports that Touchdown Jesus has shown Charlie Weis the door. According to the report, and to approximately noone's surprise, the coach who authored a 6-6 season for the Domers has been fired.*
>
> *Weis, who refused to do any interviews after the Irish lost on a gimme touchdown to Stanford this weekend, did say earlier in the week that he figured his days might be numbered. Turns out the coach who said "6-5 is not good enough" for Notre Dame found out that 6-6 was no better.*
>
> *The team will have to decide later today whether that 6 wins is worth a bowl berth as the team votes on playing postseason ball at the end of the 35-27 Weis era.*

Now the pressure is on Athletic Director Jack Swarbrick to land a solid replacement for an institution of college football that hasn't been a national contender for 15 years – and a string of failed coaching hires.

The next head man will have to clean up the miserable mark against quality schools – zero victories under Weis can't cut it. Of course, Notre Dame couldn't even beat Navy reliably anymore, either.

November 30, 2009

Weis will not be retained as Notre Dame football coach
University of Notre Dame head football coach Charlie Weis will not be retained, University director of athletics Jack Swarbrick announced today.

"We have great expectations for our football program, and we have not been able to meet those expectations," Swarbrick said. "As an alumnus, Charlie understands those goals and expectations better than most, and he's as disappointed as anyone that we have not achieved the desired results."

Swarbrick recommended the dismissal Sunday night to Notre Dame's president, Rev. John I. Jenkins, C.S.C.

"We have established an evaluation process for all of our athletic programs that, in the end, results in a recommendation from Jack to me," Father Jenkins said. "I accepted Jack's decision and look forward to working with him on selecting a new head football coach who is the very best choice possible for the University and especially for our student-athletes.

"I am most appreciative to Coach Weis for his service to Notre Dame and our community. He and his family have my prayers and best wishes."

Weis spent five seasons as Irish head coach from 2005-09, with his teams achieving consecutive records of 9-3 (Fiesta Bowl appearance) in '05, 10-3 (Sugar Bowl appearance), 3-9, 7-6 (Hawaii Bowl victory) and 6-6 in '09 – for an overall 35-27 mark (.564).

Swarbrick announced that Rob Ianello, the Irish assistant head coach/offense, wide receivers coach and recruiting coordinator, will assume responsibility for football operations until a new coach is hired. Ianello has spent the past five seasons on the Notre Dame staff and previously was part of football staffs at Wisconsin (1990-93, 2003-04), Arizona (1994-2002) and Alabama (1987-89).

Chapter 21 Coach Brian Kelly: 2010-2017+

Coach # 31

Kelly is ND's Head Football Coach (2017+)

2010	Brian Kelly	8–5
2011	Brian Kelly	8–5
2012	Brian Kelly	12–1
2013	Brian Kelly	9–4
2014	Brian Kelly	8–5
2015	Brian Kelly	10–3
2016	Brian Kelly	4-8
2017	Brian Kelly	

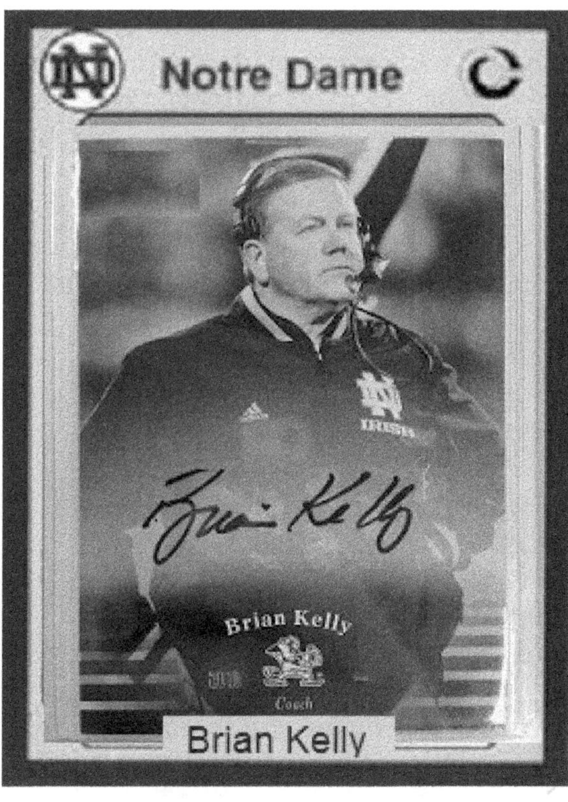

Assumption writes re: alumnus Brian Kelly

We now all have the opportunity to read about the last coach of the modern era, as I present the Brian Kelly Era of Notre Dame Football. The lead article comes from his alma mater.

Many of us already have deified Kelly as one of the future great immortals, not unlike those greats, who have brought national championships to Notre Dame. I hope that his day will come, but like others I have major concerns after a 4-8 season.

I for one am happy to wait. I had been very pleased that Coach Kelly was on the job for all the Notre Dame faithful. Brian Kelly is a fine coach. Notre Dame has done well and will do even better under his leadership. But, he must address big flaws with the ND defense and the offense must begin to score points. One does not have to be a huge expert in the football realm to make those suggestions.

I tried to give the other Brian Kelly an ND book and have a quick dialogue with him but his staff protected him. He did not seem to be intrigued or amused that we both had the same exact name other than the middle initial.

So, I must confess, my information like the information about all other coaches in this book is from consensus research. My needs did not meet the importance threshold test for an interview with Coach Kelly. I have not given up on Kelly as some but I think it would help if he talked to more people who are his friends and he listened a little more and was a bit more open to other thoughts than his own.

To kick off this chapter, I have found an independent newspaper article that I will share. My chapter format has been consistent in this book in that at the beginning of each, we discuss the hype about the hiring of each new coach, using words written at the time, and then we close out the era with words about the opinion of the pundits and sportswriters at the end of the era. There will be no closing article in this chapter of course as Mr. Kelly is the current head coach of Notre Dame Football.

Ironically, it was easier for me in my research to find ND archival features about Frank Leahy and Jesse Harper than it was to find a usable piece about Brian Kelly's hiring. Even the first page of an article from my local paper that I have had hanging in my Sun Room is inaccessible in the archives. It is from our local Paper, the Times Leader. it was placed on the wall by my friendly Anstett neighbors, you cannot really read it well below and that is OK, but you can get the essence of my neighbors' message to my wife and me.

SPORTS

Kelly gets job of rebuilding Irish

The article copy I have in my sunroom (above) is Part I of II and I do not have Part II. My loving neighbors placed my face in the space in which the coach's face had been. They put my beautiful wife Pat's picture on the top left to make sure I would not mess up the ND team. Of course, this is very funny for those who walk into my sunroom and notice.

This is my 65th book. You would like the others also. It normally takes me about a month to write a book that is reasonable sized (250 pages) and it takes at least another month to prepare it for publishing / printing. Right now, without front matter, this book is already 482 pages and I am hoping for no more growth. I cannot afford to print 100,000 at $2.00 per book so I get charged about $10.00 per book for about 500 pages when I print about 50 at a time.

Today is March 16, 2016, as I edit this paragraph. There is a major Irish holiday tomorrow. I began writing this book about Notre Dame on January 30, 2016, my birthday.

I spent several hours at the beginning of this chapter trying to find a Chicago or LA or NY article on Coach Brian Kelly but when I found this online article from Kelly's college alma-mater, I was very pleased and I stopped researching. It is a nicely written piece about Coach Kelly's appointment to Notre Dame's head coaching position. It was written by the college from which he graduated, Assumption College:

https://www.assumption.edu/news/brian-kelly-%E2%80%9983-named-head-coach-notre-dame-football-team

Brian Kelly '83 Named Head Coach of Notre Dame Football team

Assumption alumnus and former defensive coordinator Brian K. Kelly '83, who recently took the University of Cincinnati Bearcats to two consecutive Bowl Championship Series appearances and a perfect 12-0 regular season in 2009, has been named the 29th head football coach at the University of Notre Dame.

Notre Dame's president, Rev. John I. Jenkins, C.S.C., praised Kelly in an announcement on the school's website. "I am absolutely delighted to welcome Brian and his family to the Notre Dame family. He brings to us a long and successful career as a head coach, and I am confident that he will have even greater success here. I'm also very pleased that he has put considerable emphasis on excellence in the classroom and that his student-athletes graduate at a rate well above the norm."

As an Assumption football player Kelly played at middle linebacker for the Greyhounds and graduated from Assumption College with a B.A. in Political Science. His football career at Assumption included 19 tackles in the final game of the 1981 season and he captained the two of the most successful club football teams in Hounds' history for Hall of Fame Coach Paul Cantiani '73. Kelly earned all-conference honors in the New England Collegiate Football Conference as both a junior and senior and left with a school-record 314 tackles (currently seventh). His record 214 assists stood until 2005 when broken by Chris Grogan '06.

Kelly served as defensive coordinator at Assumption for four seasons under Hall of Famer Bernie Gaughan, raising the team's level of play before leaving to coach for Grand Valley. At same time, he coached women's softball and ushered the Assumption team to 20-plus and entrance into the postseason regional rankings. Kelly's winning ways were recognized when he was named to the Assumption Alumni-Athletics Hall of Fame in 2006.

A native of Chelsea, MA, Kelly graduated from St. John's Prep (Danvers, MA), where he starred in three sports: football, hockey and baseball. Brian and his wife, Paqui, have three children - Patrick Liam, Grace Marie and Kenzel Michael.

Notre Dame's webpage has the official announcement.

http://www.und.com/sports/m-footbl/spec-rel/121009aaq.html

2010 Coach Brian Kelly Year 1

The 2010 Notre Dame Fighting Irish football team was coached by Brian Kelly in his first year as head coach. This was Kelly's first season as Notre Dame's head coach, after leading the Cincinnati Bearcats to a 12–0 regular season and a BCS bowl berth.

In 2010, Notre Dame's regular season schedule was ranked the most difficult schedule in the nation with a Team Opposition Record Percentage of .6529. This poll was published by the NCAA and it only included wins against Division I teams.

Nothing good happens overnight. Yet, after the Weis record the prior three years, Irish fans were very pleased with a coach whose aim is pointing in the same direction as the thought processes of the ND faithful. When Kelly arrived, everybody may not have been singing Cum Bye Ah, but most were chanting: The Times—they are a changing! They had to change, and in fact, they have changed already and the future until 2016 looked even better!

Notre Dame finished the first Kelly season with a very healthy 8–5 record. Better than that, the Irish defeated Miami (FL) 33–17 showing that their resurgence was not a fluke.

Brian Kelly replaced Charley Weis on Dec 10, 2009 in time to work hard to bring in recruits to help the team. Two of the Irish's bright spots, Jimmy Clausen and Golden Tate chose not to play their final years and declared for the 2010 NFL draft. Graduation was another factor that caused a number of players to move-on. Weis had a good team… but.

Being hired in the off-season, if there is such a thing anymore for a collegiate head coach, Kelly's first mission was recruiting. In his first attempt at recruiting a class for Notre Dame, he was quite successful with 23 signed commitments from high school players across the United States.

Five early enrollees included Quarterback Tommy Rees, Wide Receiver Tai-ler Jones, Cornerback Lo Wood, Cornerback Spencer Boyd and Safety Chris Badger. Things were lining up for a successful Irish run.

Kelly liked Junior Dayne Crist as his QB for 2010. Crist executed well in completing 59.2 percent of his passes, for 2,033 yards, 15 touchdowns and 7 interceptions. The QB then suffered a major injury against Tulsa, the ninth game, and this ended his season. Tommy Rees, a resilient, dedicated, hard-working, but young quarterback came in for Crist, finishing the Tulsa game. Rees was very effective but could not deliver a victory as the Irish lost L (27-28)

2011 Coach Brian Kelly Year 2

The 2011 Notre Dame Fighting Irish football team was led by second year head coach Brian Kelly. Every year Notre Dame's football program competes as an independent. They are not affiliated with any conference. But in 2015, ND agreed to play five ACC games each year as other ND sports teams had become integral parts of the ACC.

This particular year, 2011, Notre Dame had a better regular season than in 2010. However, they finished with the same overall record as the team's venture into the Champs Sports Bowl led to a defeat by a rejuvenated Florida State Team L (14-18). Two years and yet Coach Kelly was not producing big stuff.

Joe Montana's son, Nate Montana left the university in February 2011, with a transfer to the University of Montana. I hope Nate does well. Additionally, junior guard Alex Bullard transferred to his hometown state of Tennessee to play for the University of Tennessee.

This second year, Brian Kelly did very well in his recruiting efforts. He had a full recruiting class with 23 prospects for the ND football team. The list included the addition of five early-enrollees: defensive end Aaron Lynch, outside linebacker Ishaq Williams, offensive lineman Brad Carrico, quarterback Everett Golson, and kicker Kyle Brindza.

Dayne Crist was healed and again ready for QB duties and the well-experienced sophomore Tommy Rees was also ready for action as needed. New guys. Freshman QB Everett Golson and Sophomore QB Andrew Hendrix were also ready for duty as needed at this critical offensive spot.

The Citrus Bowl

On December 29, 2012, the 8-4 unranked Irish were invited to the Citrus Bowl in Florida against Florida State. They were defeated in a close matchup L (14-18). Notre Dame was ahead by two touchdowns and were pitching a shutout. The Irish looked like they had the game, when all of a sudden in the second half, momentum changed. They lost. Neither playing nor coaching seemed to make a difference.

The Irish could not stop the negatives. The Seminoles rallied from a 14-point second-half deficit and used a pair of touchdown passes by EJ Manuel and two field goals from Dustin Hopkins to earn their fourth straight bowl win and their second under Jimbo Fisher.

2012 Coach Brian Kelly Year 3

The 2012 Notre Dame Fighting Irish football team, led by third year head coach Brian Kelly, played home games at Notre Dame Stadium. They competed as an independent. Despite starting the season unranked, the Fighting Irish finished the regular season at 12-0, and #1 in all major polls. Manti Te'o kept the Irish defense in control of most games as the Notre Dame finished the season with the number one defense in the country.

ND gave up just 10.3 points per game. They played in the BCS National Championship Game with a chance to win their first national title since 1988, but were defeated by the Alabama Crimson Tide. Alabama's Coach Nick Saban had a different winning philosophy than Coach Kelly. His philosophy was train the team to win and then win at all costs. ND was embarrassed at the poor performance.

Brian Kelly had gone undefeated and untied 12-0 in his third season prior to the bowl game. This was a tremendous accomplishment. Most of his predecessors, who had won national championships in their third years as Head Coach were not expected to play or win a bowl game. Yet, they won. Kelly did not!

QB controversy at ND?

The multi-talented Everett Golson was Brian Kelly's designated starting quarterback for 2012 and he did a great job most of the time during the season. Pundits who have examined Junior Tommy Rees's performance in 2012 suggest that there would have been no magic, no 12-1 stellar season, if backup Rees were not available to come off the bench to save the Irish against Purdue, Michigan and Stanford. These were major relief roles and Rees was on target in each of them. Rees should receive an ND medal of honor!

Rees survived and pulled the Irish to victory in really tough situations in this season. Golson led the Irish for most of their touchdowns and his athleticism helped him squirm out of situations in which the Irish would have otherwise been stymied.

Notre Dame Coach Brian Kelly speaks with quarterback Tommy Rees during the game against Michigan in 2012.

In terms of recruiting, this Kelly class was a bit lighter than others in the US. Coach Kelly received 17 commitments in his second full recruiting class. Those included commitments from three early-enrollees: defensive tackle Sheldon Day, quarterback Gunner Kiel, and cornerback Tee Shepard.

Michigan was next game at home. For the second game in a row, Notre Dame's Tommy Rees came off the bench to spark the Notre Dame offense in a 13-6 win over the Wolverines. Rees was drawn into action when Everett Golson was ineffective against the tough Michigan defense. Kelly substituted Rees midway through the second quarter.

BCS Championship Bowl

For such a great season, #1 ranked Notre Dame got to play #2 ranked Alabama in the BCS championship Bowl at Sun Life Stadium in Miami Gardens, FL. Alabama coach Nick Saban outcoached the neophyte Kelly. Saban did not blame the six-week wait to play this game. But there are those on the Irish side that said it took the edge off the Irish and they were defeated by the Crimson Tide L (14-42). Coach Kelly should have had them ready. Coach Saban had his team ready and firing at every play.

Before a record Sun Life Stadium crowd of 80,120 that definitely included more green than crimson, The Crimson Tide's star running back, Eddie Lacy, ran right through the Irish on a 20-yard touchdown run before the game was 3 minutes old.

This capped off a punishing 82-yard drive that was the longest of the season given up by the Fighting Irish. That was the complexion of the game until it ended with an Alabama victory.

2013 Coach Brian Kelly Year 4

The 2013 Notre Dame Fighting Irish football team was led by fourth year head coach Brian Kelly. Notre Dame played all its home games at Notre Dame Stadium in South bend, Indiana, other than those in their Shamrock Series. They compete as an independent.

Everett Golson, to the chagrin of his fellow teammates, was out on academic suspension for the year. Senior Tommy Rees stepped in as the starting 2013 quarterback. The Fighting Irish finished the 2013 regular season 9-4. They were # 21 in the coaches' poll and # 25 in the AP. ND was invited to the Pinstripe Bowl at Yankee Stadium and they defeated Rutgers W (29-16)

2014 Coach Brian Kelly Year 5

The 2014 Notre Dame Fighting Irish football team was led by fifth-year head coach Brian Kelly. The Irish were two different teams this season. Team 1 played the first six games with all players well and ready to play. Team 2 lost half of its defense mostly through major injuries and yet, they went out each week and did their best. However, in a depleted condition, Team 2 often did not do well enough to bring home the victory.

ND started the season with a 6–0 record, ranked as high as #5 in both the AP Poll and the Coaches' Poll. They suffered a major setback with many player injuries in the second half of the season. They lost five of their last six games. They finished the regular season at 7–5.

The Music City Bowl Notre Dame v LSU

Notre Dame had a tough end to its season losing four-straight games. What a great feeling as a team that worked hard through adversity to close the 2014 campaign to gain a victory over LSU in the Music City Bowl. Both quarterbacks, Everett Golson and Malik Zaire played and both were at their best as was Kyle Brindza, who contributed the winning field goal.

Music City Bowl Highlights—Kyle Brindza hit a 32-yard field goal as time expired to beat LSU.

The Irish had a tough time closing out games this year, especially with a depleted defense. It was an issue and so it had to be particularly satisfying for Golson, Zaire, and Brindza.

2015 Coach Brian Kelly Year 6

The 2015 Notre Dame Fighting Irish football team was led by sixth-year head coach Brian Kelly. As always, the team played its home games at Notre Dame Stadium in South Bend (aka Notre Dame) Indiana. Notre Dame continues to compete as an independent, though there are those that expect that in the future the Irish may complete a transition to be part of the ACC. Perhaps that is in the future. Perhaps it is not.

What a great team ND put together under Brian Kelly for the 2015 season. It can be argued that the 2015 team is the most explosive offense that Brian Kelly has coached at Notre Dame. But for four points in two games, the 2015 season would have been dramatically different.

During the regular season, the Irish were one of twenty-one schools in the country to average 200 or more passing yards and rushing yards per game. The Irish had fourteen plays of over 50 yards during the season. This ranked 13th in the country and was a Notre Dame school record. The Fighting Irish were fun to watch.

During this season, ND also had two touchdowns of over 90 yards. C.J. Prosise contributed a 91 yarder and Josh Adams gave the Irish a 98-yard touchdown. In 126 years of previous Notre Dame Football games, the Fighting Irish had only two such runs before 2015.

The 2015 running game was dominant in its success against opposing defenses. At 5.76 yards per carry, the Irish ranked fifth in the country. Finishing the regular season averaging 34 points per game, including a 62-point effort against UMass, the most points in an ND game since 1996; the point output was phenomenal.

Ohio State has always been a great team. Urban Myer's team was as great in 2015 as those of the past but they had lost a late season game to Michigan State, which kept them from winning the Big Ten

Championship. Notre Dame had also lost a big game against Clemson earlier in the season and then again late season against Stanford. Add up the Irish loss total in the regular season and you get four points…just four points. How much is two plus two?

The ND 2015 season ended on a heartbreaking note, as the Irish were defeated by Ohio State University in the Fiesta Bowl by a score of L (28-44). The resident Indiana Irish have a few things to prove to their neighbors in Ohio as ND has not beaten the Buckeyes since 1936.

Brian Kelly had another great recruiting class. He received 24 commitments in his fifth full recruiting class including one five-star, Alize Jones. The class included student-athletes from 13 different states.

Fall 2016 Coach Brian Kelly Year 7

2016 Results

1. at Texas	L 50–47 2OT	2. 1Nevada	W 39–10
3. Mich State	L 36–28	4. Duke	L 38–35
5. at Syracuse	W 50–33	6. at NC State	L 10–3
7. Stanford	L 17–10	8. Miami FL	W 30–27
9. at Navy	L 28–27	10. Army	W 44–6
11.Virg Tech	L 34–31	12. at USC	L 45–27

The 2016 Notre Dame Fighting Irish football team was again led by seventh-year head coach Brian Kelly. After a regular season in which the Irish lost just two games each by two points, with a number of starters back, Notre Dame was expected to compete well during the 2016 season. Coach Kelly had another fine recruiting class which bodes well for the future. Notre Dame accepted 23 commitments for 2016, including two 5-stars: Daelin Hayes and Tommy Kraemer. The class included student-athletes from 11 different states, and one Canadian province

Some fine recruits are heading ND's way

In preparation for the next three or four years of Notre Dame Football, Brian Kelly and his coaching staff made some good moves on national signing day, February 3, 2016, by inking 24 players in what is known euphemistically as a recruiting class.

The 2017 signing day on February 1 was almost as good. Notre Dame signed 21 players to its 2017 recruiting class. All 18 known commitments prior to today had put pen to paper and on signing day, Kelly added three more, who decided on Wednesday.

After a tough 4-8 season in 2016, it was nice to see a strong off-season also as Brian Kelly added defensive coordinator Mike Elko and linebackers coach Clark Lea to his staff, along with the hiring of special teams coach and energetic recruiter Brian Polian. These are good signs for the future. Something had to be done and so far, so good.

With Kelly returning his focus to the offensive side of the ball and new offensive coordinator Chip Long brought in to help with the play-calling, he will be guiding a group that has arguably the nation's best offensive tackle in Mike McGlinchey, perhaps America's best offensive guard Quenton Nelson and two more returning starters on the offensive line in Alex Bars and Sam Mustipher up front.

The team should have plenty of speed and playmaking ability in the backfield and at wide receiver to spread the football around too.

Defensively Elko inherits a group that just needs to be put in a position to consistently succeed. Many criticized former defensive coordinator Brian VanGorder for running a too complex scheme. Van Gorder had a tough time getting young players ready to play. Moreover, the system did not permit players such as Jaylon Smith to be in position to be productive behind the line of scrimmage.

Elko comes with a reputation of being a great communicator regarding his system and overall, the Irish should be highlighting a talented group of linebackers and defensive backs by enabling them to play faster.

247Sports has suggested that if guys like Daelin Hayes, Jerry Tillery, Khalid Kareem, Julian Okwara, Elijah Taylor, Jonathan Bonner and Jamir Jones blossom as they should with the new system. Notre

Dame will go from a defense that struggled to get any kind of push to making consistent plays in the backfield.

Kelly is very pleased with the recruiting class which wrapped up February 1, as it will supplement a roster that was short on experience in 2016 but now has all those trials and tribulations to grow from. Fans are hoping the bad stuff is in the past.
The Fighting Irish 2017 class finished No. 11 nationally per the 247Sports Recruiting Rankings, which ties the second-best mark Kelly has had in seven full recruiting calendars in South Bend. That is good. only the 2013 class that included Smith finished better at No. 5. Combine the 2017 efforts with the 2016 class (#13 in the nation) and it's a group a program should be able to win a lot of games with.

Soon again, it will be time to play Notre Dame Football.

Despite all the hype from 2016 that is similar to this year, Coach Kelly and Coach Van Gorder could not make it happen in 2016 and he finished the season with one of the worst records in ND history. There was a clear problem with the defense and we all know that by the end of the year it was not solved. Hopefully by the start of 2017 for ND fans and supporters, it will be well solved.

Like most true ND supporters, I want The University of Our Lady to do well in everything. This is my second very positive book about the University. I am working on a third book about great ND players.

Many people who read my books about ND either already are big supporters of ND. Others, by reading a Brian Kelly (not the coach) book, may get swayed with the magnificent ND legacy. I write my books to tell the truth and to highlight the team in College Football that I love the best. I'd like ND the institution to appear to be as gracious a university as there ever might be--ever.

It would be nice and I think more helpful to ND than not for those who I have contacted about my very popular Great Moments in Notre Dame Football book, would respond to my messages even if the University does not want books written by non-ND graduates to be sold in their bookstore. Just saying! It's just the polite thing to do. Additionally, I think ND should be nice to everybody. It would help the Notre Dame image and overall, it would help recruiting. It surely cannot hurt.

As I close out this chapter and this book, I regret that there is a very well-intentioned Notre Dame alumni group that is really upset with athletics and various key personnel at the University such as the Head Coach and the Athletic Director. From my own experience, I personally know that the Sports Information Department is not very responsive to requests for assistance in the building of books that are destined to deliver very positive messages about the University. I can't figure that one out! Why? I can only guess.

In 2017, these alumni took out a new ad in the South Bend Tribune. The ad is called the "Four Horsemen of Failure," which outlines how the group believes the football program has failed under athletic director Jack Swarbrick and coach Brian Kelly. The "Four Horsemen" is a famous nickname given to the legendary backfield under Knute Rockne in the 1920s. We highlight the real four horsemen in this book. I think ND Administration has let this go too far.

I would recommend some major dialogue between the warring parties. I can personally appreciate the frustrations of the alumni group as I have had similar frustrations in dealing with the huge bureaucracy at the institution. Yet, I really do not like an ad that denigrates the Four Horsemen or ND in general. I would like everything positive.

Rather than dig in and fight back, for the good of the University and the Football program, I would recommend that the Administration reach out to this group and have the discussion that might end the hostilities and it might even produce an action plan to help all parties involved. Notre Dame is too precious of an icon and an institution and a football legacy to let mere mortals tarnish its reputation.

Like most Notre Dame supporters; this author hopes that Brian Kelly and Notre Dame make a great comeback from 2016. Amen!

LETS GO PUBLISH! Books by Brian W. Kelly (Sold at www.bookhawkers.com; Amazon.com, and Kindle.).

Great Coaches in Notre Dame Football The best coaches in any football prrgram

President Donald J. Trump, Master Builder: Solving the Student Debt Crisis!

President Donald J. Trump, Master Builder: It's Time for Seniors to Get a Break!

President Donald J. Trump, Master Builder: Healthcare & Welfare Accountability

President Donald J. Trump, Master Builder: "Make America Great Again"

President Donald J. Trump, Master Builder: The Annual Guest Plan

Great Players in Alabama Football From Quarterbacks to offensive Linemen Greats!

Great Moments in Alabama Football AU Football from the start. This is the book.

Great Moments in Penn State Football PSU Football, start--games, coaches, players,

Great Moments in Notre Dame Football ND Football, start, games, coaches, players

Four Dollars & Sixty-Two Cents—A Christmas Story That Will Warm Your Heart!

My Red Hat Keeps Me on The Ground. Darraggh's Red Hat is really Magical

Seniors, Social Security & the Minimum Wage. Things seniors need to know.

How to Write Your First Book and Publish It with CreateSpace

The US Immigration Fix--It's all in here. Finally, an answer.

I had a Dream IBM Could be #1 Again The title is self-explanatory

WineDiets.Com Presents The Wine Diet Learn how to lose weight while having fun.

Wilkes-Barre, PA; Return to Glory Wilkes-Barre City's return to glory

Geoffrey Parsons' Epoch... The Land of Fair Play Better than the original.

The Bill of Rights 4 Dummmies! This is the best book to learn about your rights.

Sol Bloom's Epoch ...Story of the Constitution The best book to learn the Constitution

America 4 Dummmies! All Americans should read to learn about this great country.

The Electoral College 4 Dummmies! How does it really work?

The All-Everything Machine Story about IBM's finest computer server.

Brian has written 104 books. Others can be found at amazon.com/author/brianwkelly